Uncle Setnakt's Nightbook

This book is offered to my Patron Set, who gave me all I needed. I hope that these words inspire other humans to Remember the Pact they made with the Prince of Darkness to live extraordinary lives. As we Come Into Being as Wonders, the Work of Set is Wrought through the Angle of Victory.

Published by
LODESTAR
P.O. Box 16
Bastrop, Texas 78602

www.seekthemystery.com

Table of Contents

Introduction

In the year 1988, I was writing a short story about the Salem Witch trials. I made a chart of the events, the "evidence," and the hysteria. I tired of my work and turned on the TV – to the Geraldo Rivera *Satanism in America* special. As I listened to "occult crime experts," I saw the same logical errors and fallacies that led the women of Salem to their deaths. One of the Satanists asked the logical question – if the experts knew who were committing these atrocities, why didn't they arrest them? Geraldo cut to a commercial. I was amused by a sensible voice from the side I expected not to be sensible. I wanted to find out more. The man was Dr. Michael A. Aquino. He had founded the Temple of Set. At the time I had a suspicion of "occult orders" -- most occultists I met were dogmatic, egotistical, and a little neurotic – and that was the best of the pack. However, I had been touched by a Mystery, and part of me wanted to know more. To my vast surprise Dr. Stephen E. Flowers not only knew the guy – he was a card-carrying member. (He showed me the card).

I investigated. I read tons of anti-Temple of Set material. I talked to members and ex-members. Finally in 1989 I joined on Holy Saturday of that year.

I found what had called me. The Need I had to order and express my psyche into the objective world matched the philosophy, the community, and the practice of the Temple of Set. It benefited me, and I was glad to benefit it.

Seven years later I was High Priest.

Something called you to pick up this little book. Maybe you are a member, maybe you are a collector of all things dark, maybe you have a Need. Maybe you are buying the book to sell it to a used bookstore so the real buyer will find it in a couple of years. You are part of the Work – and it's up to you to decide whether you lead as a free and sovereign human or as a sleeping slave. The kicker is . . . I don't care. I am not out to recruit an army. I am furthering my understanding of my Self and the Cosmos and my Patron, the neter Set. If I act impeccably, my words will find the Mind waiting for them. That Mind will, in the fullest of time, give me answers to questions that I cannot answer by myself. To give me those answers, that Mind will have to transform itself by reason and Dreams, hard work and crazy flashes of insight, dazzling acts of magic and patient struggle. The actions of that Mind will lead it to questions that it cannot answer, and that Mind will talk with friends, or Teach, or write, and send forth its questions to find other Minds. In the long run, by this chaotic process, the world will by changed into a place of greater freedom and power.

Human beings have two ways of passing on information. One mode is genetic. You carry the information from your father and mother, and they from their fathers and mothers back to some primeval human ancestor in Africa. The other mode is what we Setians call the Gift of Set. Our carnal selves can be traced back 190,000 years, based on the Omo Kibish skull (as well as genetic timeline projections). The markers for Behavioral Modernity (those behaviors that separate us from our primate cousins) seem to begin at about the same point. Speech, kinship systems, singing, sexual customs and the like are based on humans' abilities to teach one another. Copying the behaviors that succeed cretae that form of external memory called "culture." This would be the so-called "Second Replicator" suggested originally by Richard Dawkins in 1975 and which has gained increasing attention since the late 1990s due to Susan Blackmore and Dan

Dennett. The second replicator system is the means by which human culture transmits, grows, drifts, mutates, and otherwise undergoes Darwinian selection. The second replicator predates the genus *Homo*, but with the arrival of our current carnal form, it took over evolution – not only in the massive brain size but also determining the fate of the species. The human ability to create and transmit such life-space ideas as art, science, technology, ethics, spirituality, and magic in refining and evolving forms frees humans from the merely biological. Humans have been slow to realize this – on the one hand it frees from them from Judeo-Christian ideas about the nature of history as God's revelation and on the other should allow them to pick such notions from humanity's past that are the best for human flourishing. The Setian sees the essential, nonbiological evolving aspect of humanity as the great force -- the divine -- in us. As other religions have focused on governance (Christianity), survival (Judaism), conquest (Islam), denial (Vedantic Hinduism), Setianism focuses on evolution. The Setian is faced with two conclusions.

Firstly, real change in the world has always been the work of small groups which have practiced self-development. The approaches to exciting and inspiring the human and training her mind are manifold and often use the notion of an idealized Self – called God (or Goddess or Tao). Change does not come from the masses, but from the small group who are altering culture as they alter and improve themselves. Cultural life-spaces must be redesigned and then presented to the rest of the world. Whether the small group was the American patriots that lead the revolution or the European Surrealists that changed the art world, the formula is the same change the Self (Microcosmos) with interaction with a charged, small group (Mesocosmos) to improve and renew the world

(Macrocosmos).

Secondly, real change in the world begins with the breaking away from cultural norms. People interested in change must deprogram themselves, loosen prejudices and opinions, and seek to develop their new ways of thinking (and therefore of Being) from first principles. This seems to manifest both as a quest for good ideas that aren't manifest in the current idea-space and a quest for methods of making those ideas more active in the cultural transmission to come. Or in less grandiose terms, the magician digs up the best of the past and creates a more hopeful future as a weapon to overcome the ills of the present.

The first realization requires the need of a Temple. We do not gather to worship our Patron, the Prince of Darkness. There would be no meaningful Gift we could give him, no sacrifice, no hymns in His honor. We gather to create and teach the ways for a better world. Our tests for that world where the nonbiological life-spaces would yield more pleasure, power, and a deeper understanding of the universe are simple – we look for bringing these ideas into greater manifestation in our lives and report our progress and struggles with one another. We have to create a group, a meso-cosmos, where our life spaces can evolve and mutate. But to test our ideas we need the world and all its friction. So we test our lives against the world, while creating a life-space that evolves by our efforts. We neither seek nor need the monastery, the retreat, the commune. We need the world, and we need each other's nonbiological evolution to further our own. Our "worship" of the Prince of Darkness is in the form of emulation – we create a better nonbiological life space and pass it on to others. We can't create what we want by book learning. We have to test, communicate, and transmit or lore because of the very evolutionary aspect it posses.

The second realization pushes us against the standard form of the occult subculture. We begin by rebelling against many societal conventions. Yet we do not rebel against the notion of ethics, the nonbiological moral practices that humans have learned to safeguard the passing on of culture. We confuse certain people because we are not movie Satanists evilly cackling over some cruel deed. But we do reject symbols of our society and take a stand against its hypocrisy. We choose darkness over light, struggle over peace, awakening over denial. The ideas we seek are not found by learning more fanciful explanations of the universe, nor accepting the prepackaged thoughts of others. We prefer the real past to occult fantasies. We assume that knowledge from outside our culture is hard to interpret. We believe that it is difficult to get rid of emotional baggage. We accept that we will make mistakes along the way and that our leaders are not all wise gurus, but simply good at the art of cultural transmission.

In this book I have collected several articles published in various handbooks and publications of the Temple of Set as well as certain articles published elsewhere. I have included inspired texts and letters I have given certain select groups within the Temple. I have done this to transmit a picture of our inheritance so that it may interact with other ideas and philosophies in the world. As a thinker I know that dialogue between idea systems can lead to Darwinian selection – our better ideas will not only grow stronger, they will be transmitted. As a magician I know what I cast into the world will come back to me bringing new resources. As a clergyman I know that my words will help some of you find a new connection with your secret soul. And as a cynic I know in the main this book will be left on the bathroom floor next to well-thumbed copies of *The Far Side*.

I would like to introduce five aspects of Setian practice, which may help you navigate through this book. I will talk about Setian Magic, Setian Cosmology, Setian Philosophy, Setian Community, and Setian Religion. After that I will give you some tips on using this book in ways to increase your personal power and pleasure. For those of you who only want the magic right now, I will label each section.

Setian Magic

The Setian has certain core beliefs about magic. The system, whether linguistically based like the runic system or substance based like Hoo Doo, is not the issue. The issue is: does the system embrace a self-empowerment aesthetic, clear signs of mastery, and appeal to the magician that uses it. The goals of magic are power, pleasure, understanding, and self-transformation upon self-chosen lines. Magical deeds (such as healing) may be done for others, but it is seen as being powered by a sense of self. If I heal my friend or kinsman, I please myself. If I create greater social justice in the world, I empower myself. I do not serve god nor scripture with my deeds of magic.

Magic is a non-ordinary event. It is not an inevitable or biological process. It causes events both in the objective universe and the subjective universe of the magician that would not have happened otherwise. The manifestation of magic does not contravene physical law; it alters the end-state of either chaotic physical systems or – much more frequently – the possibilities of human life. Outside of the cinema the magican does not wave his wand and a pot of gold appear. Magic can effect events non-causally – there is no rational path of action from the magical event and the manifestation. Magic is not, therefore, "undiscovered science" or some other modernist cliché.

Magic is difficult to do well. This notion places the Setian against the clichés of the occult world that magic is "easy" or "natural." That the magican must work for change is his or her salvation. Nothing would destroy mankind more quickly than if human will could be easily amplified. That the human must change himself in order to will more skillfully or wish more wisely is the evolutionary manifestation of the Gift of Set. By "tempting" humans with power that can only be obtained by self-development, the human seeks out his or her Teachers, and works on him- or herself. The movie version of an average human gaining a wish-granting item is an outward realization of the biological truths of our species or, in Setian terms, an affirmation of our pact with Set: Great Is The Might Of Set, Greater Still He Through Us.

Magic is the art of changing the subjective universe so that a proportional change occurs in the objective universe. The magical act is not "powered" by energies external to the magician nor by his or her biological energies. Magic does lie in the nature or expense of the ritual equipment – save that these may have an effect on the subjective universe – nor is it powered by sacrifice of any living thing, nor by relics, etc. The act of magic coming from a single psyche reflects the needs and wants of the individual and has always placed the magician or ritual specialist outside of society, since its collectivist goals are more attuned to such gods as that society may invent.

The magical event is a willed and conditioned perception of the changeable world being made to reflect the eternal, timeless world. In this magic is a truth process – see below.

THE WORKING
The Becoming Side of the Self
(Signals Sent and Received)

The Change in the Pysche   The Change in the World

The Eternal Self

Here is an image of Setian Magic. The aspect of the self that is available to the

magician, her thoughts, feelings, body, etc., has a need. She expresses that need in a form

that, A) expresses that the need has been met ("I am healthy!") and, B) is pleasingly

encoded to those subconscious pre-rational parts of herself that separate the part of

herself in the world of becoming and change and the eternal (but unexpressed) parts of

herself. If you prefer Plato, the Form of herself. The Self responds by sending signal

back that has two edges – one in the outer world and the other in a change in her psyche.

The Egyptians had a word for this, *Xeperi* – "Two things have come into being."

Let me explain the concept of the edges of an event. Most people either believe

in magic as a vast source of power or dismiss it for the reason it would take far too much

energy to manifest. Consider the following event. An old friend of mine had great luck

with dice. When games were going were badly for him, he would wish for the

appropriate die roll and, *voila*, there it was. This happened with such frequency we

suspected him of cheating, so that one or the other of us would toss the dice for him. The winning rolls still came up, although a little less often. The modernist viewpoint might attribute this to telekinesis or perhaps his cueing our bodies in subtle ways to toss the dice. The amount of energy to change dice falling through the air would be staggering. When my friend would be asked about his ability he claimed it was his "lucky ring." The two phenomena, his feeling of luck and the die rolls, are actually not separate things. It is one event manifesting both in his subjective universe (he feels lucky, his need to win is manifest) and the objective universe (double sixes again). This can only be perceived as a single event viewed from two places. The magic-using self is able to see the universe as a oneness wherein subjective symbols and wishes are as real and connected to the whole as are random events controlled by gravity, time, energy, etc. This unity of the magical universe is the same phenomena our Right Hand Path brothers experience as mystic bliss. The other point of view that sees this event as one thing with two edges is the magician's secret soul. Certain objections should be occurring to my readers here.

I will deal with the religious objection – the notion of a soul – later, but right now the question of "If Mike could make dice rolls play out that way, why couldn't he win the lottery?" Well, the event that would have a lottery win as one edge is a very different event than doing well in a game. Secondly, one might object that this would be a trivial use of power. Although I might argue that it is up to the magician to make such value judgements, my common sense would tend to agree with you. Magic has two very separate purposes. The first is for the empowerment of the self in the everyday world. Magic will save you from poverty (sometimes), give you advantages in business and legal matters (often), and heal your body and those you love (frequently). But magic serves a purpose for your secret soul as well. It broadens your awareness of itself. With

13

each deed you begin to know your soul, and that knowledge has a cumulative effect on your actions. The magician will find his life filling with virtue and strength where there was none before. He will also find himself impelled to seek after the mysterious.

My more clever readers are now asking, "Does magic only flow one way – from the magican firstly toward his or her soul?" Magic flows in two ways. Your soul is always seeking your attention. This may manifest in the strangest of places. You may have been someone that has always scoffed at the Tarot as a form of divination. You can spot the cheap psychological gimmicks of most readers and understand that others are actually self-deluded into thinking the truisms of the cards are a genuine message. Yet one day at that "Psychic Fair" at some roadside hotel that your cousin dragged you to – you get the reading that changes your life. Many humans have such moments, and interpret them in whatever mythological/cultural framework they know. They are not fully "Awakened" by their soul but at least get enough information to find a good or avoid a bad marriage. The Setian understands that her soul wants to contact her, and so she is Receptive. Not superstitious playing with divination sets, or reading horoscopes, but learning to find the few but important omens in her life. None of the parts of the above diagram are static. The changes in the psyche are changing our lives every moment. This is easy to verify – compare a "good" day with a "bad" day. Changes in the objective universe are changing our position all the time. Your magical Working for wealth may be creating one sort of event, but changes in the economy as a whole will likely have a bigger effect.

Since the Setian sees process as dynamic there are two important ideas to consider. Firstly, you do not control everything. Many magicians like to see every event in the universe as being aimed at them. After months or years of such paranoia, the magician burns out. Such people are bad at the practice of magic. If you were to send a letter to the king asking for a favor, you wouldn't send off ten more letters before he has answered the first one. Or if you feel that every event is a magical one – that is to say, having an edge in your subjective universe and one in the objective universe – your megalomania would soon make self-development impossible. Secondly, the universe you live in is neither wholly random nor wholly fated. Some events are expressions of your secret soul; others have no subjective/self-changing edge. Your life is neither determined by your soul, nor free from its influence.

The question that arises is, What does this mean for group Work? Is a group of magicians who are performing a ritual together is simply several individuals who simply happen to be trying for a common goal? Or is something else happening? There are two things to consider in this case: Firstly, a group Working is very likely to have a massive effect on the psyche of the magician in the chamber. Hearing the voices, chanting to the music, smelling the incense, seeing fires blaze are very useful ways of encoding information to one's soul. Secondly, the message sent to the secret soul is important. It is not merely a Wish for money or power or wisdom – it is a message that the self in the world of becoming has found allies and Teachers. The response will affect the group, the meso-cosmos, of the magician. Even as the group is doing its human best to work out ideas and improve its lot, the answers from magic will aid the group in unusual and not directly causal ways. The Workings of the Temple are not just a group of magicians (of various levels of skill) seeking greater power and pleasure for themselves – they are an instrument to improve the dialogue and interactions within the group and its place in the objective universe.

Now, magical practice in the Temple of Set can take varied forms. What Setian A does with a Voo Doo doll may achieve the same goals that Setian B does by carving runes or Setian C with cyber-magic. Most Setians learn a form of Western ritual magic as a training aid. The terms "ritual" or "ceremonial magic" conjure up a smoky image of portly men in Golden Dawn robes mispronouncing Greek and Hebrew. An interesting entertainment, perhaps, and certainly something to do before TV was invented. The purpose of ritual is to impress a direction on the Matrix of Darkness. The Matrix of Darkness has two poles. It is "dark" because the contents are magical, unknown, and – to the untrained preceptor – frightening.

One pole is that part of yourself from which unexpected thoughts, feelings, and actions arise. How often have major life changes come from what seem to be the least of whims? "I read that book. I went to that movie. I ate at that restaurant -- and I met my beloved, changed my religion, or decided what I wanted to major in at college." From that internal Dark comes forth things, clothed in Darkness, that change our lives. The inner darkness is not infinite, although we may wish, like Lautréamont's character Maldoror, that it were so that we might enjoy endless change and metamorphosis.

The other pole is that part of the Cosmos we call the future. There, too, things are not tied down. There, too, the unexpected thing comes forth, and we are changed. Sometimes these unexpected things are vast and transpersonal – like a war. Other times more focused – like an idiot that runs into your car. Here, too, possibilities arise. The future is not infinite, although we may wish, like E. E."Doc" Smith, that it were so, that we might enjoy endless progress. But it is from these two apparently separate things that we can make Change.

Now, we can follow the prescribed rituals of another, and try to make ourselves and our world into another model. The Catholic Mass is one of the best examples of ritual designed to do this. It has kept the Church going, despite the forces of civilization and hazard. This type of magic is trying to impose the Known – the Light – on the darkness and is hence known as White Magic. Or we can begin by seeing the true nature of that which we would Work with. If we've got a better handle on Darkness, we can get a better result. So we can impose Darkness on Darkness – impose Change on that which Changes. This Black Magic is more potent for the simple reason that it is more resonate with the forces of change. One Black Magician can do what a hundred White Magicians cannot. This does not lie in the elegance of his rituals, nor in the secret knowledge that she possesses, but in the nature of the Cosmos as a place of darkness. In this great and darkling Void, all is ready for our Creation.

Setian Cosmology

Most of the religious and magical systems of the world make a wrong assumption about the nature of the objective universe. In most systems cosmic law is reflected in the phenomenal universe (for example: Judaism, Islam) or the phenomenal universe is cosmic law itself (for example: Taoism, Confucianism). That tree over there is trying to tell me something about the shape of my soul, or the Nile river reflects a cosmic truth (or IS a cosmic truth). This can lead to nature worship or to simplistic folk sorcery. If the universe we observe and cosmic order are linked, it would be easy to believe that everything in the universe has the potential to aid or teach us, as its placement reflects divine will and special creation. Therefore, all things – both me and not-me – are linked

17

because of divine will, and my purpose would be to harmonize myself with the universe and to seek models of my purpose from its substances and phenomena. Salvation must always be at hand because we are part of a greater It.

The Setian begins with the problem of perception. Firstly, I do not perceive the universe directly. My sense impressions are filtered through my body, restricted by my upbringing , and modeled by my mind. I am not experiencing that tree over there. I am experiencing *my mind's model of the tree*. God did not put the model there; I did – although many of my actions were not volitional when I learned about 'trees." If I draw inspiration from the tree, it is conditioned by my experience – "It is a Texas live oak, one of the lucky ones not infected with the "Decline" – an oak wilt that hurts live and red oaks. My wife and I have made love under it. My cat Big Pig likes to sharpen his claws on it. Its shade is nice today." I can be inspired by its beauty. Because of my education I may think of Zeus' Oracle at Dodona, world- trees in Aztec and Germanic mythology, and Charlie Brown's Kite-eating Tree. I am not the tree; however, the perceptions of the tree are me.

The items of the universe are not placed there for my enlightenment; therefore, I have no creator god to thank. The items I create in my mind are possibly useful in my enlightenment. My subjective universe does not merge with the objective universe any more than a map merges with the territory. Setianism is a dualist school.

My subjective universe can model things incorrectly – "I thought Bootsy Collins would say 'Yes!' when I invited her to prom." My subjective universe can model things differently for different reasons. When I am writing a "hard science fiction" story, I model the universe in terms of eleven-dimensional membrane theory. When I am writing a ritual for the Order of the Trapezoid, I model the Universe as consisting of nine elements, beginning with Ice and Fire and ending with Venom and Earth. My subjective universe can model things that do not exist at all (for example, see my space opera book *The War with the Belatrin* available from Wildside Press). My subjective universe can model, create, synthesize in manners beyond the objective universe. The objective universe – every particle, every field of force, even the space-time continuum itself – can be derived and measured in terms of yes-no questions. It is consistent and repeatable and maybe treated as a computable problem. One can explain the observable universe best in terms of science and reason – Setians refer to the observable universe as the "natural universe."

The subjective universe shows different properties than the objective universe. It can be manipulated to produce thoughts and questions than transcend the computable/predictable universe. The natural order does instruct the Setian in the ordering of those parts of herself that are beyond that order. The Egyptian god Set, who stood apart from the ordered universe, is seen as the divine patron of this part of ourselves. As Dr. Michael A. Aquino said on the *Oprah Winfrey Show,* "We believe that this quality [to oppose the natural order] in the human soul that makes it different from all other life forms…was deliberately inculcated in humanity in its distant evolutionary past by an active agency that is acting in defiance of the universal norm."

Setian Philosophy

Western magic has been Neo-Platonic since the Renaissance. In fact, when Cosimo de Medici hired Marsilio Ficino to begin the Renaissance by reviving Plato's school as the "Florence Academy," he had Ficino first translate the *Corpus Hermeticum* and then the complete works of Plato. Magicians began with a working view of the material world as not quite real and influenced by a more true world, the world of Forms. Setians magical practice is applied Neo-Platonism – by changing things in the ideal world (the subjective universe) change will occur in the manifest universe. Setians have always been deeply Neo-Platonic. The complete writings of Plato are on our reading list, as well as a helping of Plotinus.

The Setian in many ways goes against the grain of current relativism which dominates the major intellectual core of such movements as Chaos Magic. However, the Setian is a child of Satanic heritage and does not trust prepackaged truth. Scriptures and cult leaders do not appeal to Setian modeling. This brings up three important issues – comissability in Setian thinking, the nature of the role model as a guide to Initiation, and the philosophical justification of the School. I will begin by discussing by the first two ideas – comissability and the notion of limits in regard to initiatory role models. In the former idea I am influenced by the French philosopher Alain Badiou, and in the latter by Ipsissimus Stephen Edred Flowers. Both ideas seem t o be commonly held in our culture, although neither seems to have had much rigorous examination.

We live in a fragmented world. There are no ruling paradigms that order our society. The visions of religion, civic good, and science have limited effect. The average human has a cafeteria philosophy – "I'll take most of my ethics from Christianity, a scoop of Marxism, an afterlife vision from *Ghosthunters*, and some cosmology from Darwin and *Star Trek*. The postmodernists see no problem in this as long as some process is involved. Truth for the postmodernist is a thought construct.

Alain Badiou broke from his French postmodern tutors in asserting that truth is real, eternal, and unchanging. But he did not break from their emphasis on importance

and energy of individual process. The energy of life and its gains are as a result of truth

processes such as Art, Science, Love, and Politics. To these the Setian may add Magic.

As one discovers truth, one gains in Being. Truth lies outside of truth processes.

However, truth is inherent in the operation of the procedures – that it to say, one pursues

these processes in good faith to obtain truth. Some truths will be of a personal nature (for

example, in the Love and Art processes); however, each of these truths point to a larger

eternal verity. A person faithful to a truth process does not construct truth, but acquires

the means to introduce what she has discovered into the world. In other words, truth is

not merely a contemplative reality, but a call AND means to action.

From a Setian perspective this reflects the process we call "Xeper." As a sentient

entity discovers truth, her own actions will reflect this truth in the deeds begun in the

worlds inhabited by the Setian. I Have Come Into Being And By My Coming Into Being

The Way Of Coming Into Being Has Been Established. This dual process reflects the

individual discovering her own truths as opposed to absorbing the manifest image of her

host culture/society. It allows for a person to be in a multi-layered dialectic with the

world (shades of Althusser) but still aligned with Platonic notions of the Truth.

Badiou gives a strong caution against tying oneself to one truth process. He

warns specifically against suturing one's self to a single truth process. One should not

look simply to science for truth, nor politics, nor even love. Such a suture denies the Self

as an observer/dialectician. If all your truth comes out of someone else's box, you are not

a self. The self that cannot exist in dialectic is not a self. Or, in Setian terms, for the Self

to exist (Set), there must be the Other as a constructed reality which must be deconstructed, rebuilt, or conditioned (Horus). Badiou's warning against a single suture seems to me to be a secular restatement of that puzzling line in the *Book of Coming Forth by Night*. "The text of another is an affront to the Self."

Badiou's notion goes against the grain of social constructed behavior. Humans, good primates that we are, love to adopt "truth" in big prepackaged sets. Badiou points out such large-scale adoption of a viewpoint is detrimental to the Self. We too often see humans that feel compelled to adopt every aspect of a certain utterance. My more occultish readers could compare this to the First Beast's warning against the "the demon Crowley." My own interest in Badiou is a case in point. Politically, he is firmly a Maoist, and I pursue the truth process philosophy with the aid of Adam Smith and Thomas Jefferson.

Yet Badiou does not advocate for *fracta* and fragmentation as a goal (in this he is in strong opposition to Postmodernists in general. See Leotard's writing on fracta as a source of energy). Suture can occur and at this point when different truth processes converge, the Self finds a place of integration with the objective world. For example one could find sutures between Love and Art in the novel (see my *Endless Honeymoon*), or one could find a suture between Politics and Science when one reasons the importance of teaching evolution in public schools. Such sutures are called Understanding in the Setian jargon, and a coherent web of such sutures would be seen as one of the characteristics of the Grade of Magister Templi.

During his Runa Talks twenty years ago, Dr. Stephen Edred Flowers discussed a similar idea in the notions of limits and role models in the Quest for Runa, itself a sacred version of Badiou's truth processes. Both as Edred spoke of it, and with the new interest in Wyrd within the Temple of Set we will be revisiting, we need not reinvent the path of every single truth process. We can see what explorers have done and emulate them, as long as we place the proper limits on our emulation. Edred spoke of three levels of models. I will discuss these and add a fourth.

The human level. We meet a living human teacher and follow him or her. This has the great advantage of being the easiest to follow. The struggles and victories of the teacher are easy to see. Did he go to college? Maybe I should go to college. Did she travel? Maybe I should visit the same places. Did he write books? I should try that.

The heroic level. We find a culture hero and emulate them. This has the advantage of showing certain virtues in a very clear way, but is harder to follow. We may learn that Beowulf exemplifies Wyrd when he comes to slay Grendel – and decide that, if we intend to be more than what we seem, we must discover what things are possible for us and not for average humans. But heroic role models have greater Will (capacity to Do things) than us. We will most likely not be killing monsters in the fen.

The divine level. We pick a god to emulate. This method is as available to the Right Hand Path (What would Jesus do?) as the Left Hand Path. The god's quests are very clear, and we may draw on Secret sources of strength as we follow them. The god's path is clear (and especially important for the concept of Runa) *ordered*. Odhinn not only has his five quests; he has them in a given order.

I would add a fourth level: the fictive level. This might seem to be the same as divine level in that it also follows a human construction. However, the divine level has been field-tested in many human psyches and has changed in its power as a story because of the magical interaction with many humans. One may draw great inspiration from

Doctor Who, but our good Time Lord doesn't have the whole strength and nobility of a culture behind him.

Dr. Flowers stressed the importance of limits when following these paths. Just as Alain Badiou warns against the self suturing itself to a single truth process, Flowers pointed out that total emulation is both self-stifling and sometimes just plain dumb. Your human role model might drink to heavily; that does not mean you have to crack open the bourbon bottle because you are trying to write like Faulkner. Your hero may engage in acts that are morally reprehensible to you; you do not have to kill a dog to be like Cuchulain. The limits on following the divine role model should be clear.

For the Setian truth not only can be found in many venues, it must be pursued in many venues. The eternal and invariant truths that the Setian discovers must exist in comissability in her, and from this blend she will bring new vitality into her world. The paths and Doors are yours alone; the Truth beyond these doors is the same; and the way you introduce it into your world creates the unique joys, spaces, and opportunities of the world. The teachers, both living and mythical, can give you strong hints about the finding of truth and introducing it into the world – this is what is passed, as we say, "from Mouth to Ear" – but find many Teachers and find your own mix so that you fill your world, not with your teacher, but with the Good, the Beautiful, and the True.

Justifying a School is an easy task for a Right Hand Path religion. The student, in order to improve himself, must seek submission. In the Left Hand Path where the end goal of the practice is a sovereign self, Schools must be justified. In order to find a School, the following thing has to be true: the Seekers desire challenge rather than reassurance. If one tests oneself against self-chosen standards, the self cannot discover its blind spots and misunderstandings. This type of challenge is, for the most part, avoided in the occult world, which exists as a vehicle for the brainy but insecure self to gain the permissions to spend life reading weird stuff and listening to scary music. Schools provide Recognition, which is a fuel for self-development. Anger, Pride, and Pain are good fuels until something better comes along. But the problem is they are hard on the organism, on one's relationships, and on one's hope for growth.

The need that takes their place is the Need for Recognition. This is different than "fame" or even "notoriety," as Charlie Sheen fails to understand. Recognition is a three-part formula: You need to find some source worthy of Recognizing you. For example, it is easy for me to sell fiction to a semi-pro 'zine, but the *New Yorker* has still not glanced my way in 25 years. Secondly, you have to produce something worthy of Recognition. Thirdly, you have to Work to improve both you and the Recognizing body so that the Pride and Energia you have gained by being Recognized spurs you on to meaningful goals.

Now, it is tempting to translate Energia as "energy," the word British scientists coined from it, but a better translation is "Functioning." When the Energia of an organism, a business, a psyche is increased, it functions at a new (and previously Unknown) level. You functioned at a higher level after high school or college or marriage or your first good job.

When I was first a III° in the Temple, the average member was a college dropout in his twenties (I was older at 29), there were four or five people abroad, and people dropped out after four years. Although the spiritual aspects of my Recognition were for real, the non-spiritual stuff was easy – I had written books, and I was a magician with

25

decades of practice. So in order to make my Medallion something that was a Talisman instead of a trophy, I had to change. I went back to school and got my BA; I bought a home; and I traveled to some foreign Conclaves. I also had to change the Temple. I sponsored Pylons in Finland and Australia, wrote books for Setians, tried to increase the hard sciences and logic in the Temple.

I found in the Temple people more advanced than me, so they could Recognize me. I Worked and worked and Played hard. I took my moment of Recognition and made it a Force moving forward in time. I have done this with areas in my life besides the Temple, but it was here I learned the formula.

Setian Community

Over the years I have been amused by the black market sale of Temple materials such as the *Jeweled Tablets*. The tablets are like reading the novelization of a good movie – entertaining but in no way a trade-off for the real thing. It is easy to sit and read; much harder to find the courage to find people to interact with face-to-face. The human factor provides not only challenges and supports, but also it enables the psyche to unfold. It is much easier to change your subjective universe when you can see others in the same quest. It feeds the soul with the knowledge that change is possible and desirable and fulfills the non-natural need awakened humans have to learn and teach. The Setian community provides three very important resources: a Victor-Turner-style *communitas,* a Freemasonic networking group, and the challenge of Conclave.

Victor Turner took van Gennep's analysis of rites of passage a step further. Van Gennep focused on the individual. He is isolated, undergoes change in a liminal environment, and then is reintegrated into the community with new powers, prestige, and responsibilities. Turner looked at groups undergoing Initiation. People undergoing change process at the same time can both share experiences and discern the meaning of phenomena in a liminal environment. When you have followed Alice's rabbit, you find a very strange world indeed. Synchronicities and miracles show up, strange opportunities arise, and you have the chance to work on your emotional life and issues in a more direct manner than conventional therapies offer.

In a traditional religion the initiate is given prepackaged explanations for everything – in Setianism the initiate works with others to figure out his self and the Cosmos. Reality is not spoon-fed but discovered in an atmosphere of rational dialogue where others, who have and are experiencing the liminal world of magic, can offer insight and support. Turner found that people going through liminal experiences form close bonds – whether they are a group of Aboriginal boys becoming men, troops in boot camp, or a couple becoming married. This comes as a great surprise to most Setians because lifelong interest in the forbidden has made them loners.

Setians learn to trust other Setians. Not because a rule from above forces them into any kind of obligation or required hospitality, but because of the *communitas* phenomena, Adepts (Second-Degree-plus) learn about the character – especially strength of Will, creativity, and honesty – of their fellows. As such, Adepts in similar lines of work begin to form useful social networks and business alliances. Setians tend toward work in the creative arts (with writing, music, filmmaking, and art leading the way these days), academia, and the military and police fields. Each of these areas attracts the sort of person that wants to figure out how the Cosmos really works and then control aspects of the world that will increase her pleasure and power. Thus, the Temple's insistence on the practical side of magic and Initiation also expresses itself in study groups and associations for writers, musicians, artists, academics, women's empowerment, and other areas. This has both practical and magical benefits for its members.

The Temple has a yearly gathering. Its Conclave has been in San Francisco, Toronto, London, Berlin, Austin, Helsinki, Honolulu, Sacramento, Porto, Munich, Los Angeles, Las Vegas, Savannah, Belfast, Edinburgh, etc. These gatherings offer a practical challenge – "How can I get there?" – as well as unique experiences of magical sightseeing throughout the world. This has a massive effect on younger Initiates in their twenties who may be experiencing world-travel at the same time. It also provides for large-scale Workings with as many as a hundred participants. There are Setians in every continent except Antarctica, although some of our eco-warrior types have been in expeditions fighting whaling there. Since other Setians have performed rites in nuclear submarines and under Arctic Circle ice, the Temple can boast to having enchanted the entire world. Conclave keeps the Temple of Set from being simply a set of far-flung electronic mailing lists.

Setian Religion

The Temple offers no creator god, no doctrinal teachings on the afterlife, and advocates virtue-ethics rather than an imposed moral code. It can, in many ways, not be seen as a religion in a conventional sense. Before I discuss the religious duties of a Setian, I'm going to toss a couple of quotes into the mix. The first is from Jessie Berring in John Brockman's *What We Believe But Cannot Prove*:

> A group of children who were tested on death comprehension reflected on what it might be like to be dead with references like "sleeping," feeling "peaceful," or simply "being very dizzy . . . ." Younger children are more likely to attribute *mental states* to a dead agent than older children . . . .It seems the default cognitive stance is reasoning that human beings are immortal . . . .

The second quote is from Karen Armstrong in *A Short History of Myth*:

All mythology speaks of another plane that exists alongside our own world, and in some sense supports it.

Setians in the first degrees of Initiation need profess no belief in the existence of beings other than themselves. They are not asked to "believe" in magical practice, but required to show talent in this area. But Setians of the last four degrees – Priest, Magister, Magus, and Ipsissimus – are expected to have knowledge of an entity we call Set.

Setians see Set as a being both transcendent and immanent. Set is seen as the Patron of those aspects of the human being that suggest properties not bound to a deterministic universe. We speak of these properties – imagination, self-reflection, free will, magical powers, love and hate (beyond what is required to function among other primates), aesthetics, curiosity and so forth – as the Gift of Set. In most cultures (although not consumerist America) a gift is a contract that binds both giver and receiver. Why does Set give his Gift?

When young Michael Aquino was a Satanist I° in Vietnam, he performed an illustrative working. This is a magical re-enactment of a psychological or cosmic phenomenon. Aquino took on rewriting Milton's *Paradise Lost* from the demons' point of view. The demons were cast as the givers of the "Black Flame" of self-awareness to humans – a Gift that would lead (some of) them to revolt against the cosmic tyranny of JHVH. Despite a copy being blown apart on the battlefield, Aquino was able to finish the book and mail a copy to his mentor, Anton S. LaVey. Parts of it were worked into Church of Satan liturgies, but the theological idea of an entity in revolt against the cosmic norm and in a way related to us by the Gifting of Free Will didn't fit well into the Church of

Satan's Atheism with monster-movie aesthetics. Aquino's Working of Imagination could be a textbook case of Henry Corbins' notion of the imaginal:

There is a mode of knowledge which is intuitive, divinatory, combining the action of imagination and feeling, and which as such is the mode, essentially, of religious knowledge" (Henry Corbin, *Temple and Contemplation*)

A practical approach to the Prince of Darkness grew from this willful use of cognitive imagination or, to use the terminology of the Church of Satan and the Temple of Set, "Greater Black Magic." If we see the Gift of Set as a willful action that is an action of procreation, we see ourselves as having a potential to come into existence as Set did – through an act of self-creation using those parts of the psyche that are not bound by the laws of the physical universe. This leads to two questions: What was Set's motive in Giving the Gift? What is our ethical response to this Gift?

In traditional theology gods make men for the sake of worship. This notion belittles both god and man. Set is driven by necessity to create other minds in the universe. As psychologist Stephen Kosslyn has demonstrated minds do not arise from the action of our neural systems, but from the interaction of other minds. We humans, like our spiritual ancestor Set, extend our reasoning abilities and regulate and constructively employ our emotions through the minds of others. Minds do not grow by seeking unity with one another, but by interacting with one another. Set extended his mind, not by observing the clockwork of the universe, but by creating other minds in the only meaningful way – by giving other minds free will. Without free will other minds are not something to interact with, but simple extensions. Humans "serve" Set by refusing to serve.

The Gift in humans may be rejected. Humans may choose to deny individuality and seek union with the Cosmos – either by worshiping it in a Right Hand Path religion or studying it through the truth processes of science or art. Or humans may embrace the Gift and perform the action of exchange – using the Gift in such a manner that enriches the Coming Into Being of other Gifted beings. What Set asks of humans is to live extraordinary lives. By their deeds and speech, humans extend the reasoning ability and emotional sweep of one another and of Set. Since Setians perceive the Gift as being beyond the deterministic cosmos, they can use this Gift in various ways to transcend that Cosmos – not only in emotional responses (finding someone to Love), not only creatively, but also magically, causing things to occur in the universe that change its unfolding in ways that transcend its programming.

Humans religious duty is to understand the cosmos by using the tools of reason, and by altering its evolution. Setians call these actions Understanding and Being. These tether the Setian psyche to the Cosmos. Understanding, whether it comes form of the joys of science or simply learning the heart of another human being, keep the Setian from drifting inward to solipsism. "Being," or willfully changing the programming the part of the objective universe so that the unfolding of the Cosmos is changed, causes the actions of a Setian to continue in the objective universe long after he or she may be gone from that plane.

Most Setian activity is an oscillation between withdrawing from the universe (to seek and understand the Self) and return to the universe to make forceful changes in accordance with the Setians' desire. For some Setians if such actions are resonant enough with Set's Purpose of furthering the Gift in other humans, the Setian may perceive Set.

This perception of Set consecrates the human as a Priest or Priestess. This is not unity with Set, but a profound moment of empowerment wherein the human becomes liberated from the deterministic universe and takes on more of the characteristics of Set. The human comes into his inheritance. In this way the human's actions are less entangled with the momentum of the world. In this Mystery, Set is seen both as a transcendental figure, lying outside of the Cosmos, and an immanent figure who is interacting with His Priests. Set does not grant wishes or intervene in human affairs, but by creating a way of knowing Him, allows the human to achieve a specific and personal connection bound in space and time.

The goals of the Setian are like his Left Hand Path cousin in the Indian tradition. The Setian likes the withdrawal (nivritti) and return (pravitti) of the yogin. The Setian can obtain the bliss (bhaga) of Self-love, magical powers (siddhis), and liberation (jivan-mukti). The Setian's love (bhava) of his or her possible self and their love for the Giver of self-awareness leads to the devotion (bhakti) of leading a life that will inspire others to acts of self-creation. A Setian shows his love of Set by seeking pleasure, wealth, liberation, and ultimately immortality. The Setian needs to both understand and demonstrate to others the nature of consciousness, both through actions that defy arbitrary taboos as well as exalt consciousness though creativity. Every action that inspires others to greater deeds of self-creation is a moment of return.

Many find the actions of return to be too difficult. They find the withdrawal necessary and spend a short career in the Temple, leaving as an Adept. Thousands of people have passed through our doors this way. The harder part of the Work, expressing one's transformation in objective terms, appeals to the few who become our Priesthood.

The core of the Temple is small and growing but far exceeds the number of Priests and Priestesses of Set that ever lived in any historical period of Egypt.

How to Use This Book

When I began this book, I intended to write a sort of miscellany – gathering some articles from various publications and venues. I have written several hundred thousands of words about Setianism, and I wanted to share some of these words in a collected form both for Setians and non-Setians. I realized, however, that this action of return needed context. So I have added a few words in italics at the beginning of some of the pieces to help the reader understand the original intent of the words.

The book deals with interactions with Set (in *The Book of the Heb-Sed)*, interactions with the world (interviews and articles), articles for Setians (from the *Scroll of Set* and other sources – ritual texts, fiction, poetry and even college papers (to show Setian thinking is manifest in all aspects of an Initiate's life). The book is best read in small doses. The ideal reader will read a section, pause, and ask herself what she thinks of it. Are any of these ideas usable in my life? How would I test Setnakt's assumptions? As a collection of small writings, this book will work well for book clubs. It will also work for bibliomancy. Ask loudly, "What does Uncle Setnakt say in my current situation?" and open the book at random.

When you have read the book and mulled it over for a while, the following ritual may help you to insights. Gather a pitcher, a glass that is special to you in some way, a black candle, a bell, a piece of bread, a writing implement, and a piece of parchment. Fill the pitcher with a pleasant-tasting drink

Ring a Bell Nine Times for the Nine Wishes you are about to make

Light a Black Candle with these words: "In myself a flame of consciousness burns. For the flame there is only one Good – to burn longer and brighter. My experiences are the fuel, and I can gather other and better fuel. For the flame there is only one Evil – to go out. I welcome Setnakt's words to make my flame burn brighter and hotter and longer. I offer my deeds and words to the Flame-Giver for a day, that It may Teach me more about the Flame's Good. By this Flame I Wish to Understand myself better with reason and dream, desire and magic. I Wish that for Pleasure, Liberation, Magical Powers, and I Wish the same for Setnakt for his help with my Flame."

Place your left hand on the pitcher and say, "I have Wisdom within me that I have forgotten. I call it to memory. There is Wisdom outside of me I call to me from the furthest reaches of the Cosmos. There is Wisdom I will create and share with those I Love; I call forth its Coming Into Being."

Pour yourself a glass from the pitcher, say these words, and drink deeply. "For some, wisdom comes bringing Chaos and looks evil. Hail Vama Kali! Hail Hekate! For some, reason if full of Light, Lust, and Magic. Hail Apollo! Hail Dionysus! Hail Hermes! For some, Wisdom comes with a price. Hail Odhinn! Hail Prometheus! And in its truest form, it reveals the Self to the self. Hail Satan! Hail Shiva! Hail Saturn! Hail Set! Eleven is the number of Magic, Energy tending toward Change."

Take the bread in your hands, say these words, and eat it.

"I have read Setnakt's words. Now I will learn how one word leads to another word and nourish myself with my Wisdom. My dreams, my memories, my desires, my fears that I have overcome, my wonders that I will make – these become my immortal body freed from the clockwork universe. I eat my body and Become who I am."

Sit down and write the four questions you most wonder about in life. Then write down four things you really wish for. Say these words:

"In order to have universal knowledge, one must have power to hold this knowledge in one's heartmind. With these eight Wishes and the Wish-Granting Gem given to me by the Prince of Darkness, I will use what I have read and gain the Power to Know these things."

I add one question; write down the following:

"I will know the one thing that the Prince of Darkness Desires that I know."

"I send these Nine Things into the Fire. They vanish from the world and will reappear in my life in a year's time. I will have my wishes and my answers. I will prosper from Setnakt's words. The Flame-Giver shall gain his Nine Wishes; for as I do, It does."

Light the paper with your candle; burn it thoroughly.

Say, "I return the Black Flame to its Eternal Hidden Home."

Blow out the candle.

Ring the Bell for the Nine Wishes that the Prince of Darkness has made.

Say,

"The Work is Wrought through the Angle of Victory!"

The Book of the Heb-Sed

Less then two weeks after my Recognition to the Grade of Magister Templi, I received The Book of The Heb-Sed. *I told my Teacher Magus Stephen Edred Flowers about the Reception and otherwise kept Silent. I began a series of Workings in the Temple related to the idea of the Egyptian rebirth festival which Pharaohs underwent in the thirtieth year of their reign. The Workings lasted for the Years XXIX and XXX, during which time I Received a Command from Set to Re-Utter "Xeper" from the Order of Setne Khamuast, and I became High Priest. Here is a commentary I wrote for a few Initiates I gave the book to in the Year XXX.*

Book of the Heb-Sed

October 3, XXVIII (1993)

I had just been Recognized to the Fourth Degree in Sacramento. Ipsissimus James Lewis had performed the Ceremony. I had returned to my hometown of Amarillo to be with my mother, who was undergoing surgery. Mom had downplayed her illness and not told me that she was going to have the same sort of operation that had killed my father ten years before. Mom was deathly pale and drifted in and out of consciousness. When she was awake, she talked about fate and destiny, which are pretty odd topics for my mom. Although she later had an amazing recovery, things were pretty touch-and-go right then.

After a long day of sitting by her bedside, I excused myself to the parking lot of the hospital. I thought about the place. It happened to be on the section of land where her father had been a tenant farmer in the late Twenties/early Thirties, part of the Frying Pan Ranch. Heck, just north of where I stood was the small cave where she and her brother were trapped by a rattlesnake. In 1979 I began using the *same* cave for my neo-shamanic activities. Four years later my father died in the same hospital where my mother lay now. A lot of Wyrd for a small piece of land. I looked to the stars of the Thigh of Set, and I said, "If you have anything else to teach me, please tell me now. I don't know if I'll be back."

Words started falling like big, fluffy snowflakes into mind. I had never had such an experience. I drove a couple of miles to my mother's house and wrote them down on a yellow legal pad.

The Book is not a prophetic book such as the *Book of Coming Forth by Night* or the *Book of the Law.* It belongs to that class of Egyptian literature called *Sboyet*, or Wisdom literature that describes the Cosmos and gives moral precepts. I distributed it first to my Teacher, Magus Flowers, then later to the Masters of the Temple, then to the Priests, and finally to a very few Adepts. Using its principles as I Understood them, I began the Heb-Sed Working of the Year XXX to revitalize the Aeon of Set. Some of its byproducts have been my occult books, the Soa-Gild, the Order of Setne-Khamuast, and a growing fascination of Setians with time.

So in the jubilee year we are to meet again in Luxor, and through the Form of Playfulness does one X Become three, and an ancient formula open in a way as yet unknown to you.

When I got the book I knew Luxor had a big Temple, but I didn't know much about it. I knew there was link between Set and Amun – both in older sites like Ombos and Oasis sites like Kharga. Everything else I had to research.

Luxor has one of the oldest Temples of Egypt, Karnak. It belongs to the Hidden One (Amun). The Thirtieth Year (XXX) continues the pun from *The Book of Coming Forth by Night*. I had no idea that I would soon be re-Uttering the Xepera formula.

The Karnak Temple is a huge complex. Over 80,000 Egyptians worked for it or its fields. That would be one out of ten Egyptians. The Temple was mainly constructed in the Eighteenth and Nineteenth Dynasties – with most of its construction by Setian pharaohs of Dynasty XIX – and was used for nearly a thousand years. Its major festival was the Opet, an annual rebirth festival. The Pharaoh came and Opened the Mouth of the Amenopet, who lived in a totally hidden shrine. After calling down to earth the eternal hidden principle of Rebirth, the Pharaoh was empowered to perform an exchange with the more visible god of the temple Amun, who lived in a better known hall. The king offered pure (wab) water, and Amun made him pure (wab). The king offered fresh blossoms (renpyet), and Amun made him blossom (renpi-ti). The king burned incense (sendjer), and Amun made him a god (s'nedjer). The basic formula of becoming Set, who Opens the Mouth of the Gods, and then enacting the Hermetic "as above so below" went on here for about a thousand years. (See Lanny Bell's *The New Kingdom "Divine"*

Temple: The Example of Luxor in Temples of Ancient Egypt edited by Byron E. Shafer for more details.)

The first shrine at Karnak was a Heb-Sed shrine of Senusret I. Amenhotep III had placed blocks from that shrine in his own Heb-Sed shrine in the temple complex. His son Akhenaten had built a Heb-Sed shrine to block further building on the great Amen temple, which derailed the project for a while, but Seti I wrecked Akhenaten's shrines, hacked off names, and used the rubble to shore up the walls of Amenhotep's shrine. The first re-use of stone was to fuse the old with the new, the latter to kill Akhenaten's shrine – it's all in the placement.

Hatshepsut had added two obelisks to the complex celebrating her Heb-Sed and a large Pylon gate showing the god Set teaching her archery. When she became unpopular, the gate was taken apart.

R. A. Schwaller de Lubicz, the Magus Aor, based much of his study on this Temple – and created the books that shaped the early modern Temple of Set's ideas about Initiation and Egypt. "Aor" means Light in Hebrew, "inheritance" or "Thigh" in Egyptian.

Thou alone knowest that the Fourth blooming of Set has happened, and I command you to speak of this sparingly lest vigilance be relaxed. Always those of the Stone are tempted to the way of Hafiz.

Obtaining the Stone means receiving the Fourth Degree. Hafiz, the great Islamic scholar, never organized his teaching. Once one obtains Being, it is Needful to organize your teaching so that you do not Forget. If the Master does not make his teaching transpersonal, he will not make it strong enough in himself. If he does make it

39

transpersonal, Set's will is injected into the Cosmos and forces people to act on something beyond their accumulated past actions. Blooming (Renpyt) is a Renewal (Renpyt). The other three bloomings have been in the Archaic Period, the XIXth and XXth Dynasties, and Late Antiquity – about every 1500 years mankind seems to reach out to Set. *Ewige Blumenkraft*.

Thou has yet learned to open to me and as a foolish child seeks to avoid what the living Aion has prepared for thee, but this is true of all trapped in the cycles knowing not that they are the makers of time.

My dilemma as a human magician is that I can ask Set for Advice but then Hear what I want. The power of my accumulated actions – my Horus-side – may not empower me to Hear/Understand/Act on that which I have called to Earth.

The Aeon sets up situations in the world where the Horus-side and Set-side can Act as one. However, learning to see its subtle net of synchronicities requires a high level of awareness. One of the magics that all humans know is giving meaning to time – all Sleeping humans are unaware they have this power. If humans became aware of this power, they would be much happier.

Only my Jackals can Open the Way and great is the cost to them, and the living Aion often knows them not choosing them as sacrifice to its capricious goals.

The Egyptians called Ursa Minor Set's Jackal, and the clearest form of this god might be Sed, the jackal god who rules the Heb-Sed. There are people who are so deeply obsessed with digging up mysteries that they forget their day-to-day lives – examples might include MacGregor Mathers, Jack Parsons, and Ronald Keith Barrett. Jackals are not merely good or compulsive researchers, they are forced to work out their personal problems by causing everyone around them to enter into huge Workings lasting months or years. Often times bringers of woe to their families, and certainly great pains-in-the-butt, these people revive magic that sleeps but Shapes the world and load it with personal significance. Despite Gerald Massey and Kenneth Grant, "Shugal" is not *Hebrew* for jackal, nor does it mean "howler." Instead it means "burrower," referring to the grape-eating Syrian fox. The Hebrew word *shu'al* (through the Persian *schagal)* becomes our jackal, Grant's formula of Shugal = 333, is not indicated here. The gematria would be 331. Sorry to disapoint the Grant fans, although Setian Cabalists may note 3+3+1 = 7, the number of Set. The only gematria I have found for this book is 30 = Yod He Yod He = It Will Be, the formula of Neheh, and 28 Kaph (vau) Cheth Power or Teth Yod Teth Clay. I will discuss these numbers below.

Yet despise not the living Aion for it has no Archon save for the sign of the seven stars and the boiling waters. I have given it my Freedom and the power to Create its Advisers and Testers. It is dear to me and I have hidden Treasures for it in places you cannot imagine.

The Aeon isn't out to get you. You can't blame your bad luck on it; however, it gives those touched of it Freedom to make any circumstance an empowering one. In the Ritual of Opening the Mouth there are two figures, the Un Ra (Opener of the Mouth) and Semer-F (Friend). The Un Ra smites the corpse with three objects: the Seb Ur, the Thigh of Set made from meteoric iron; the Ur Hekau, a scepter shaped like Set; and the Pesh Khent blade, the tail of Set. The Un Ra is the stand-in for Set; the Semer-F who has Horus hair, is the stand-in for Horus. The formula is simple – the shocks of life may be turned into objects of Power – the Seb Ur gives authoritative speech (Hu) and army rations (also Hu). The Ur Hekau gives the oldest and strongest magic. The Pesh Khent bring a sense of permanent identity. In this scenario Horus is a friend, because he sets up the playing field. There is a fourth shock as well, before these well-known ones. During the Setian Renaissance, a Vision/Dream aspect was added to the litany. The sem priest has a vision (Qed), and after the vision tells craftsmen how to carve the Ka- statue. The sem priest warps himself in a leopard skin (iself a symbol of Set) , has a vision, awakens, says he has seen his father in all of his forms, and tells the craftsman how to shape the statue. He addresses each side of the block of stone as "My father" and then tells the craftsman which grid to cut (literally which "spider") and what contours to make (literally which "shadow"). Set's stand-in shapes the Ka, by visiting the farworld. (Scenes 9 and 10 in the Ceremony) Set has shaped your ka, so that the Shocks you get during your life can Awaken you.

Beware of this knowledge for you do not know its letter and measure and will seize dross. And doing so will cry, "Woe!"

It is easy to think that, since the Aeon creates its own advisors and testers, any tough situation is advice or testing. Sometimes we just don't need another learning situation – and if we put ourselves through too much, we've got no one to blame but ourselves.

Know that this too is a test I have set for you, for all of you who read these words. These are not profound visions of ringing words. These are simple things, the Roots of Stars, that I reveal to you and one other.

Simple to read; hard to know. This seventh verse mentions stars, showing that it is Set of the Seven stars speaking.

In its time and measure but not foreordained and foreweighted. Consider this, yet seek not Perfection for in imperfection canst thou do what the Forms may not and they too are but gem hues thrown forth by the Flame, thou knowest, but whose beautiful and terrible NAME only I can speak and then only in the cycles of My making, greater and more grandiose than those you now know how to make. Yet you will rise into these Cycles making them more myriad and manifold wondrous in your glorious strangeness. For you are the Children of imperfection made Perfect in your struggle. Love struggle and beauty for these Forms I always send forth first by speaking the NAME of my Beloved.

When Set starts up a world/age – he speaks the Name of the Black Flame, Victory. People desire it, form an image of it (Beauty) and work/fight/scrabble for it (Struggle). This sets up Life. We can create worlds the same way. One of the Forms of that Name in our time would be Indulgence, which creates Beauty and Struggle on a primal level in the human being. I once heard Robert Svoboda describe tantra, as the "art of discovering what you want and what you need to do to get it."

Those two could create all beauty of a sterile kind, oh Ovid, but I seek not to make shadows. Learn this Secret my Children and the Fourth Blossoming will be a rose to my Beloved's bower. Fail in this and you will join the endless crystals on my star shelves. Thou art indeed neither the oldest nor the last.

Life/Walhalla could be just unnatural desire and struggle against the inertia of the cosmos. Religion would then be simple self-improvement cults, or compensation cults – but Set is seeking something more. He does not want his Children to be ruled by Visions of Beauty they Struggle for. He wants us to Become like Him and transcend this world into cycles and time-ways beyond this world.

And your bones are of iron, and the double-headed wand is yours, and the NAME as perfectly as it may be Understood in time is yours, and the admonitions and the words of the prophets in their Books are yours. Yet you have still to seize upon greatness. Think not that this is easy.

The first three items are part of the Opening of the Mouth – the adze, the knife, and magic wand. The Books are of the First and Second Beasts and correspond to the Qen of the Sem priest. But even with these Treasures, we have not yet done what we might.

I know not disappointment, but Sadness I know for that is a state beyond you. Sadness is a puff of smoke between the Flame and the Shadow, and it is permitted to know it. From it is the Kharga wine.

Sadness exists between the world of Life and Black Flame. Overcoming cosmic sadness makes the Kharga Wine – the wine of the Oasis of Kharga known as the Ink Sutekh, the "Gift of Set." Kharga was also a big site for *homo erectus,* who left many of his hand-axes there. This eleventh verse refers to Will.

Know that having given the gift of freedom I know not what will become of thee. I exist between the possibilities of absolute knowing and the absolute Unknown and here I Work things through the centuries. Find this place of power and you will have the powers Belial hinted at but only dimly perceived.

Thou must change the nature of Perception itself -- this is the Great Work. One speaks for what is perceived in the veils created by the Flame. One spoke of the perceiver seeking to be perfect like the Flame. You are not pots to be fired.

Not yet.

Set does not know our future. But we can change the nature of Perception (in Egyptian Sia, literally "grasping," so that we can understand our life choices better. The Temple does not possess a perfect technology for this but may have such a method in the future. The verb Xem can refer to performing addition or to firing pots. The imperative "Xeper Ir Xem" could be rendered "Become Perfect!" The Hebrew word Tyt or clay has the gematria of 28, the number of verses in this book. The notion of pots, which are made of clay, shows up in the center of the book at verses 13 and 14.

Change the nature of Perception and you can solve the dilemma of Perfectibility. Be Proud of your pieces of string, and of seashells gathered on the beaches of foreign worlds, of what is Beautiful and worthless. Be afraid of what thou hast overlooked.

The Egyptian stellar afterlife held that one Became a star. The Akh was a blend of the Ba, the imperfect soul of Becoming, and the Ka, ageless impersonal soul of Being. This is different than Western Magic's idea of the Higher Self/HGA that is perfect and the poor human part of yourself. Only when the "higher" and "lower" are blended are you Pure, Fresh, and Deified. When you achieve this, all of the minutiae of your life become sacred, especially the souvenirs of Play.

There are Eyes thou knowest not of, windows which maybe found. Do not fear them for they will open to each what only the great Amung you have opened. Thou knowest not! Thou knowest not! Yet I Set speak to thee.

More magical Traditions will be unearthed by Setians. We will Open the Mouth of more Gods – and we will have a much higher level of Initiation. The idea that the average Setian hangs around four years, barely scratches the surface of Setian magic (and doesn't try anything else), and makes no real changes in themselves is gone. Long Desire is Coming Forth.

There is in this not a Word, but an infinitive waiting not for thee to proclaim but with these words for another to explain.

Only in this and in the Wall that Becomes a Door will you know that it is by my hand. And yet it is for each to find this. Only when these words open for each may scenes from another time and space be opened.

I suspect certain things but will not say them.

Thou did make the rent with the Spear. Becoming is the Way.

During the Spear of Wyrd Working in Hollywood, I took the Damned Spear and cut a hole into the realm of the psyche so that I could write about it. Boy that *one* has come back to me. Because of its connection with Loki, the OTr is the only Order that tricks its members; it hands them the controls of the Universe and says, "Go ahead, ask for it!"

Think not that thou knowest this because it is simple. In the simplest things I dwell.

The simple truths of one's life are one's personal runes.

At the times and places I have created are opportunities, but I do not lay them through time. I know not of Destiny having bequeathed that power not to the Living Aion, but directly to my children. For it is a true Sign of Love to create for one's descendants what one sees in the Beloved Flame. And the Flame whose Hidden NAME means Victory has given me a gift by giving to my Children what she

sees in me. Struggle. Struggle overcomes Fate.

Set procreates not by knocking up our mothers (no pigeon for the virgin), but by Willing that subjective beauty become part of their world. The Black Flame gives a Gift back to Set by giving his Children an inborn Vision of Set. Thus Set is both beyond us and within us.

And in those two circling round and round and roundabout again are the Secret pathways between Shadow and Flame made. And in these two and contemplating these two are points far apart in time and space made contiguous. This is a by-product of my Word and Seeing it clearly a new beginning, a Heb-Sed for those lost in the wasteland. Thus I create a new soa-gild not as an Order but as a secret - creation arising already in my Priesthood.

A simple thing this seems. Water in an Oasis is simple.

The interplay of Struggle and Fate creates paths directly to/from the Black Flame. One can interact non-locally with space-time through one's struggles – or, to put it another way, my battle here can help your battle over there if both are born of Xeper. When someone has transformed him- or herself enough to see this in action, a new level of interplay takes place.

One of my favorite quotes about the eb-Sed comes from Bryon E. Shaffer, "Elements of the ritual are known, but their exact sequence and content are a mystery (which the kings intended) and a topic of scholarly debate (which they did not)." Prince Setne Khamuast, who took the Heb-Sed to great sophistication, linked it with learning. On the inner doorway first pylon gate of the Ramesseum in Thebes, he portrayed his father Ramesses II setting enthroned at the sed festival. This scene that welcomed one to one of the one world's first libraries called "the healing place of the soul" showed the link between certain kinds of knowledge and renewal.

The Heb-Sed is the combination of two political events into a rebirth event. The political events were the "Appearance of the King of the North" and "Appearance of the King of the South" – where the king ran by a series of lunate markers – sort of an Egyptian rose bowl. "Hurray, the king is strong! We can go kick some Libyan butt!" It was probably an annual event – the annual rebirth later became the Opet, which actually used more flowers than the Rose Bowl, and needed 80,000 workers to pull off each year. Disney, eat your heart out . . .

The Heb-Sed combined the two races and added a sensory deprivation chamber so that the king's effective soul could then run through the sky.

It takes years to prepare for a Heb-Sed. Statues have to carved, buildings built, etc. The rite itself had many parts – purification (the king had been born pure but needed to regain purity) – and a good deal of magic – the foremen of magical crews and the "amulet men from Upper and Lower Egypt." The king visited the shrines of Set and Horus and received the four arrows of victory. The king shot arrows in four directions to protect Egypt and raised a Djed column. During these actions he is accompanied by a wolf-headed Wepwawet. Then the king is confined in a tiny space, wrapped in a symbolic placenta. Just as he had run through a magical model of Egypt, he now ran though the sky in a guided visualization.

R. O. Faulkner writes in "The King and the Star Religion and Pyramid Texts" (*The Journal of Near Eastern Studies* 1966, pg. 130) the relevant spell of this confinement:

O, king, free course is given to you by Horus, you flash as the lone star in the midst of the sky, you have grown wings as a great breasted falcon, as a hawk seen in the evening traversing the sky. May you cross the firmament by the waterway of Ra-Harkarhti , may Nut put her hand on you.

The Opener of the Mouth took the king out of the symbolic womb. Naked, save for his penis sheath, he would run the race that took possession of Egypt.

I imagine you're saying "So what?"

Here's what. In the Solar afterlife, prayers were said over your dead body to unite you with the sun. In the Osirisan afterlife, spells were said over your dead body to fool the stupid guards of the farworld into thinking that you were Osiris. In the stellar afterlife – you had to do the work while you were alive – work which included both practical things, like running a huge festival, and magical things, like learning how to have out-of-the-body experiences while buried in a fetal position wrapped in a cow's hide. The best quick guide to the Heb-Sed is Greg Reeder's "Running the Heb-Sed," *KMT Magazine*, 1994.

Soa, or Za, means a working crew. The reference is to the crews of Setian priests who tended the Oases and made magic to help desert-crossers. Set's priesthood died along the Nile in the XXIIth Dynasty – Setian priests were in the Oases even at the time of the Roman emperor Hadrian. In the Old Kingdom, there were five Zas – Horus, Set, Thoth, Green, and Little. On building projects they worked two days on the north side of a project, had a day off, then two days on the south. This works out that each Za gets ten day off in a month of 30 days, and a perfect work year is 360 days.

An Egyptian month had 30 days. Perhaps from the thirty toes of the scarab beetle, which explains the scarab spell in *The Book of Going Forth by Day* being number XXX – but more likely to make the right number of days for a 360-day year (plus five out-of-time days, the birthdays of Osiris, Horus, Set, Isis and Nepthys)

A Heb-Sed had 30 years.

Magistra H pointed out to me the Lunar and Saturnian aspects of the Heb-Sed festival.

As a child, a month is a long time. For an adult, months race by. To an immortal thirty years race by. The "month" of Saturn/Kronos is 29.5 years.

In the Year XXVIII when I received the Book of the Heb Sed, I wasn't thinking about "months of years" -- I was 35, and the Temple was 20. I certainly didn't think about the number of the year (28), nor did I count the number of paragraphs (28) in this Book until recently.   It has been said that the Khepra beetle's eggs take 28 days to hatch, which is why the First Beast made it his symbol of the Moon in his Tarot.

This is a network of Being through which much will be Seen.

Thou thought these words were to your glory, but they are not. Thou will put them away for years and return to them.

But when the tool is made clear the craftsman will be ready. Not just so for you, but to any who unlock this Mystery.

HU HO HA HUM

From Life to the Living Aion to Inspiration to the new Contemplation. What you

suspect you will not speak of.

The mantra with its following translation sums up the Initiatory path as revealed throughout the Book. It is influenced by both Indian and Runic roots, but holds a mystery – Life is continually opening Secret paths to the Black flame. HU is almost the same sound as Contemplation and a key to paragraph 22. Twenty-two is the Number of Bonds with Set: Do What Thou Wilt Shall Be The Whole Of The Law. Great Is The Might Of Set, Greater Still He Through Us. Hu is the Egyptian god of performative speech. Performative speech are those speech actions which change reality. For example if you say "I do" at your wedding, it changes things. If you say "I do" while walking in the park, nothing changes. The concept of "performative speech" came from grammarian/philosopher J. L. Austin (see his *How to Do Things with Words*).

Hu is the power that is given by Opening the Mouth. It puns with Hu, the word for food. Hu, as a god did not have a big cult in Egypt, but he had a whopping big statue called the Sphinx. Sri Harold Klemp, Spiritual Leader of Eckankar, notes, "Hu is the ancient name of God, a love song to God. When Soul has heard this sound, Soul yearns to go home." Eckankar uses the singing of Hu's name as a spiritual connection to the Heart of God. They sing the name Hu to draw closer to the Divine Being. I would say that "Hu" is the sound of the Ninth Angle releasing energy into the First Angle. (When Gini Scott Graham wrote her book about the Temple of Set, *The Magicians*, she renamed us the "Temple of Hu.") Hu is born of the blood of Ra's penis – when the King of the Gods is initiated into his Za-gild and circumcised, he gains the power of "performative speech." Khafre choose to carve his face as Hu, so that he could rule Egypt forever. The Egyptians themselves forgot this son of Ra, but Hu spoke to them – for example, choosing

Tuthmose IV to be king. The Sphinx's magic has attracted myth and story every time it reappears from the sand – Edgar Cayce, Madame Blavatsky, and current Egyptosophists have had tried their spells on it. It was and is a god of dreams, or as the Egyptians say "Resew(t)" an "awakening in the farworld."

Ha is an obscure Dynasty VI god, "Lord of the West."

THERE ARE OTHER PARTS OF COMMENTARY HERE AVAILABLE ONLY WITHIN THE TEMPLE OF SET

Of other things I am Silent.

Interview with *Egregore Magazine*

Talking with "Set Is Mighty"

It is Man the Magician who leads humanity toward the Unknown. Magic seeks to translate energies from one state of existence to another in accordance with an intention of the operative intelligence. So does science. The difference between Magician and Scientist lies in methods and materials, which sometimes are not so dissimilar as might appear. A circle-dance and a cyclotron have much in common. The symbolic tools of Magi and Mathematician both operate through Inner dimensions to cause Outer effects. Modern science has evolved far more ritual procedures in its techniques than ancient magicians ever dreamed of, and they all come from the same source – Man's curiosity concerning the Cosmos and what he has to do with it; human attempts at growing into Godhood. Ritual is a major tool of Magic and science alike for patterning the consciousness of its operatives so that calculable results may be obtained. Unhappily it is a sadly neglected tool, ill cared for and misunderstood.

-Badiou, A., *Peit manuel d'inesthétique.*

Meeting Don Webb was strange. I had expected a man that names himself after a XXth Dynasty Egyptian Pharaoh, Setnakt "Set Is Mighty," to have Egyptian jewelry or tattoos. Or worse yet, to have a Gothic aesthetic that would have matched a man thirty years his junior. Instead he wore an Hawaiian shirt and gifted me with the current issue of *Fantasy and Science Fiction,* in which he had a story. After he got his chai and made small talk about the dryness of Austin weather, we got down to business. He broke off occasionally to meet other people in the coffee shop and had a tendency to wander off into Austin stories. "All Texans are storytellers. Texas is a continuous magical narrative that we tell ourselves. Like all sorcery, ten percent sublime Truth and ninety percent bullshit. We only have problems with Texans that forget the ten percent, like George Bush." He asked me to send him transcripts by e-mail so that he could be more accurate with his quotes. "I have a reputation of being smart. Sadly, that may not be in the ten percent."

Per Webb's request, I allowed him to make frequent use of capitalization, which he feels reflects the archetypical nature of the topics discussed, and I feel reflects a clinging-to-occult style. We disagree where additional capitals lie in the ten-ninety percents.

Q.   How is Setian magic different than other magical systems?

A.   Setian magic is about managing synchronicities Setians, like most Western magicians since the Renaissance, are Neo-Platonists. We see change in the subjective universe, the realm of Forms, produces change in the objective universe, the realm of common perception. We understand that Desire is the key to changing the realm of Forms and that the manifestation of that change is an event with at least two "edges." One edge is the effect on the subjective universe – how does the magician feel and think about herself and the Cosmos after the event has occurred – and the other edge is the effect in the objective universe.

Take a simple example. Setian Boniface needs some money to go to Conclave. He creates a prosperity rite. He chooses the language of American Hoo Doo, for various personal reasons. He might just as well have used Runic magic, or sigil creation, etc. The rite conveys information to his unknown self – the timeless self that exists outside of the manifest realms. His desire has been strong, and the unknown self sends a message back. One side of this message is overhearing a great job opportunity while waiting in his dentist's office. Another side is having the confidence and daring to act on the overheard information. He gets the job – and this affects him in many ways. It creates a sense of empowerment; it causes him to grow more disciplined in manner; it causes him to deal with some of his baggage by being exposed to a new emotional environment. On the Objective edge, it gives him more money, opportunities for professional growth, and an airplane ticket to Munich. The event isn't a simple "make a wish and get a treat" happening. It changes him and requires balance and artistry to incorporate the change into his life.

The Setian realizes that Initiation may be defined as thinking the right thoughts at the right time, puts great care in managing these synchronicities – she knows the "dangerous" side of Black Magic (that is to say magic done for the Self) comes in the moment that she sees her own Will manifesting inside her and beyond her.

The Setian differs from the Chaos magician (and most Thelemites) that "belief is everything." The Setian does believe that Truth exists and that it is invariant; however, she does not believe in a single method to learn Truth by.

Setians must engage in what French philosopher Alain Badiou calls "truth-processes" – methods by which the self acquires truth. Badiou lists Science, Art, Love, and Politics – to which the Setian would add Magic. This is a Remanifestation of an older idea. For example, in the third book of the *Picatrix* there is an interesting dialogue (after an Apotheosis spell!), wherein Hermes asks Socrates how magic is like philosophy. Socrates replies that it is "Perfect Nature" and goes on to explain that the Magician becomes aligned with his Perfect Nature (here seen as a planetary spirit) in the same manner the philosopher is empowered by Truth – "It is this which opens the gates of the science; it is by this that the unknown is known; it is this which affects the open and hidden dimensions of the world. " Our method reflects these same intents, which Aquino rediscovered and I have provided a firmer scholarly link to through the Work of the Order of Setne Khamuast.

Q.   How does Desire play into Setian magic?

A.   The Right Hand Path in its purest form – southern Buddhism – rejects desire as the force that causes the Self to believe itself separate from the Cosmos. Dr. Aquino's magical theology elevated Desire to a central role – in his *Ceremony of the Nine Angles*, he described the Ninth Angle as being a flame that burns to the glory of desire. We embrace desire as the source not only for individuation, but also for meaning-making. As a consequence the Setian experience is one of gradually causing all lesser desires to be subsumed into one great desire for Becoming, of manifesting the sense of order of the unknown, timeless self into the chaos of this world. Each feat of Becoming is designed not to quench Desire, but to lead to a state of functioning in which stronger and more complex desires may be obtained. This differs from the Church of Satan's immanent path where Desire is seen as an expression of a mortal being subject to carnal decay – such desires are fleeting and ultimately fail with carnal self. The Setian seeks to refine and discover her Desire so that the Unmanifest part of her Self will exist in the realm of Becoming long after the physical part has failed.

One of the aspects of my High Priesthood had been to emphasize the importance of Life-work, finding a cause in the world that you infuse with your Will so that it serves your psyche much as the ancient Egyptian mummy was said to serve the Ka of its owner. One of my experiments with this was my part in the Recognition of Lilith Aquino's V° Word of Arkte, which consecrated her Life-work in the realm of animal protection into a vehicle of her Will that will endure on this world in a way much more magically potent than simple fame (or an expensive tomb at Forest Lawn). My use of her Work as a teaching moment of the idea of Initiation would be an example of VI° Work.

Q. What would you say are changes in the formula and practice of Setian Initiation that you brought into the Temple?

A. I draw much more strongly on anthropology and the social sciences than my predecessor did. In particular the work of Arnold Van Gennep and Victor Turner. Gennep provided a model of Initiation of Isolation-Liminality-Reintegration. The Temple of Set, because of our roots in the Church of Satan, which emphasized hedonism and social criticism (reactions to the Society of the Spectacle), were very good at the first two steps. Most Setians, horrified by the mindlessness and hypocrisy of society, had voluntarily withdrawn form it in some way – whether the simplistic adoption of a "Goth" or "Industrial" lifestyle or something as radical as subsistence farming. Once the forces of the human macro-cosmos are withdrawn, the forces of the Self become manifest. Strange things happen and the "Chinatown" phenomena that Robert Anton Wilson likes to write about. In the liminal state the arbitrary rules of the intersubjective universe are exposed as arbitrary, synchronicities abound, and magical might is confirmed by strange signals and omens.

Setians tended to park themselves in this phase of the process. They enjoyed weirdness for weirdness' sake, which lead to two problems. Firstly, most Setians burned out after about four years, just wanting a 'normal" life. Secondly, there isn't much power-taking in Liminality. You live paycheck to paycheck in your apartment at the beginning of the process, and you are still there at the end of the process. The third phase, Reintegration, means you take your transformed self back into the world, working at a stronger and more complex level. I helped Setians understand the goal of magic is not more magic, but to take areas of the world they initially loved but were estranged from. Setians began much longer stays in the Temple; education became a more recognized goal. Six percent of Setians have PhDs, which is a very different profile than when I joined, and most Setians were college dropouts (as I was at the time).

Victor Turner, a successor to Van Gennep, talked about the effects of Initiation on groups. Turner argues that groups of people that undergo initiatory processes at the same time form close bonds. As High Priest I utilized this by announcing themes the Temple could work on. I would chose broad, open-ended ideas (like the Ankh, the Monolith, etc.) and encourage people to explore this ritually. Strong friendships developed in the Temple, and without any enforcement or manipulation from the leadership, some of the economic synergy of Freemasonry came into being as well as a higher level of philosophical dialogue within the Temple. I modified the institutional structure of the Temple which had Pylons, groups of people exploring basic Setian Initiation (usually on a geographic basis) and Orders, groups of people that study and refine the Teachings of a Magister Templi, to also include Elements, group who co-operate in specialized study or coordinated social, political, cultural or magical actions upon the world. Examples would include groups for musicians, writers, martial artists, women's empowerment, graduate students, etc.

Q. What was the effect of the Utterance of Runa in the Temple?

A. In the Year XXIV, the Council of Nine Recognized the Runa, Word of Magus Stephen Edred Flowers. I had joined in XXIII, and I was at ground zero. The effects of Runa were huge, and I would like to point to three areas. During my High Priesthood, and especially in my actions of the Third, Fourth, Fifth and Sixth Degrees, I strongly taught Runa in the Temple. The three areas I wish to focus on are, firstly, that Runa ended modernist conceits that magic is undiscovered science; secondly, Runa emphasized an objective balance to subjective inquiries; and thirdly, Runa has emphasized objective results.

The Church of Satan's aesthetic largely comes from *Weird Tales* and *Unknown* – Twentieth Century fantasy magazines fond of the "magic is undiscovered science" approach. Since the Church of Satan emphasized magic as an expression of individuals rather than a tradition, magical theories did not involve traditional beings and forces. Magic was thought of as energy liberated from the psyche and subject to scientific laws. This differed little from New Age beliefs, and the Temple was attracted to the pseudo-sciences and simplistic popular metaphors of the Seventies and Eighties. Flowers' simple observation that systems that had worked in the past would work again partially drew attention to traditional approaches, and his academic background drew Setians to linguistic and anthropological theories of magic – particularly Dr. Stanley Tambiah's linguistic model.

The Temple has always favored a subjective approach to the subjective universe, influenced by one of Aquino's favorite philosophers, arch-idealist Fichte. The notion, which remains a central part of LHP ideology, is that the best guide to me is me. However, as humans we may shy away from what is painful to us, or difficult to understand, because of lack of experience. When a symbol system is chosen to help understand the daemonic and emotional selves, the magician must examine his blind spots. Flowers points out that symbol systems that have stood the test of time – the Runes or the Tarot, for example – will alert the magician to lacking areas in his development. If someone learning the Tarot says, "I don't get the Moon," it points to a blockage in their nature that can be explored and addressed, leading to both healing and empowerment.

Lastly, the Runes as an historical artifact communicate across time. Master carvers carved the stones, set them in public areas, and to communicate across generations. The notion of a masterpiece has become part of Setian culture. The Temple had thirteen published writers when last I checked, unlike the days when it was Dr. Aquino, Dr. Flowers, and me. The Temple now also has artists with galleyr shows – not just folks that show up at Conclave with pictures about the devil – jewelry makers, Setians creating retreats, etc.

Q.   What is your magical anthropology?

A.   When I joined the Temple, it relied strongly on Initiatory material from other systems. One of the books on our reading list was Peter Ouspensky's *The*

Psychology of Man's Possible Evolution, which outlined a three-center man – the stomach/physical center, heart/emotional center, and brain/mental center. I changed this model and provided an approach for each of the four centers.

The carnal center is the physical body. I suggested that it is, firstly, an altar to the psyche and that the Initiate must explore and broaden the ways her body can know pleasure. Secondly ,taking a tip from Indian Left Hand Path (particularly Indian alchemy), I advocated finding forceful ways to reverse the processes of entropy, disease, and old age. This is physical antinomianism.

The emotional center is the emotions we have been trained to feel, plus those that arise from our authentic experience. I advocated examining and removing material that is not your own but which had been forced upon you, using Crowley's methods to pairing images and sensations with their opposites. For your own material, seek to deepen it, and, taking a tip from Assagioli's Pyschosynthesis, work to make sure your emotions follow you, not that you follow your emotions.

The intellectual center needs training in logic and critical thinking on the one hand and training in creativity and lateral thinking on the other. The average person attracted to the occult is not a critical thinker, since the magical state is not a rational one; this has lead to the sad state of the occult sciences these days where to be a magician is (justifiably) equated with being a gullible fool.

The daimonic center is the result of such magic as you have perceived coming into your life. The other three centers may be said to exist in three parallel lines. We often mistake an emotion for a bodily sensation or an idea for an emotion because we have not learned to be self-observant. The daimonic center may be seen as a line running orthogonally to the other three. I advocate increasing the daimonic center through play and observation. The *daimon* of ancient Greece was seen to be a being below the perfected gods but beyond the limits of humankind. When the daimonic center is aligned for self-evolution and powered by a love of magic, all other centers (if working properly) will flourish in many ways – getting mysterious boosts from an interesting and beautiful life. My four-fold system also helps Setians understand the lack of coherence in the self and the need to Self-Create the Self. Xepera Xeper Xeperu.

Q.   What do you mean by your statement that "Magic is a Truth process"?

A. Most religious and philosophical systems understand that humans begin in ignorance. We are given a model of the world based on sense perception, received ideas, and notions deliberately crafted to make us feel or "think" in a certain way at a certain time. In our postmodern world there is no central paradigm that holds intelligent people together. When one stands against such a world by asserting that one's own reality is more authentic than the spectacles presented to us, intelligent people are presented with the choice of assuming either there is no reality save what we believe or that Truth is hard to get at. Chaos magicians choose the first; we choose the second. Setians distrust prepackaged realities (even those coming from other Setians) – so you can't hand them a text and say "read this!"

Setians are given a Need. In order for their magic to Work, they must discover real principles behind themselves and their cosmos in order to know what changes are possible and what are the most efficient methods of achieving those changes. The Setian seeks Truth he can verify by experience because each Truth leads to an empowerment of the Self – "Perfect Nature" from the *Picatrix* above. Humans have several areas wherein the process of dealing with ideas – Seeking after Forms – can yield Truth to them. Amung the Truth processes are Art, Love, Science, Politics, and (for the Setian) Magic. The "Truths" yielded by the processes are experiential Truths. For example, you can understand when I say, "It is better to have loved and lost then never to have loved at all." However, if you have had the experience alluded to in the words, your understanding is based on gaining Truth; if you have not had the experience, your understanding will be an intellectual one only. Truth processes expose the psyche to a reflection of itself that transcends the known levels of the four-fold human. At times the Truth processes of different sorts may come into a play – a successful love spell may yield Truth in the realms of both Magic and Love. Badiou calls these moments "sutures," when you gain Truths that hold you together. I prefer the Setian term Remanifestation, which refers to the deeper re-experiencing of a state already known on some level of being. These moments knit the human together and can be seen as a personal manifestation of Ouroboros or Leviathan.

Q. How are Gurdjieff's Work and the idea of "sutures" related in Setian practice?

A. Gurdjieff 's great gift to the Left Hand Path is to point out that the "Self" does not exist of its own. He helped make humans aware that, rather than a single Will working upon itself and the Cosmos, humans are a bundle of little wills. Such a collection makes change impossible on the human level – and the notion of immortality more of a curse than a promise. Gurdjieff used exercises in precision and self-awareness, cutting across the human centers, to create an artificial sense of Self that might grow into true Self with time and continued effort. My method is to use ecstatic perception of Truth to unify the parts of the Self. Unlike Gurdjieff, I propose there is a Self, however Unmanifest, that communicates with its Remanifested parts, mainly through Wonder.

In Gurdjieff's system, humans must find a School that directs the correct energies (Shocks) that welds the parts together. In my system, only those humans who by self-grace have begun their own Self-Creation can be aided by the School. Neither I, nor the Temple of Set, can teach a Self to Self-Create. We see this as a holy mystery, the Gift of Set. I teach that it is possible to pursue certain activities in the presence of others with similar pursuits and useful situations can arise that lead to the moments of suture. Just as the Setian learns to manage synchronicities, I have taught methods of group work to the Temple of Set that lead to large numbers of humans experiencing those synchronicities at the same time and therefore being able to have meaningful dialogue about them in a greater community dedicated to discussing methods of self advancement in all forms, from financial to spiritual to health, etc.

Q. What is the Work of the Order of Setne Khamuast?

A, The Order is named for the world's first Egyptologist and librarian, Rameses II's fourth son – Set-Is-Beautiful, A-Power-Manifests-in-Thebes, I began my magical order at a Working with the Order of the Trapezoid in the British Museum. The aim of the Order is to reclaim workable Initiatory and magical formulae from Egyptian, Middle Eastern, Greek, Mesopotamian, and African sources. Dr. Flowers has a threefold method which he used to remanifest the runic systems: Objective Analysis, Subjective Synthesis, Enactment. I added a fourth element Teaching. My students look for the best data they can find on a religious or magical system. Once they feel they have understood the system in its own terms, they take what they find beautiful and re-create it in culturally meaningful terms for their current needs, then they enact the magical system until they get results. Lastly, they must teach what they have done – firstly, inside the Temple and then into the greater world. Some have published as Setians. Others choose to put forth their findings in other ways – for example, essays in archaeological journals or even in Left Hand Path training manuals that do not have the ToS imprimatur. Others still have made their fourth phase of manifestation art and video.

One example of the Order is my best-selling *The Seven Faces of Darkness*, where I took the spells involving Set-Typhon from the Greek Magical Papyri and reworked them for use for the modern magician. On the one hand it provided a good basic spell book, but on a deeper level it enabled a modern human being to experience the magical essence of Set in the context of his life while understanding how this essence has expressed itself through time. The historical aspect of the Work of the Order gives the Self a suture that only comes from understanding that the world the Self is manifesting into is conditioned by those very magical currents that awakened their daimonic centers to start with. Using historical magic not only claims for the Self the very forces that made it, it Teaches the Truth of Self-Creation. This sort of suture, this experience of magic as a truth process, can only come through reenactment.

Q.   What is the purpose of your Initiatory writing?

A. The simple answer is to find people who are undergoing the Xeper process and help them find the Temple of Set. Self-Creation is always, at first, a daimonic affair. When you begin going against the stream of the world, you are attracted to images of revolt. This is your daimonic center awakening you. For example, when Europe began its Renaissance, it wasn't merely reason that created the new way of looking at the world. On a daimonic level the images of the old gods were needed – for a good example of this, see Godwin's *The Pagan Dream of the Renaissance*. People need certain images and magical formulae to ease the Need their daimonic centers possess – and unless that need is met with a blend of intellectual and emotional supports, you simply have human beings in pain that spend a few years spray-painting the word "Satan" on the backs of buildings until their fire of self dies down and they become the dead souls that maintain the world of illusion.

Most of the people that read my books won't seek out the Temple, but depending on how the great Need for my darker memes are, they will spread these ideas into the world – on the one hand making more art and material for Setians to draw from and on the other contributing a more free society that supports the notion of Self-Creation, which is the long-term goal of the species, whether you see it as Nietzsche's Over-Man or Ken Wilbur's integrated human. Setians may get there first, but my love for mankind prompts me to help others get there, too. In this I reflect the Will of my Patron. Great Is The Might Of Set, And Greater Still He Through Me.

Interview With Fringeware Review

I edited an issue of Fringeware Review *on magical antinomianism and the Left Hand Path in particular. Fringeware was a click-and-mortar bookstore in Austin, Texas, dedicated to Waking people up and giving them a good time. It sold erotica, brain toys, conspiracy theory stuff, and a great selection of literature. It has some nice traces left on the Web, especially the archive at The Laughing Bone*

https://sites.google.com/a/laughingbone.com/www/fringewareephemera

I initially was going to interview Dr. Michael Aquino, but he demurred – so I interviewed myself. I think I was tough but fair.

Set is Mighty:

An Interview within the Fane of Darkness

by

Don Webb

When I began the assignment of putting together *Fringeware Review #666*, I wanted to interview a real, radical practitioner of Black Magic. Not someone who was going through a Goth phase or whose connection with the Prince of Darkness was a fashion statement. I interviewed a "bishop" of the Temple of Set, an international initiatory organization in its nineteenth year of operation (by contrast, the Golden Dawn only lasted ten years). My bishop chose to be interviewed under his magical name of Setnakt, an Egyptian nominal sentence meaning "Set is Mighty." His titles are Magister Templi, Herald of the Order of the Trapezoid, and the Grand Master of the Order of Setne

Khamuast. The interview took place on October 16, which according to the Calendar of Cairo is the day Isis and Nepthys weep, for Set has slain Osiris. This is also the anniversary of Belzoni discovering the tomb of Seti I, the Pharaoh whose name means "Set's man."

DW. So what is Black Magic?

S. Black Magic is the process of changing one's subjective universe so that a proportional change will occur in the objective universe, depending on the passion and precision of the operator. The White Magician believes in some force outside him- or herself that can be manipulated. The Black Magician revels in his or her isolateness, knowing that they are ultimately the god of their own creation. The "black" of Satanism, the color of revolt against god, has become the "black" of Setianism – the color of the self-created god. Our crystallization of this process is in our watchword of Xeper (pronounced "Khefer"), an Egyptian sentence reading, "I have come into being." Our role model is Set, the principle of isolate intelligence.

DW. Do you worship Set?

S. Do you worship "Freedom" or "Evolution"? No, of course not. Let us say that Set might be viewed as a friend who represents the essence of the Left Hand Path to us. An individual's attitude toward Set is as dynamic or evolving as the principle of isolate intelligence itself. Of greater importance is the individual's attitude toward him- or herself, a mix of self-love and dissatisfaction that impels them to transform their lives into a process of Initiation, or structuring more and more of their activities to reflect and challenge the god they seek to become. Our symbol, the inverted Pentagram within a circle, has two points raised signifying the we hold Change and Creativity over rest and preservation.

DW. So why the trappings of conventional evil? Black robes, meetings at night, the love of diabolical imagery?

S. Antinomianism is important. We begin by breaking the social conventions. Breaking these small fetters gives us both the practice and the energy to break the greater fetters – those self-imposed limitations which hinder our development. Because of dedication to civilization (like Plato says in the *Phaedrus:* "You must forgive me dear friend: I'm a lover of learning; and trees and open country won't teach me anything, whereas men in the town do"), we honor the laws of men. There has been a great deal of nonsense written about "Satanic" crime, and despite this being debunked so well in *In Pursuit of Satan* by Robert D. Hicks and other books, people are more likely to ascribe criminal intent to us rather than face the greater challenge we give society. The challenge to think. When we make people think, we are expanding that principle of isolate intelligence. The ultimate good of that principle is its preservation and expansion.

DW. You have this string of titles you gave me. I'm always a little leery of titles and authority generally. What is all this? The "Order of the Trapezoid"?

S. When you contacted me for this interview, you described yourself as "Contributing Editor of *Fringeware Review*" and mentioned that you had over 200 articles and stories published, in six languages, I believe you said. I think all effective people are prideful of being in some ways. The important thing in the world is not the title, but the effectiveness of the individual. If an intellect is not to be dissolved by the cascades of eternity, it must create and cause change. In order to cause change, it must change itself. The Temple offers a graded structure to test one's skills against, but that's only for training purposes. The real test of the magician is , how many titles he can get but the twofold challenge of changing his or her subjective universe and the objective universe around him. The Temple's degree system is an illustrative Working of the principle that isolate intelligence is not omnipotent; it must work to produce changes in the universe. This again reflects our lack of worship to an omnipotent god like the fictional Jehovah but emulation of a finite force (like Set) that is opposed to divine mindlessness.

Orders represent specialized study groups in the Temple. I would imagine our best-known Order is the Order of the Vampyre, mentioned in Norine Dresser's book *American Vampires*. An Order represents an attempt to explain and further the initiation of a Fourth Degree, a MagisterTempli; it is a remanifestation of their initiation. The Order of the Trapezoid existed originally in our evolutionary predecessor, the Church of Satan, as a secret society to produce world change. The Order still serves this function of changing social and political reality so that the magicians and philosophers of today will not be meat for the burning stakes. But, in addition, the Order of the Trapezoid investigates certain aspects of time, and cognition, in order to influence the past and future as well. Beyond this, I cannot say and merely refer the interested individual to Stephen E. Flowers' book *Fire and Ice*, wherein some of the electrical practices of our Order are discussed.

DW. You're not fooling me with this. I know that the Order of the Trapezoid has a pretty sinister heritage.

S. You mean you think we're Nazis. The order in its present form was re-cast into the world by Michael Aquino in a Working at the Hall of the Dead of Himmler's Castle. In fact, he consecrated an SS blade. I know because I've used the dagger myself in magical Workings. Considering the Order has gays, Jews, and blacks among its membership, if we're Nazis, we're pretty damn bad at it. No, our agenda has nothing to do with racial or biological "triumphs of the will." Breeding programs are for domestic animals. The ruthless desire to change the world, we may share with the Nazis, but we aren't interested in racial or national lines – nor does the crude power of the boot fascinate us. The greatest magicians are like flute players in the desert night. Unseen we walk among you, and when you feel that you are working your own wonders, you are working ours.

Of course, we are not egotistic enough to think that we ourselves are not products of the magical workings of others. One of the benefits of the Temple is its 300-book reading list, which can help the seeker discover the forces that shaped him and her (and therefore begin to pull their own strings). One of the ideas associated with the principle of isolate intelligence is that it is not omniscient; it must work hard to see clearly. Question everything you encounter. In fact, here's a gift for you. When encountering anything, try this formula: Awaken, See, Act. The first assumes you've fallen asleep, the second that it takes work to find out what's really going on, and the third is that, knowing, the real you *must* act on it. Now, if you want become a philosopher, try this formula on a situation you believe you are familiar with.

One of the most interesting aspects of the Order of the Trapezoid is its exploration of geometry and architecture. There is precious little work on the effect of certain angles upon consciousness; although certainly the eerie phrases of H. P. Lovecraft's fiction might provide the useful hint or two. With the coming of recreational mathematics, such as programs to generate fractals for your home computer, there are whole varieties of magic only now being invented, and you can be sure that the Order of the Trapezoid will be there, in fact, *is* there.

DW: Does Set do something for you? Answer prayers, grant boons?

S. The mythological lens we have created to view the Real processes places Set in the position of a Giver of the Gift of isolate awareness. We would say that when life reached a stage of sufficient complexity to hold this Gift that the Gift became manifest here. Set's only Gift to us is the awareness that we are apart from the Cosmos and responsible for our own decisions. Followers of the Right Hand Path try to destroy this Gift by seeking unity with the cosmos. We honor the Gift by reveling in our selfhood. Remember that the

Egyptian god Set slew two opponents. Firstly, Osiris, the principle of death, and secondly, Apep,the principle of divine mindlessness. Our choice of Set is part of an illustrative working of our principles. We seek independent immortality and self- deification through the practice of magic in an initiatory schema. The Gift of knowing our separateness is all we need. It is perfect, that it is to say, complete.

DW. What about mystic revelations?

S. I think Umberto Eco's remark in *The Name of the Rose* that mystics seek to communicate with the forces that we, the magicians, control, sums up our approach to mysticism. There is a place for direct knowledge, what Plato called *noesis*, but that pinnacle is only to be sought after much training in logic and rationality. Greater Black Magic contains the secret of obtaining *noesis*. *Noesis* is hard work, not something in a capsule or in reading a cheap paperback.

Xeper is the change that takes places through the long search for the mysteries of the Self. If you think of the knights of the Graal, Xeper would not be the Graal, but the long road traveled. Fortunately, an application of your mind can sometimes give glimpses of that which is often sought but seldom found. The principle of isolate intelligence can inform or teach those possessed of it. The glimpses are only useful as targets for what the psyche can become. Strengthening self-awareness comes not through isolation and meditation, but through exposure and expression of the self. Even Crowley knew that. In the *Book of the Law*: "Ye shall find them at rule, at victorious armies, at all the joy: and there shall be in them a joy a million times greater joy than this."

DW. Do you think the world would be better if everyone joined the Temple of Set?

S. Absolutely not. The Temple – like all human institutions – is created as a tool for our own development. If it's not the tool for you, don't even think about it. It may be a damn fine screwdriver, but what you may need are pruning shears. The Temple provides a place for discourse for people seeking after the mystery of their own becoming. I wouldn't recommend it to anyone who hasn't tried more conventional philosophies and finds them wanting. I think Gurdjieff was probably right, that humans need a School in order to "escape" from their self-imposed trance, but as Schools go, the Temple is fairly rough. No guided curriculum, no spoon-fed lessons. The real prizes in life are the ones you win for your self. To give more (if possible) would be to take.

We provide forums for discussion, opportunities for group magical work, and a really great get-together. After creating the space, all the magic rises from the individuals.

DW. So how can I have a Setian experience? How do I find the Temple of Set?

S. I don't know if you want a Setian experience, but the real seeker is always welcome. The presence of isolate intelligence in the flesh is necessary.

Like most secret societies, the Temple of Set is very hard to contact. You would have to look up our phone number in the San Francisco phone book (under "Churches: Satanic").

Or you could write for our General Information letter from the Temple of Set, POB 470307, San Francisco, CA 94147. Some of our members also post on alt.Satanism. If you really want a Setian experience, find some dark quiet place, and see if you can still your mind from all the ads you heard on TV last week. Then ask yourself, calmly and clearly: "Am I ready to foreswear mindlessness, accept the pleasures and pains of existence, to seek after the mystery of my own creation? Do I dare my own answers, or do I accept the answers of others?" If you decide that the text of others is an affront to yourself – but more importantly if you're filled with a sense of wonder at yourself and the Cosmos – maybe you should write for the General Information Letter. If you decide that it's better to stick with the scriptures of your fathers, I wish you well, because I wish happiness for all men save those who would torment and hinder me. If you decide that you feel silly for even taking a moment of your life to ask about it, you deserve the life you get.

DW. *I didn't know what to make of this man. I hade expected talk about incantations and magical formula, or why Set was a better god than YHVH, or at least something about Heavy Metal music. Instead, he made me think about my life, and I do not know that that made me happy. And yet, I have to say that the men that have ever really made me think are too damn few in number.*

Concerning Words

I wrote the following to help the Temple of Set evaluate Words, the magical tool of Magi. The Gift of Set has many facets. As humans align themselves with that Gift, some humans will come to see one aspect of that Gift as a doorway to experiencing the Gift while in the flesh. If the doorway can be articulated as a single word, and that word has certain properties, the Council of Nine may Recognize it as a Word by a unanimous vote. The Work of the Magus is the combination of his or her Work as a Magister Templi and the Will of Set. Set may be seen as an immanent deity in the whispering of Words into the ears of potential Magi.

This article reflects my understanding of Words, the Utterances of Magi, in the context of the Aeon of Set. It is neither more nor less than my understanding and should not be viewed as a Temple document. I hope other Masters may wish to focus their own thoughts on this matter.

The article will deal with five things: the Reception of the Word, the Magus/Maga, the nature of a Word, the Utterance of the Word, and the Understanding of a Word by Masters of the Temple. It will focus on Setian practice but will have comparative examples from magical systems of Late Antiquity, the Indian system of sonic theology, and European and American philosophical systems. It is not written to evaluate any particular Utterance or concept that may be Coming Into Being. It does not address the concept of a Word outside of Setian thinking and practice except tangentially.

The Aeon of Set is the Working of the Prince of Darkness upon the Earth at this time. Its primary components are human beings, who both individually and interdepedently refine, evolve, and spread Xeper by thought, word, and deed. A

principle component of this Working is the Temple of Set.

One of the more obvious ways the Temple of Set aids the Prince of Darkness is by

the Recognition of Words, which are easily accessed imperatives for actions that are seen

to refine, evolve, and spread Xeper across space and time. The Temple is not an infallible

source of Recognition, nor can the Masters of Temple completely foresee the effects of

adding another tool to enhance free will.

The founding Root of the Temple is, was, and shall be the Utterance of Xeper by

Michael A. Aquino. The principle of Xeper holds the notion that an Idea that is becoming

manifest as an evolving idea has the Power to create its own field to grow in. It will

displace other less vital ideas and will require of the humans who use it to engage in self-

development in all areas of Being. The task of the Temple is to distinguish

useful concepts and tools from Words. The former bespeak the wisdom and excellence of

the humans who have created them from their struggles. The latter represent an

enlivening influence from the Price of Darkness though a human. The latter must be

subjected to great scrutiny and testing. This process of scrutiny provides very useful

material for the continued development and empowering of the Masters of the Temple.

The Reception of a Word

The Prince of Darkness is not *deus absconditus*. He is perceived as aware of the

human struggle and capable of Divine Intervention in such ways that do not hinder the

evolution and expression of Free Will. He provides Gifts, which are seen as amplifications of his Gift to the human race of Self-modifying Isolate Intelligence. This gifting is accomplished by the giving of Words to enable motivated humans useful imperatives to aid in their own quest for immortality, power, and pleasure.

The Prince, through magic, presents Words to certain humans at certain times. As each Word represents an unbinding of the conditioned order of the Cosmos, its effects can be estimated and guessed at – but all of the consequences cannot be known. Each human takes in certain risk as he or she adds to possibilities of Becoming.

Words are not the property of the human who Utters them. The human, and his or her methods, are part of the meaning of the Word. This distinguishes the life teaching of a Master of the Temple. A Master's Teaching is a Remanifestation of him- or herself. A Word is the Remanifestation of the Will of the Prince.

Amung the tests that a Master must use in testing an Utterance is discovering the story of its Reception. Each Word will have a unique path of Coming Into Being, and that path will be resonant with the Master's apprehension of the Prince of Darkness.

The Magus or Maga

The Magush was the Persian fire-priest. Zoroaster had determined that there was not a Cosmos full of Gods. There was one god – the God of the Mind. Every concept in the divine world illuminated a portion of this god, just as the human had a Self that wore many faces (from greedy to Noble, wonder-filled to angry). The symbol of the Mind in the physical world was the *fire*. The fire-priest, because of his knowledge of the Cosmos as well as the force that displaced the laws of the Cosmos as needed, was a perfect example of what Victor Turner calls the *ritual specialist*. In other words, the fire-priest knew what you needed to do to Change things.

The notion of a dynamic divine world symbolized by *fire* entered the Greek world through Heraclitus, who also invested us with the philosophy of Becoming. The Magush became the Greek "Magos" and our word "Magus."

The Magus knows how to bring about Change at a price.

He or she can teach you to perform magic, but you have dedicate your soul to his or her Word. When you pay your price, you gain a new Tool for manifesting and expressing your psyche – and all you manifest or express will further the Will of the Prince of Darkness,

The Magus or Maga can only Hear the Word if he or she has a great Need for it. The struggles of the Magus to understand the Word are the magical sacrifice that empowers it. The need to understand (and therefore Experience) the Word requires more than one human's experience. The Magus is therefore compelled to speak. The process of Recognition may empower the Magus by drawing attention to his words and deeds but is not necessary for the Magus' Task.

Philo of Alexandria, wishing to portray Moses as being more important than Plato, said that a Magus needed a Word, a Book, and a Law.

Since Aleister Crowley, the Law has come to be seen as an imperative phrase that tells Seekers something they must Do but also describes an existing Process in the Cosmos. It is both prescriptive and descriptive. The Utterance of a Law does not bring any new thing into being, but brings an anticipatory Awareness of that thing. To use that problem from your beginning philosophy class – if there is no one in a forest to hear a tree fall, it does not make a sound – the phenomenon that described the law did not happen because no was listening. But now that the Law has come to humans, they will not only listen for the phenomena, but will be out felling trees.

The Book of the Magus is that collection of magical techniques that can allow the Seeker to perceive certain aspects of the Word which cannot be accessed by ordinary consciousness. This includes mystic communions, noetic understandings, or "hands-on" experience with the Creation of the Universe. Setian jargon for the latter is Greater Black Magic.

In many mythological systems – Hebrew, Aztec, Germanic, Egyptian, etc. – the universe is presumed to be full of chaotic stuff before a conscious god acts upon it to Create the ordered Cosmos. In such systems the god's Plan would be equivalent to the Word, Book, and Law – and it should be noted that when the god has done these Deeds, the Cosmos will still contain Mysteries for him, which will provide the material for his further conscious development.

In other systems – the Vedic and the Gnostic, for example – the universe is Created by the Word. In these systems the Word would equate with the Magus' Word, and the Book and Law are those things that come into being as a sort of operating manual.

Either mythological model can be used to understand the Setian view of the Magus as Creator and the Word as Tool.

The Nature of a Word

A Word is a twofold thing. One part is a label for a group or constellation of ideas. For example we all "know" what we mean when we say, "Capitalism," "Communism," "Democracy," and "Racism." We use some Words to define who we are, and others to define who we are not. We can gain motivation when we think about Words – because Words separate us from the mechanical universe. A rock never worries if it is a good enough Capitalist, nor does a locust think badly about ants to be Racist. All Words are ways that human beings align themselves with movements – and as such with the power and limitation of groups.

At their worst Words can lead to sleep. For example, we all know other people that are so self-identified with their label "Mormon" or "Democrat" or "Feminist" that they have ceased thinking. We also know people that think a good deal about their label and – by bringing it to their highest level of thinking – shape themselves and their world in good ways (or at least in ways that appear good to them).

Words are also a magical act. In a psyche-centric religion such as the Temple of Set, the Word of an individual's self-creation is the word of cosmic creation. The sentient observer and actor is what is created, and his or her actions and perceptions of the Cosmos create his or her world. Purely philosophical systems see the contemplation of Words as a method of purifying the soul, or even causing an Ascent into powerful regions. Such systems generally look upon ritual enactments of the Words as a "lower" or "superstitious" system. Most magical systems usually think that Words are keys to power only through a magical technology. The Setian system (in many ways harkening back to Chaldean theurgy) sees both approaches as complimentary and necessary. Thus we are neither wholly magicians nor philosophers but a unique modern synthesis cast forth as a Left Hand Path school. In a later article I will address why this synthesis not only is, but must be, manifest in a Left Hand Path School – even though the term itself (from the Sanskrit *vama marg*) is less than a thousand years old

Words do not have to be new concepts. All Words represent principles that are part of the multifaceted process of individuation. Words have to be something that is Needed in the world as a living and evolving concept. On a human scale, Words are concepts that need to be activated in the world. They cannot be so broad that they are too large to define – such as "Justice" or "Liberty" or "Meaning." They should exist as part of natural language; if they are simply made-up nonsense, there is no chance of exploring the Word beyond the Magus' writing and saying. The act of seeking out the meaning in context should itself provide an enriching process for the users of the Word. Words do not have to be from an exotic lexicon (i.e., they do not have to be Greek, Norse, Egyptian, etc.), but they have to be from unusual discourse so that they may be appreciated. This is an example of the Setian idea of the magical tool. You could use the knife you carve the turkey with to be your magical dagger, but the Inspiration a special tool will have will increase your power. Likewise, common language may suffice for holding most of the straightforward meaning of the Word as a philosophical imperative, but the full magical force of the Word needs something that sets it aside from average discourse.

The Utterance of a Word appeals to the approach of Reason over Tradition. The Word should provide new thought that displaces older patterns and destroys/renews a Tradition. The mythic model is that of Jesus, who came to fulfill the law, and thereby create a new law. Words are resisted emotionally because they threaten Tradition. Words are tested by seeing if they further Reason. Words have areas of growth and friction (that leads to strength) on all levels of reality. In the emotional realm Words challenge long-held beliefs and also create and destroy alliances. (Matthew 10:35). In the intellectual realm, Words (like mental concepts) must be tested by reason and debate – and will grow when one human seeks to teach/share the word with another. In the physical realm, writing, broadcasting, etc., must spread the Word. This requires money, effort, development of talents and so forth. In the daemonic realms the Word must cast out collections of energy from other Words - and must provide such magical experiences that those who rally under Its banner shall be able to empower and protect their numbers against the forces of stupidity.

The Utterance of a Word

The world is filled with self-help and how-to-do-magic books. It seems that almost every struggle or problem you may have has been figured out by somebody, who will gladly tell you what to do in order to fix your sorry self, blast your way to mega-bucks, or finally hook up with Bootsy Collins. And, wonder of wonders, the authors of these books just plain know better than we do. They have articulated a formula; does this not make them Magi?

We do not live in a purely intellectual universe where only ideas count. Nor do we live in a world of things where no ideas have any place. We dwell in a reality that is both physical and mental, not two realities. Change in the one reality comes by the interaction of planning and deed, thought and hazard, trial and error. The Magus does not float outside of the world, dropping helpful hints to us mere mortals. The Magus struggles, has victories and defeats – and in order for both him and us to profit, we must watch, judge help, wonder at, and occasionally be glad we aren't her or him.

The Utterance of a Word consists not only of the Magus' words, but also of his deeds, his Signs, and his Wonders. We have to watch and evaluate. We have to decide if it will further us to be part of his Rituals. We have to decide would it help out our friends or family if we exposed them to some (or all) of the Word. We may decide that we want to buy a copy of his book for the library of our college, or we may decide to challenge him to a debate on an e-mail list, or we may decide to perform our own Illustrative Working to see if we can see what he Sees. Some will be moved to resist the Magus, and his Utterance may grow stronger by overcoming an obstacle. Others may fall in love with him, or take him to Thanksgiving dinner, or put a blog about his ideas in their native Korean.

All things become part of the Utterance, which soon grows beyond the control of the Magus. Some will purposively not understand and by spreading their misunderstandings set up patterns of resistance that the Magus' followers will deal with for decades. Others may misunderstand but feel so righteous in their misunderstanding that they challenge the Magus on his own Word. Others will mock the idea of a Word as the Will of the Prince of Darkness, and still others will accept that notion with such blind religiosity as to hypnotize themselves.

The Temple seeks to aid the human with an Utterance. It can help him or her to Understand that the Word is or is not from the Prince of Darkness. It can provide resistance to its Coming Into Being by the formal Recognition process – Words are nominated by the High Priest and need a unanimous vote of the Council of Nine.

The Master of the Temple Understands the Word

Words are easily accessible imperatives. They tell you to Do something. The Master of the Temple is involved in integrating, understanding, and expressing himself. The Master has achieved a level of self-sufficiency from the Universe. The Master can take the universe on his or her own terms. To grow, the Master must cause the Universe to relive certain aspects of his life. This is an extroverted form of samasati meditation. Allan Bennett had taught the First Beast this method. In Remanifesting his or her life, the Master experiences triumphs of the art of his existence.

The Master, having reached a level of self-understanding neither falsely proud nor falsely humble, can reliably receive magical communication from the Cosmos. The Master can evaluate mysterious signs without self-serving or facile explanations.

An apparent Curse falls upon a very few Masters. The material of their lives does not supply them with the knowledge, luck, or magical method they need for a particular Need. This Need, for example, the crisis of the Church of Satan in Year X, causes the master to Seek an answer. This process is an act of magical memory wherein one discovers the moment a certain Sign was presented to him or her. The reception is a Willed deed wherein a principle presented to the human is made into a channel for the Prince of Darkness' Will. The moment of first "hearing" is not what makes one a Magus – Aquino did not become a Magus reading Budge; Crowley did not achieve the grade in Cairo; Flowers was not elevated during his car ride in the Year IX. When the outer stressor forces the Master of the Temple, he or she must abandon what has been their life (i.e., Words kill Tradition) in order to deal with the outer world.

Other Masters have the ability to evaluate the Word. They can judge magical signs. At their best they are not moved by their feelings toward their fellow human (Magister Billy-Bob has been a member twenty years; this is a reward," or "I hate that woman; she spilled Jell-O on my shoe at the San Francisco Conclave"). The Master evaluates the Word on two poles. "Can I use this Word in my own life?" and "Can I understand this Word in the development of the philosophy of the Temple of Set?" This level of dual thinking personal-greedy/impersonal-wise is one of the marks of the Master.

There is an allure of the Grade for those not in it. When watching a football game, we do fancy ourselves the one carrying the ball – when he makes a touchdown. We may not envy him when he is tackled, fumbles, or has no personal life. For those possessed of the Grade, there is little allure. It is humbling. All of your students seem to Understand things better then you, all of your failures are known, and no feels that they have the least barrier toward criticizing you. The imbalance of becoming an expression of the Will of the Prince of Darkness has a heavy toll. The Master of the Temple has the relationship that people dream of when they seek to become magicians. The Magus has bought his ticket. At the best, he is riding on a roller coaster. At the worst, the *Hindenburg* or the *R101*.

Questions to Consider

Interacting with a Word is a process of discovering principles of consciousness,

Self-discovery, releasing of magical energies, and communing with the Will of the Prince of Darkness. You can learn a great deal by discovering that a particular concept is a good tool and not a Word. Some Words will open to you at once; others will be very slow to reveal themselves to you. The Words that are the Sun and Moon to your best friend may be tiny, dim stars for you. Here are some questions that may help you in determining if a certain utterance is or is not a Word:

1. Is the Word (and its Law) descriptive? Can you see example in myth, history, and people you know wherein the principle described helped them get ahead in the Cosmos?

2. Is the Word (and its Law) prescriptive? Does it tell you something you should Do? Can you see a situation in your life that the Word would point a path of action?

3. Is it simple enough to grasp quickly but subtle enough so that one could spend a lifetime working out its refinements?

4. Does it resonate with and expand the philosophy of the Temple of Set?

5. Would you feel comfortable with the idea of performing a ritual to help you Understand the Word in your life?

6. Could you describe its philosophical principles to someone without using the jargon of the Temple of Set? Words are a medium by which the Will of Set interacts with the

world. Not only should they be accessible to all levels of Setians, but they should be understandable to intelligent people.

7. Can you understand (at least in broad terms) how it relates to other Words of the Aeon?

8. Does the Word exist as an idea on its merit and not simply a subsection of an existing Word?

9. Once you have Heard the Word, does your mind and heart return to it often? Are your dreams, deeds, and thoughts drawn to it by no effort on your part?

(A nod to my Teacher)

Hsueh

I always encourage Setians to see themselves as the beginning group of what will become a world religion. I fight against the notion to see us as the last fruit on the Crowley tree, and one of my methods is to introduce the "Words" of Magi that do not appear on Crowley's list. In this early writing (note that is pre-cell phone) I discuss the Word of Confucius.

Confucianism is concerned with Harmony as a means to Liberation. For the Confucian, the way out of the toil and disappointment of everyday life is to learn a series of mental disciplines to effect Harmony. The Confucian trains himself to know the path of greatest Harmony. Once this very tough training occurs, a certain creative species of freedom descends upon the practitioner. No matter what bad thing the world hands him, he is able to choose a path that matches his skills with the needs of the task. This type of lifelong training is called Hsueh. Hsueh is usually translated "Learning" although it can be translated "imitation" or even "development." The thing to be imitated is usually the exemplary experience of the master. The Confucian knew that true Initiation only rarely came from books but was found by the Eye, Ear, or Hand. The preferred method of book learning was to read the autobiographies of masters.

The Setian too seeks this sort of Liberation. He or she must cultivate the mental disciplines that allow him or her to change every situation into one of pleasurable challenge. All of us in our magical quests have the fleeting idea that someday everything will be all right, our loved ones won't die, our cars will never be in accidents, and we will never know a minute's ill-health. The chances of all things working so well, even in the lives of the most powerful magicians is so small as to be nil. So what the Setian must seek to do is to cultivate the habits of mind that tend to turn day-to-day life into a form of Play. This training includes cultivating a sense of humor – one of the most obvious manifestations of the Black Flame in the world – reading the biographies of men and women we admire, and lastly, paying attention to how we got out of difficulties.

The latter may look so unmagical as to be ignored. We're great at writing up how we do the Vorspiele, but often miss the point on real-life power. Let's say your car broke down recently as did Priestess W. We got out of the situation so easily, that it was worth making magical notes on.

1. The car broke down in a very busy road, but next to a large parking lot. I got out and started pushing immediately – no time for denial or worrying.

2. Priestess W--- was out of the car and calling AAA within a minute. She didn't ask if she could use the phone.

3. We inventoried the car for fun things to do. Like all smart people that respect themselves, we had books to read.

4. We worked out a strategy for accomplishing our original mission of feeding a friend's cats and dog. This required a little lateral thinking; we had to break through ideas that we had to go to the auto repair place, which would be closed, or back to our house, which would make us have to start again.

5. After feeding the livestock we called a cab, and a pleasant, funny, good-looking cabbie drove us home.

6. Total time for the problem: 45 minutes. Time to have done the deed without problem: 25 minutes. In fact it didn't stop any of our later activities.

Now, what's worth studying? One, we didn't waste time on denial. Two, we had ways of avoiding boredom and anxiety at our fingertips. Three, we made it into a problem-solving exercise (How do we feed the animals and get home?). In short, we did good, and we rewarded ourselves for it in various ways. The rewards are as important as the recapitulation because they install the habits of mind that make use of the luck the magic generates.

Now, if we had had an awful evening, it wouldn't be worth programming it into our minds. If we were occultniks, we would merely be proud of power – the tow truck was ten minutes away, the cabbie so nice, etc. But as magicians who seek Liberation - from the Subjective anguish from the World of Horrors as well as Luck in the Objective realm, this was a time for Hsueh.

You can probably think of a similar adventure in your own life, and can share this idea with your Pylon.

"When engaged in Hsueh one must keep on pursuing and searching until one arrives at a spot completely roadless and blocked from all directions: only in such a place can one gradually find the true beginning of the road. The road has to be found by one's self." Ch'en Chia-mo (1521-1599)

If you want to read more about the concept of Hsueh, try *The Confucian's Progress* by Pei-Yi Wu, Princeton University Press, 1990.

Lovecraft

In the early days of the Church of Satan, editor Mike Resnick suggested to Anton LaVey that he should use his vast collection of Weird Tales *and* Unknown *to spice up Church of Satan liturgies. Anton asked Magister Caverni Michael Aquino to create a pair of Lovecraftian rituals for the* Satanic Rituals. *Aquino's rituals offered the notion that some humans simply had more Otherness in them, which is why they were drawn to the Dark. This is an example of the imaginal Work that Aquino started with the* Diabolicon *furthering the notion that we humans are the Children of Otherness. With Aquino's Lovecraftian Work in America and Kenneth Grant's Lovecraftian musings as part of his Set-Typhon Work in the United Kingdom , Lovecraft became part of the Left Hand Path in the West. I have been in Lovecraft's thrall since my brothers gave me* The Colour Out of Space and Other Tales *the day they found out they weren't going to Vietnam. I have written many tales in the Lovecraftian vein. In this article I discussed Lovecraft as my Hero in the Hero-Emulation practice of the Order of the Trapezoid.*

Howard Phillips Lovecraft

Knight of the Primacy of Imagination

". . . More luminous for thee the vernal grass

More magically dark the Druid stone

And in the mind thou art for ever shown

As in a magic glass;

And from the spirit's page thy runes never pass."

From "To Howard Phillips Lovecraft"

by Clark Ashton Smith

I have been drawn to, transformed by, and in all ways enchanted with the life and literature of Howard Phillips Lovecraft (1890-1937). His mode of life and art – the former determined by the latter – were and are objects of scorn and puzzlement. He did not hold court with the ways of the world, but despite a short life, chronic poverty, illness, and only the worst of all possible literary venues, managed to create an effect on both low and high culture in the English-speaking world, introduce new philosophical concepts, and determine the magical aesthetic of the Order of the Trapezoid. That his works are treated as "real" by occultniks of the poorest stripe and by money-grubbing sensationalists who created the "Satanic panic" of the 1980s would have been for him (as it is for me) a source of greatest scorn for the human animal.

I am drawn to Lovecraft for his bravery, his antinomianism, his understanding of the transformative power of the object (especially the book) that linked the realms of imagination and reality, his sense of the cosmic, and finally, above all, a unifying of his insistence on the primacy of the imagination. Now, I beg my readers to note that this is only the *briefest* introduction to Lovecraft's fictional themes and practice and their influence. I hope that if his words have moved you, you might seek out some of the books I suggest.

Lovecraft's fiction was primarily presented in *Weird Tales* magazine, which published all but four of his major pieces. A secondary source of income for Lovecraft was the revisions of the manuscripts of other authors who were primarily *Weird Tales* writers, which enabled him to salt their mines with references to his own imaginative universe. In addition to these streams, several writers, beginning with Frank Belknap Long, began using and contributing to Lovecraft's Mythos. The effect that this had was truly Weird on his audience. With each issue of the magazine the names of the deities would begin to have an effect on the readership. These names would begin to have evocative/emotional effects on the reader – which were strengthened by two narrative strategies. Firstly, the names of strange gods were presented in an inconsistent form – sometimes benign, sometimes terrible. Even Cthulhu, Lovecraft's best known bogey from "The Call of Cthulhu," receives benign mention in "The Strange High House in the Mist."

This evasive/evocative approach, which Lovecraftian critic Steven J. Mariconda (following the critical lead of Wolfgang Iser and Stanley Fish) has characterized as "reader-response," is an essentially magical technique. Any magician in an initiating society is aware of how her or his thinking of the entities and names used changes with time. The second strategy, which produces a "weird" or becoming, was Lovecraft's effort at making the Cthulhu Mythos fiction appear secondary or derived. He created a number of fictional texts, such as the *Necronomicon* or the *Pnakotic Manuscripts*, as triggering devices for his readers. The trigger works as follows: the reader is reading the tale, the hero reading a text partially concealed. Suddenly, the reader has the frisson of glimpsing a partially obscured part of his own imagination. Lovecraft pushed this technique by seeding the tales of other writers with the forbidden books, and encouraging his friends to drop these references throughout their own texts. This illusion of the reality of these books convinced many *Weird T*ales readers of their existence, as well as many sampling the Cthulhu Mythos today.

Lovecraft produced copious letters, about a tenth of which have been published in a five-volume set, as well as poems and articles – but it is his fiction that has had the greatest impact on the world. His public writing career spanned 18 years, from 1917 to 1935. His first public tales were the "The Tomb" and "Dagon."

"The Tomb" is a bit of a heavy-handed ghost story in which a young man realizes that he is not part of the modern world (in which he is sickly and scholarly), but in reality he is displaced from an idealized past where he is a lusty boisterous fellow. The end of the tale is a vision of redemption that he may be buried in the tomb of the family he spiritually belongs to. The image of a sickly scholarly type was the one that Lovecraft - cultivated for all of his correspondents – in fact not a true image. The idea of a redemptive return to the past, connected with fear and pleasure, is one that fills the beginning of his work.

The second tale, "Dagon," concerns the encounter with a vast pagan sea god that seeks after the narrator. This tale represents the fundamental Lovecraftian structure – if you seek after the mysteries, they will seek after you. The tale also contains what most people fault in Lovecraft's fiction – the rational narrator writing about his demise up to the last minute. People who don't like Lovecraft say, "Why don't those people get up and run away?" not realizing that the things they run from are internal.

In 1918 Lovecraft wrote "Polaris." This product of the second year introduced the bipolar horror of the past/present. The pole star causes the living narrator to remember the events of 26,000 years ago when he fell asleep at guard duty and allowed the North to fall to the Eskimo. The star that lured him to sleep then now keeps him perpetually awake. This bipolar force impelling the past and the present is a common theme to many of the tales and is a perfect description of the force that magicians reviving the Great Tradition feel in this century. One of the greatest of them chose his magical name from this tale.

1919 saw the beginning of a fairly steady production of fiction. Of the seven or so tales produced that year, the most important is "The Statement of Randolph Carter." Presented as a legal statement to an unnamed police authority, Randolph Carter explains the death of his friend Warren. Randolph is Lovecraft – his magical persona, if you will. He witnesses his friend's descent into a tomb and discovers the latter's death by remote sensing. These images of distance shows that Lovecraft wasn't ready himself to face the depths of his own imagination. Lovecraft recorded that the story had come to him from a dream.

1920 had fourteen tales, the most important being the prose poem "Nyarlathotep." Bruce Sterling once described this as "the first virtual reality" tale. Like "The Statement of Randolph Carter," it had its origin in a dream. A terrible traveling con-man out of Egypt produces frightening and glorious visions for his audience, who find themselves transported to a strangely altered world after their encounter. Nyarlathotep is described as having risen out of the darkness of twenty-six centuries ago; that would date to the Twenty-fifth Dynasty of Egypt, when the Stele of Revealing was written. The name means "Nyarla is Pleased." There is no Egyptian god named Nyarla, but the Dogon name

"Nya," meaning "stellar," does provide a bit of a magical tickle. Above all, Nyarlathotep is a symbol of an experience that changes the one who experiences it. He is therefore seen as a messenger or initiator – a bringer of Understanding (magical knowledge) that changes he or she who grasps it.

1921 was another seven-story year. Of particular note was "The Music of Erich Zann." The nameless narrator in an unnamed city (Paris is hinted at), discovers that the mute violinist above him plays weird and unearthly harmonies that attract and also hold at bay strange forces in the night. Erich Zann attempts to pass the secret of his music to the narrator, but forces snatch the pages away. All the narrator is left with is the notion of a sound, not of this world, which resonates with another reality. It is a typical Lovecraftian idea – a memory so real it cannot be forgotten and so alien that it cannot be acted upon. In short, a sort of reverse existentialism.

1922 had yet again seven tales. The most interesting tale Lovecraft wrote in his sixth year was "Hypnos." Another nameless narrator encounters a silent initiator on the streets of London. The initiator leads the narrator through a series of dreams, where they both experience revelation after revelation. The narrator draws back from the knowledge beyond, but the initiator continues his quest. He achieves apotheosis or death -- for he is transformed into a bust bearing the name, HYPNOS.

1923 had little fiction, but for the first time Lovecraft's characters begin to be more than passive observers. "The Rats in the Wall" is a lengthy tale about a man who actively seeks to discover the secret of his ancestors. Brave and decisive, Delapoer shows a manliness in this world which is lacking in previous tales. Nevertheless, the secret of his family overtakes him, and he fulfills their dreadful pattern of cannibalism in the depths beneath the castle. The standard Lovecraftian motif of the-mythic-past-is-the-future is strongly in place here; an interesting addition is the fact that Delapoer is ultimately descended from something other than human. This begins to displace Lovecraft's characters a bit more from the world. Not only are they drawn to the past, but to a nonhuman past.

1924 was a bad year for HPL with only three tales. The best of these was "Imprisoned with the Pharaohs," which was ghost written for Harry Houdini. Houdini was the hero of the piece and therefore escaped to tell the tale without being eaten by Hrumachis, whose horrifying secret he had glimpsed beneath the pyramid of Cheops.

1925 was also sterile with a mere three tales. "The Horror at Red Hook" united his fiction with figures of conventional demonology. The purpose of consorting with demons is made clear; it is not merely the pleasures of the demon-wife, but the prospect of personal immortality that draws the magician on. The Past, the Outside, the Other – bringing these into the soul overcomes the much weaker here-and-now.

1926 was a year of regeneration. Eight stories were produced this year, three of them key to Lovecraft's artistic concepts. "The Call of Cthulhu" introduces the notion that there are beings, gods perhaps, whose life cycles and cosmic purposes are so vast that human history is a mere footnote. These vast beings sleep in a huge city of R'lyeh, which has a frightening nonhuman geometry. Their High Priest, Cthulhu, sends out dreams to cause humans to act in strange ways to prepare the cosmos for their return. Cthulhu has cultists in strange places, but can reach into the minds of others – sensitive souls like artists. Like many of Lovecraft's stories, this too began as a dream, of an artist showing a clay sculpture still wet – yet claiming it was older than Babylon or Egypt. The story is a triumph of narrative structure that would have made Henry James jealous. It is told in a series of nested tales; at the center the nesting is nine layers deep, where Professor Webb says the awful formula, "Ph'nglui mglw'nafh Cthulhu R'lyeh wgah'nagl fhtagn." (In his house at R'lyeh dead Cthulhu waits dreaming.) The horror of Cthulhu is that he is an accurate depiction of the human psyche, which has purposes larger than the here-and-now and is seldom awakened. This story is one of the best descriptions of numinous terror available to man.

The other two very strong tales which come from this time are two Randolph Carter pieces, "The Silver Key" and *The Dream-Quest of Unknown Kadath.* The first deals with Randolph Carter's urge for an ultramundane life, which he gains by acting in accordance with an entity beyond any set of space-time known as Yog-Sototh. This tale and the novel *The Dream-Quest of Unknown Kadath* both introduce the urge to go to another world as an heroic urge, and like all such urges they produce great becoming in the hero as he can obtain only *images* of his quest. In the novel, Randolph Carter seeks to discover the secret of earth's gods, finds that he is descended from them, and – even more to his horror – has transcended them by his questing. This heroic motif can be said to be Lovecraft's own quest for the fabulous as well.

In 1927 Lovecraft wrote what he considered to be his best tale, "The Colour Out of Space." This tale of a color that cannot be described is again one of Lovecraft's nested narratives. The narrator, having seen a strangely wasted area of the countryside, goes to

seek a crazy old man named Ammi Pierce, who then tells him of the destruction of the-
(ironically named) Gardner family. The color had come with a meteorite; it was a strange

living thing, alien to nature that longed to return to its place of origin. To do so it sapped

every living thing in its presence, a powerful metaphor for the estranged human psyche

which must use up all of its life to transform itself according to its innate unnatural

patterns. As always with Lovecraft, the closer he is writing to real but hidden human

experience, the more memorable his tales are. Like most of Lovecraft's fiction, the

tension exists between human interests – the Gardner family and the ultramundane,

which is indifferent to them. Here the mythic past, which becomes also the color's future,

has become perfectly nonhuman.

In 1928, Lovecraft penned his second-best-known tale, (after "The Call of

Cthulhu") "The Dunwich Horror." This is the story of two half-human brothers of the

Whately clan who have a new mission. Instead of trying to return to their nonhuman past,

they desire nothing short of opening the Earth to their nonhuman progenitor Yog-Sototh.

This tale changes longing into action, and like any religious reformers, these brothers die

martyr deaths. Wilbur dies seeking access to the *Necronomicon*, which would open the

gate to the otherness that his father represents. Wilbur's unnamed brother dies in a mock

crucifixion scene, which had been prophesied before his birth. The tale is a long send-up

of the Christianity that Lovecraft despised, with Wilbur's invisible, monstrous brother as

Jesus. It is without a doubt the funniest thing that Lovecraft ever wrote.

The year 1929 saw only revision work from Lovecraft. The tale he wrote for

Zealia Bishop, "The Mound," began the cementing together of all of his themes: the

Cthulhu Mythos gods, both of his creation and others, exist here; the idea of secret history involving the geologic layers of the earth and the nested narrative are demonstrated.

1930 had the keystone tale of the Cthulhu Mythos, "The Whisperer in the Darkness." Albert N. Wilmarth, folklorist, is contacted by Henry W. Akeley, who claims that beings from Yuggoth were tormenting him at his rural Vermont home. Eventually the narrator is lured to the home, where Akeley claims that there has been a mistake – really the fungi from Yuggoth are our friends. Akeley is hidden in darkness and begins a psychological torture of Wilmarth, mentioning every Mythos concept he can, from Frank Belknap Long's Hounds of Tindalos to Clark Ashton Smith's Tsathoggua. Wilmarth is invited to give up terrestrial life and join Akeley and others as a living brain in a cylinder – to be flown endlessly from sphere to sphere. But in the end Wilmarth discovers the whole affair to be a ghastly practical joke – since he has not been dealing with Akeley at all, but a brain in a cylinder playing Akeley's part. This story is one of Lovecraft's most unsatisfying, apparently written only to patch things together.

1931 had Lovecraft's second stab at the novel, *At the Mountains of Madness*, an investigation of prehuman ruins in Antarctica. The narrator's party discovers the frozen corpses of the Old Ones. The hero of this tale is not any of the individuals involved, but the long description of the rise and fall of the Old Ones, whose bioengineering caused all the life on this planet to evolve, and whose blind pride allowed them to be wiped out by their own creations. This is one of the first ecological novels, and like most of them will no doubt fail to wake mankind up.

1932 had two transdimensional fantasies, "The Dreams in the Witch House" –
which tied together witchcraft, other dimensions, architecture, and dreaming as methods
of prolonging life – and "Through the Gates of the Silver Key," which dealt with
Randolph Carter's brief return from the other dimensions he had spent a lifetime in. Both
posit that human life can be extended by living outside of time but that nostalgia for
human life brings the sorcerer back from time to time. These stories have a more positive
view on the bipolarity of human concerns and the indifference of the ultramundane.
Lovecraft seems to be reconciling and synthesizing the day-to-day life's pleasures and the
vast possibilities of time and space. Both of these tales were set in real-world cities,
Salem and New Orleans, as opposed to the fictional Arkham.

1933 was marked by some of his least interesting revision work, as though the
synthesis begun in 1932 took too much from his imagination.

In 1934 Lovecraft created his utopia. Typical of his distrust of humankind, it was
the nonhuman world of the Great Race. In "The Shadow Out of Time" he envisioned a
race of cone-shaped half-animal/half-vegetable beings called the Great Race. These
entities had one purpose – the pursuit of knowledge. They could send their minds into the
bodies of any species at any time and then return to report to their fellows. They were
esteemed for the strength of their mind and, as most critics fail to notice, for their ability
at fantasy. Sexless, eternal, curious, they represented all of Lovecraft's values, yet they
also return to their home to share their discoveries. This utopian vision was the final
synthesis of Lovecraft's themes.

In 1935, he wrote "The Haunter of the Dark" as a favor to the young Robert

Bloch. Set in real-world Providence, it tells of Robert Blake's discovery of the Starry

Wisdom Church. He actively seeks after the mystery of the Church and discovers that

they were in possession of an angular gateway – a dark gem called the Shinning

Trapezohedron – which opens the way for the materialization of Nyarlathotep into this

world. The Messenger and the Seeker unite. Just as in "Dagon," the worried seeker writes

with horror as the god comes to him, describing the changes of his consciousness until

the last minute of terror (or transcendence).

Lovecraft's themes dominated his life. He was like his heroes, seeking a return to

an idealized past. He avoided any intrusion in his world, kept his shutters drawn, and

avoided outside employment like the plague. On one occasion he refused a job in

Chicago since the city had no Victorian buildings. He spent far more time writing letters

than stories – and far more time idly dreaming than anything else. There are no doubt

hundreds – maybe thousands – like him in most college towns. But Lovecraft's dreaming,

and his communication of it to his friends, served as a sort of initiation. Many of his

correspondents were initiated into writing from him – Robert Bloch, Frank Belknap

Long, Fritz Leiber, and Harry Kuttner. Many of his themes live on in such modern

masters as Thomas Ligotti, Bruce Sterling, Brian C. Hands, and Alan Moore (ans lesser

lights like myself as well). One of his disciples, the late August Derleth, created an entire

publishing house to keep the master's work in print, calling it Arkham House after

Lovecraft's favorite fictional city. The films, the dissertations, the rock groups, the

comics, the role-playing games, art, even magical tributes such as "The Call to Cthulhu"

in the *Satanic Rituals*, or recent articles in *Gnosis*, could make an essay ten times as long

as this and scarcely cover the field. I'll list a few books at the end to help the Seeker. But all of this– all of it – is because Dreaming came first.

You see. Lovecraft died of stomach cancer and malnutrition. Writing, then as now, doesn't pay very much. He died, after a horrible wasting period, on March 15, 1937. Despite his great pain and emaciated condition, he charmed the nurses of Jane Brown Memorial Hospital with his politeness and courage. He spent the last few days of his life making copious notes on his physical condition in the hope that it would be of aid to future physicians.

Selected Bibliography:

The Dunwich Horror and Others by H. P. Lovecraft. Sauk City, Wisconsin: Arkham House, 1963. Most of the best work.

At the Mountains of Madness and Other Novels by H. P. Lovecraft. Sauk City, Wisconsin: Arkham House, 1964.

Dagon and Other Macabre Tales by H.P. Lovecraft. Sauk City, Wisconsin: Arkham House, 1965.

The Horror in the Museum and Other Revisions by H. P. Lovecraft .Sauk City, Wisconsin: Arkham House, 1970. this is a collection of Lovecraft's revision work that appeared under other names – a study in how to plant your fictional motifs in others' work.

H.P. Lovecraft: Four Decades of Criticism, edited by S. T. Joshi. Athens: Ohio University Press, 1980. Best scholarly overview of early Lovecraft criticism. The essays by Wetzel and Leiber are particularly recommended for their magical content.

H. P. Lovecraft: A Critical Study by Donald R. Burleson. Westport, Connecticut : Greenwood Press, 1983. This is a good historical overview to Lovecraft's life with reference to his fiction. Good information on how the fiction transformed the man; a great magical study.

Lovecraft: Disturbing the Universe by Donald R. Burleson. Lexington, Kentucky: The University of Kentucky Press, 1990. Has great linguistic analysis of Lovecraft. This is the practical manual for fictioneers seeking to use skald-craft in their work.

The Starry Wisdom: a Tribute to H. P. Lovecraft, edited by D. M. Mitchell. London: Creation Books, 1994. A collection of modern tales inspired by Lovecraft's writings. Of particular interest to magicians are stories by Alan Moore, J. G. Ballard, William S. Burroughs, Peter Smith, Henry Wessels, and Don Webb.

"Lovecraftian Ritual" by Michael A. Aquino, *Nyctalops* #13 (May 1977). This is the greatest magical tribute to HPL, an example of encoding his themes in such a way that the utopian nonhuman vision might be obtained through personal self-transformation on this Earth. These are the background notes for the Lovecraftian rituals Michael A. Aquino prepared for *The Satanic Rituals,* and the fullness of their effect on the warp and weave of reality is an ongoing area of investigation within the Order of the Trapezoid of the Temple of Set.

How we View Egypt

When I joined the Temple of Set it had the typical demographic of occult groups –
mainly men with some college, but no degree. This population is attracted to belief
systems that bolster the egos with the notion of elitism but don't cause them to question
the need to reintegrate into society by getting a college degree. I too was a college
dropout, but with four published books. With the encouragement of my wife I
reintegrated into society by enrolling at the University of Texas. In Dr. Nethercutt's
Egyptology class I wrote about the way we view Egypt by focusing on a specific papyrus,
"The Tale of the Two Brothers" This is a story about Set in his Bull form, the Bull of
Ombos. This paper shows how moderns use the idea of Egypt to further their agendas, a
practice Setians call Lesser Black Magic. I share this paper with you both for its mythic
content (it is a story of Set) but also to show how Setian thinking influences academic
pursuits. The demographic of the Temple has changed to show a more practically
empowered group, with 6% of the Temple holding doctorial degrees.

How We View Egypt: An Experiment

This is a story of a story. Like the hero of its story, this story has many
transformations. I think it has come to mean many things because it is a good story. The
story tells of Bata becoming a eunuch, a dead man, a bull, a pair of trees, a crown prince,
a pharaoh, and finally an immortal star.

Once upon a time a scribe named In-na had to write a story that would entertain a young Prince, who would later grow up to be Seti II. The kid had had a hard time of it. His dad Merneptah had had his mother killed for treachery. Then after dad died, a usurper took the throne for awhile. His older brother Sitptah had regained the throne and made the young Prince the "royal son of Kush" – that is, gave him the gold-rich region of Nubia to rule over, which had been a key to pharaonic power during the XIXth Dynasty.

Now, In-na, who worked for the treasurer, was no fool. It would be a good idea to get in good with this Prince. After all, everyone knew, Nubia one day, Ramessestown the next. So he customized the story. He took a very old Egyptian pastoral god named "Soul of the Bread" who had been assimilated into Set, the patron of the young Prince, and made him the hero. Then he made him have a bad mother that the Pharaoh had to kill off. Oh, he added that on Bata's rise to power he was "royal son of Kush." Then he wrote a whopping great tale of shape-shifting and adventure. He gave it to the royal prince. It was a learned piece, and why not – just a few years before the Prince Setne had created the world's first library, and Egyptian literary culture was doing quite well. Of course, the last thing he did was sign his name very nicely so the young Prince might remember him. (The story was flattery.)

Whether or not Seti II read it, we don't know. But somebody scribbled a shopping list on the outside of the roll: "great loaves – 17, sets of provisions – 50, loaves for the temples – 48." (The story was on scrap paper)

But the scroll was put away. Maybe it wound up, as did many scrolls, in the place of hiding the royal mummies at Deir el-Bahri. Many papyri wound up there to be sold to Europeans in the Nineteenth Century. Anyway, it was filched and sold and wound up in

Rome. A wealthy French widow wanders by and sees it. Just a few years before, one of her countrymen had deciphered the language of the ancient Egyptians, and papyri were changed overnight from fuel to a speculative commodity. Perhaps the little Italian man did not know what he was selling? It had to be worth something, it was 18.666 feet long. Madam d'Orbiney buys it cheap and attempts to sell it dear. Unfortunately, the French still had a depressed economy, and she wouldn't sell it to the filthy British, who bought every Egyptian thing they could lay their imperialist hands on. (The story was an unsuccessful investment.)

1857, d'Orbiney dies, and her relatives aren't as picky as to where they make their money. They sell it to the British Museum, and various publications come out. The British are very interested in showing that Egypt, which they run, is the source of later ideas like Judaism. This is a standard practice of empires, going back to Alexander, who wanted to promote his fabulous tourist draw of the "Seven Wonders of the World." In 1895 Charles Moldenke published his translation of the papyrus with notes (humorously) suggesting that Moses had studied at the University of Heliopolis, where he read the story and then later plagiarized it for the story of Genesis 39. This established the non-religious basis of Jewish scripture, an important Victorian rationalist goal, as well as the historical depth of the sophomore literature survey course. (The story helped paved the way for rationalism,)

The French, however, wanted to make Egypt the culture that just stole things from other cultures (hmm, I wonder who they were thinking of?) François Lenormant proved (in 1874) that the text was the Attis myth in Egyptian clothing. (The story was emblematic of the British rape of the world, which the French could have done better).

In 1913 Otto Rank, Freud's protégé, surprisingly found the tale of Bata to be the story of Oedipal conflict. Bata's mother figure had come on to him, after all, and the self-castration is the equivalent to Oedipus' self-blinding. Apparently Bata had thought about it. (The story shows Freud is smart).

This Freudian nonsense was done away with. Bernard Sledzianowski, writing in 1973, showed that the story is a healthy tale of integration. Bata was merely confronting an *anima* figure in his brother's wife. The painful transformations make him into an integrated being. (The story shows Jung is smart).

As recently as 1986 Leonard Lesko explains the story to us. Its deep misogynism reflects an Egyptian hatred of strong queens of the early Eighteenth Dynasty. (The story is useful for feminist readings of Egypt).

In 1988 the Black Classic Press republished Moldenke's paper with commentary by Runoko Rashidi, and Africanized cover art by Mary Greer Mudiku. Rashidi's commentary stresses the important aspect of the tale in context of Black liberation: "The challenge to the African world to reclaim Egypt must be seen as integral part of the Black liberation movement." Rashidi sees Bata (which he spells Batau) as an exemplary hero – a disenfranchised peasant that gains justice, and characterizes the tale as one belonging to the Egyptian masses. (The story will aid in Black liberation.)

The tale has gone through more changes than this, I merely chose a few examples. I think that people are afraid of approaching this story as fiction rather than myth. I suspect that we are loath to note the similarities between Seti II's and Bata's life – even though we live in an age when custom-mass-mailing is the rule.

What we fail to see is that the story is good. We are excited by the soap-opera scene between Bata and the wife of Anubis. We are thrilled by the barn scene where Dr. Dolittle gets his warnings from the cows. We are amazed by the story of the miraculous lake with crocodiles that Re sends to protect Bata.

When Bata takes his heart out and places it in a tree, only to have it felled by the pharaoh, we feel for him. His brother Anubis, who then searches for Bata's heart for seven years, is movie-hero stuff. The shape-changing and the revenge plot against Bata's ex-wife make a great tale. This story just plain feels different than most Egyptian myths. It doesn't have the propagandistic feel of the "The Shipwrecked Sailor" or "The Tale of Sinuhe." It isn't a burlesque of the gods like "The Contendings of Horus and Set." It isn't a spell like those in the *Book of Going Forth by Day*, nor is it like the life literature (*e.g.*, "The Song of the Harpist"). This story is like what I do for a living; it is a story.

A good story, or even those we scribblers think are good, always has a different fate than other writing. People identify with a story then come up with reasons why afterward. People join in the action, and that simply feels good. A story is exactly like a low-grade ritual. It provides images and suggestions for people to feel why they visualize the images. So "The Tale of the Two Brothers" was as much created by In-na as any story. It was part his conscious intent and part that thing we can all the unconscious, the Muses, or whatever. A good deal of that "whatever" must be culturally conditioned, born of language and history and maybe even genes, but a good deal more belongs to all of us, so that Dr. Mark Southern can recite parts of the tale three thousand years later in an overly warm classroom, and we listen to the latest remanifestation of Bata.

Well, I am finished with my tale of a tale.

Works Consulted:

Breasted, James Henry. *A History of Egypt,* New York: Charles Scribner's Sons. 1909

Hollis, Susan Tower. *The Ancient Egyptian" Tale of the Two* Brothers", Norman, Oklahoma: University of Oklahoma Press. 1990

Rashidi, Runoko. "Commentary" in *The Tale of the Two Brothers: An Egyptian Fairy Tale,* Baltimore, Maryland: Black Classic Press 1988

Velde, H. te . *Seth, God of Confusion* PdÄ 6 1967: with corrections. Leiden: E. J. Brill, 1977

Celebration of Bata

This is a ritual I wrote as a Priest of Set. I was the Sentinel of the Bull of Ombos Pylon. The Bull of Ombos was an Austin-based Pylon, which remained active for many years. Founded by Stephen E. Flowers, its first rite was the Ordination of Dr. Flowers by Dr. Aquino via speaker phone. The pylon produced two Ipsissimi and four Masters of the Temple. I share this ritual with you because it shows another way of dealing with the material that became a college paper. Setians must work in all realms: the carnal, the intellectual, the emotional, and the daimonic. The ritual is a invocation of the Egregore of the Pylon. Dr. Flowers had studied the Egregore rites of the Fraternitas Saturni and modified them for our Pylon. The Working is a synthesis of Egyptian myth and Die Elektrischen Vorspiele, *which had been the signature rite of the Order of the Shining Trapezohedron Flowers had founded to explore the "dark and futuristic side of Odianism." Flowers had disbanded the OST when he joined the Temple of Set. If you are interested in the* Die Elektrischen Vorspiele, *you may wish to look for the YouTube video* The Electrical Preludes.

* Prepare chamber

    1. Charge atmosphere

        2. Display Stele of the Bull of Ombos Pylon

        3. Drape Northern Wall in Black

* Bell 9X

* Light Black Flame / Open Gate (T***)

* Invocation of Set (R*******)

In the Name of Set, the Prince of Darkness, do we enter into the Realm of Creation to Work our wills upon the Universe. Set-Hen, hark unto us, look upon us with your transforming gaze, and go with us on this journey. Enfold us with the Powers of Darkness that we are each become as One with them as we are each become one with the Eternal Set, whose seat is behind the constellation Sokaris. As we send forth our most exalted and sublime selves, rm them with the Pentagram of Set and with the scepter of Tcham that they may defy all constraints, dismay all challengers, and cast down all that is moved to appear against them.

Let then our eyes become the Eyes of Set, our strength become the Strength of Set, our will become the Will of Set. As Sparks of Intimate Fire we are Become; as the Perfumes of the Temple we are Become; as the Stones of Foundation we are Become; as Water which reshapes the land we are Become; as Yeast that enlivens the Worlds we are Become. We dwell in the Fane of the Flame of Ba. Time bows before our will, and we are Lords of Life, Death, and Life in Death. Hear then this Doom which we pronounce, and beware the Ka which now Comes Into Being through that Art which is ours to command.

•   Calling Forth of Bata

GRAAL:

This is the elixir of the Ninth Angle. It is the beginning and end of all things. To drink this Hellish brew is to accept all the pains of existence and all of its pleasures. Take this and Drink; it was given me by an ancient dragon.

(After the Initiates have partaken of the Graal, begin strobe, but don't extinguish the candle yet so the elemental summoning and the Word of Set may be read with ease.)

Elemental Summoning:

From the North I call the pure pagan silt which offers itself anew to the Beings touched of the Black Flame, that we may experience the joys of the thousand paws which have touched it .

From the South I call the ever burning fire, which reminds us of the glory of desire and the possibility of Pylons of light and life.

From the East I call the clear air which bears the whispering voices of wonder throughout Allternity and delights us with the sweet incense burned to the Dark Lord.

From the West I call the brine of the great salt sea from which all life springs forth and through which we may send our dreams to those as yet unborn.

Word of Set: Third Part, English and Enochian

(The candle is now extinguished, the celebrant reads the Liturgy of Bata. Before the beginning of the liturgy and at each pause throughout, a blast from the Tesla coil charges the air.)

Anubis:

I am Anubis. Evil word has reached my ears of my younger brother Bata, that he has sought after those things which should not be his. I will drive him from Khemit into the wastes of the South.

(Anubis threatens Bata with the dagger. As Bata turns slowly widdershins, Anubis will lower the dagger. When at the end of Bata's speech they are again face to face, Anubis will be able to hand Bata the dagger.)

Bata:

I am Bata, shunned and feared by men. I wander the wastes of the South, nourished by my sorcery. I make stones into bread and the fruit tree bloom without water. I have made a garden of delight, and I am the serpent within it.

The fear-filled ones slay me, yet by a single drop of my blood I arise as a leopard, and with the fierceness of a leopard do I slay my slayers. I place my heart in the top of the persea tree. I teach Black Magic to men, yet one betrays my secrets to the mindless, and they chop down the tree. Yet a single splinter flies into a red ox nearby, and I am sustained by my will.

The ox is marked for sacrifice, yet the very enemies who spoke ill of me seek the ox in the night. They eat its heart, thinking thereby to steal my Power. But my will overcame them, and I became a baby in their wombs. I was born in a high place, full of craft. And I became vizier. Gave I the pharaoh wise advice and laws which have endured through the ages. But in secret I taught the Greater Law and the Lesser Law, and these too have endured.

The pharaoh died without issue, and I was named Pharaoh, and in my wise rule I preserved the gateways my searches had revealed to me. I built Temples and had carved upon the stone the secrets which would remain and act upon Earth until the coming of the Fourth Ordering. And I instituted Great and eldritch Mysteries whose power endures, although they are forgotten.

When my cycle had run, I went North beyond the Field of Grasshoppers and ascended the ladder of Set. I passed beyond that constellation now called Sokaris into the black realm of strange angles. Moving slowly through the fantastic planes, I would peer ever and anon at the race of men. The Greeks felt me and cast me in the form of the Minotaur, terrible god of the labyrinth.

I found others who dwelt beyond the curved realm, and the thundering of my hooves joined their strange bell-like baying. Hear the sound of my thundering hooves which lifts the veil between the worlds!

Through the gateways I built did my essence pour into the World of Horrors; Dee heard my hoofbeats and resolved them into Words of Power. Al-Hazared wrote of me, crying, "Ia, Shub-Niggurath!" And in the fullness of time, men plundered the tombs of Khemit and spread my strange treasures across the world, hidden Amungst simple curiosities. And I began walking unseen again on the Earth.

In Cairo I spoke to the Beast, and there were many who were crushed beneath my hooves. In San Francisco I taught of the fourfold shape which gives increase to my kind and smites those who would oppose us. Then through the Tenth Key, I came fully forth, and the men of musty mind cried, "Woe, for our time is at an end!" I roamed the Dimensions of the Temple of Set freely as I had haunted the wastes of the South. A place was fashioned for me by Polaris, and there I dwell when I am not upon the wide ways of the world.

Know then that I am Bata who wakes the dead. I am Bata who orders the World through the Ninth Angle. I am Bata whose horns scar the sky and whose feet crush the mummified remains of my enemies, and I have set a Nine-Horned wheel, with angles of dimensions unrecognizable save for the Children of Set, as a sun of guidance and vengeance in the Firmament of Wrath!

(Anubis hands Bata the dagger. Bata salutes him, then traces the Pentagram of Set with the dagger. He then returns the dagger to Anubis. The strobe is turned to a very slow setting, and the CPS tape is begun. The celebrants begin casting their webs through the Pentagram – when each feels they have cast enough, they may be still, holding the world in quiet waiting. A senior Initiate addresses them.)

There are secret governors of every age. Know you now that we are those governors, whose rulership is ordained by Set, and that naught moves save by our will.

(The strobe is turned off and the proclamation is made; lit only by the Black Flame.):

Celebrant:

We desire Power!

All:

We shall have Power!

Celebrant:

We desire Wealth!

All:

We shall have Wealth!

Celebrant:

We desire Wisdom!

All:

We shall have Wisdom!

Celebrant:

We desire Recognition!

All:

We shall have Recognition!

Celebrant:

We desire influence!

All:

We shall have influence!

(Celebrant lights a candle. Someone reads the closing.)

      What we have proclaimed in this holy hall cannot help but come to be. Bata's

hooves are heard in all quarters and all times, and we have created for ourselves a place

of reason and delight.

Celebrant:

A Set Hen!

All:

A Set Hen!

Celebrant:

A Set Heh!

All:

A Set Heh!

Bell 9X

"So it is done, and so shall it be!"

The Bull and I

I was Sentinel of the Bull of Ombos Pylon during my third degree and part of my fourth. Priests usually run pylons. During that part of Initiation, the Initiate seeks to kindle the Black Flame in others. The stresses of running a group from scheduling meetings, designing rituals, and dealing with interpersonal friction provide useful challenges. I treasured my time in the Bull of Ombos. I wrote this article when a new Sentinel took over the Bull.

The Bull of Ombos was based on a magical joke. It was founded by a University of Texas professor, because the UT mascot, Bevo the Bull, made it a sure thing that the Pylon could always see and obtain lots of material with its logo on it. The graduate library of UT had a copy of Te Velde's *Seth: God of Confusion*, and Adept Flowers and Setian Wade were able to look up stuff about this Egyptian god. They were not Egyptologists – heck, they didn't even know that Bata, the Shepherd God, was a form of Set that had special significance for the XIXth and XXth Dynasties. They just liked the idea of the Bull, and the first issue of the *Vox Tauri* had the magical formula "Bata Bevo est."

They were unaware that the words appearing on the Seal of Set, "Let then my great Nobles be brought to me" were the words uttered by Bata when he became Pharaoh. They didn't know this anymore than Michael Aquino had known that phrase came from one of the few Setian religious texts available to us when he put them around the Seal in the Year X. They damn sure didn't know that I would show up and unravel that.

Then-Priest Flowers ran an ad in the *Chronicle* for members. It said "Rosemary's baby is nineteen years old now, want to find out what he's been up to?" Temple of Set, POB . . .

I remember the ad because I saw it when I picked up my first *Chronicle*. I had moved to Austin in the Year XIX, and the ad intrigued me. I knew who Set was, and I was interested in the group, but I was afraid to write them. Not afraid that they were blood-sucking telemarketers, but that they might be people wearing silly clothes and acting like the Masters of Atlantis. I went on doing my thing.

A series of odd encounters began when I hung out invitations to my Advanced Dungeons & Dragons game. I met a guy, who introduced to me to another guy, who introduced me to then-Priestess Flowers, who was the editor of the *Scroll*. Soon I met her husband, a very intelligent, somewhat taciturn guy that had just written a book called *Fire and Ice*. The Satan scare was in high fury by this time, so the Flowerses were discreet. I only found out about their membership after watching the Geraldo special on Satanism. I told Nancy Flowers that I would like to write a fan letter to Michael Aquino and speculated on how I could get his address. She told me "I'll be seeing him next week." Then I found out that my friends had a dark and glamorous secret life.

I joined the next year, XXIII. It had been four years since I had seen the ad and decided not to write. In seven years I would be High Priest. I take my rapid growth in the organization to largely be a product of my involvement with the Bull of Ombos. Now, you might be thinking that being involved with a Pylon makes everything easy and quick. Wrong. It can be a major pain in the Initiation. It is a sure way to let the forces of your Self into your life. You will undergo a great deal of change if you perform ritual magic with a group – and the members of the group will become involved in your life – as teachers, as challengers, as students, as friends, as tragic examples. They have to. They are standing at ground zero when you let your magical bombs off in the world.

And you are standing there when they let their bombs go off as well. The interactions that you unleash will give them certain strange and mysterious roles – roles they won't want. Nobody in their right mind would want to stand in for parts of another's psyche.

Unless.

Unless others were willing to risk the same for them.

This is one of the dire and wonderful Secrets of magic. You are on an adventure with the magicians that choose you and you choose and Set arranges. You'll see it all. You'll see people that you think are without potential turn into awesome, balance-inspiring individuals. You will see people that could be like gods just slack and leave for the pettiest of reasons. You'll see nobility that will make you weep, and you'll see treachery that will make you curse mankind. I can't tell you how many times I thought of quitting the Temple because of things going wrong in the Bull.

I saw sights of all sorts, from naked altars to pregnant deer stealing corn chips from our campground to the treasures of Amenhotep III to computers used in magical workings. I saw people overcome odds I couldn't believe, and I saw greed and stupidity.

Okay, you say, you can see that all in your life anyway. Well, maybe not naked altars . . .

But I got to see these things after I had told my Soul– LEARN and REMEMBER– so each of these things leaves a mark, a hieroglyph on the scroll of my life, that Taught me much more than books could ever teach.

Every word I write is marked by my experiences in the Bull of Ombos – my ecstasy, my agony, my fear, my confidence, my sense of wonder, my sense of friendship – all made for my Soul. In this I have Sensed a possibility for other kinds of life than that of five senses and three dimensions. Although if you were to ask at what point I learned it, I could not answer you. I couldn't say it was when we were watching some cheesy vampire movie, or that day I found a special candelabra in a junk shop that was just perfect for the F.˙.S.˙. rite. I couldn't say it was that twilight on Lands End in San Francisco when I did an impromptu Lovecraftian rite with two Ombites tossing lapis lazuli in the ocean, or the night that Magus Flowers gave us a lecture on Runa amidst a thunderstorm with all the lights off. I can't say it was writing the articles for the *Vox* or getting a new Stele from Adept W. or representing the Bull at the Xepera Mundi Working at the Schrecks' bookstore in L.A. It was all of these things that changed my soul. If I have ever written anything that has helped you, you can thank the spirit of the Pylon as much as you can thank yourself or me. You should Do so. Send your magical blessing toward the Bull and ask your Self and Set to make you part of a similar great adventure. It is, my friends, not to be missed.

Imagination

Many of the candidates for the Temple of Set come from other magical traditions, and there is no need to teach them the basics of magic. However, a growing number of people are drawn by the philosophy of the Temple of Set and do not have a magical background. I wrote some articles to help in their training. This article uses some Setian jargon, such as Lesser Black Magic/LBM (metacommunication), Medial Black Magic/MBM (sorcery,) and Greater Black Magic/GBM (initiatory magic). Persons wishing to try the second exercise may use the invocation in the preceding ritual.

One of the first skills to learn is imagination.

Imagination is space, a void, a container that time fills up with the desired items.

When imagination and will are in conflict, imagination usually wins. For example, your will says, "I will eat healthy food!" Your imagination starts focusing on a cheeseburger. How it tastes, how it smells, how it feels in your hand, how the pickles crunch in your mouth . . . before long you are in line at McDonald's. When we introduce our imagination to others, we call it LBM (if it is done by direct communication) or MBM (indirect communication). When we use it to shape our wills, we call it MBM. When we use it as a receiving device to get information from our psyches, we call it GBM.

Imagination can be trained. Here are four exercises that need little time and few props.

1.   Moving people. Go somewhere that people gather (a park, a shopping mall, etc.) In your mind create a little space – like the area between the fountain and the two trees. Imagine people gathering in that region or (if is already full of people) leaving that area. Do this until you can do it fairly easily. You will discover that it is not a matter of "force" – you don't will people away – but a matter of relaxed inner seeing. This has practical application for getting good seats in restaurants, movie theaters, etc.

2.   Empowering the Invocation. Memorize the Invocation of Set from the *Crystal Tablet.* Learn to see scenes from it as you say it. Then recite it in the morning, followed by a wish for the day –"I Wish to make more money today" or "I Wish to see the motives of others more clearly today." Try picturing/imagining the scenes from the Invocation as your recite as well as scenes that would reflect your wish.   Mentally do the same exercise as you fall asleep – make your Wish a type of dream – "I wish to dream of my most magical childhood experience" or "I Wish to dream of my old age." Try doing this for four days on, then not doing it for four days. This exercise will teach you how to connect imagination with a sequence of pre-chosen images. It will also teach you how to imagine concretely impersonal and abstract ideas. Record any success in your magical diary.

3.   Scrying and character analysis. You can use your imagination to gather information about people. When you meet someone, make a good mental photograph of them. Later in a quiet moment picture them standing in front of you. Fill in as many details as you can remember. Then picture them holding a smaller photo of themselves – look at the smaller photo – is it of any angry person, a glamorous person, a nice person? This will tend to be the face they will show you. Write down your experiment, and then

see how accurate you are. IMPORTANT TIP: Until you become good at this, do NOT use it for important people in your life! Use it on your grocery clerk, a man you chat with on the train, etc. TIP #2: Your write-up need not be long. "Met Mr. Smith. Saw intelligent man in astral." This exercise helps you visualize things from the real world as well as visualizing things your total senses are picking about people.

4.   Shifting perceptions. We all see what we have been trained to see. If your look at a rose bush, you focus on the roses. Try seeing some detail that is unimportant. For example, look at the leaves of the rose bush. Look at the part of the book jacket without writing on it. Look at the plate around the food. Then try a few minutes later to visualize what you just saw. This exercise causes the imagination to become analytical. You can take apart and recombine worlds in ways other than you have been programmed to do. Practical advantage to this exercise is that you will become an expert in finding lost and misplaced objects

Now, later when you find yourself wanting a cheeseburger, you can understand how magic works on you.

The Aeon of Horus And Us

The Temple of Set was founded in 1975, one hundred years after the birth of the First Beast, Aleister Crowley. In the Book of Coming Forth By Night, *Set relates his Aeon to that of Horus. Crowley's Work has brought about a celebration of the human will – drawing from Nietzsche and William James – blended with a rebirth of magical practice and yoga. This blend freed the human both emotionally and daimonically, enabling the Self to see itself freed from its Matrix. Some of the early aspects of this show up in the Work of Frater Achad, Kenneth Grant, and especially Anton LaVey's Utterance of Indulgence. The neo-Platonism and Pragmatism that marked the philosophy of Michael Aquino allowed him to become Crowley's magical heir and Utter a Word more centered on Self.*

Crowley's Word of Thelema (= Will) needs other humans to contest against or harmonize with. "Xeper" focuses on the withdrawal to Self, oscillating with the shaping of the world in light of what has been found within. Many Setians come from a Thelemic background, even more read books composed under that banner, and the unfolding of the world currently owes a great deal to the programming of the world by the First Beast. I have written a short study of Crowley; The Fire and the Force, *for the interested reader, Here I discuss some of the relationships between the Aeon of Horus and us.*

In the cosmology of the Temple of Set, we are given a picture of two gods: Set and Har-Wer. Because of the map given in *The Book of Coming Forth By Night*, we map these neters onto primal gods of ancient Egypt as well as the ideas of Ipsissimus Aleister Crowley. In our task of self-knowledge/self-creation we are most interested in the God of Self-Creation, Set, but are drawn to the notion of Set's first creation, Har-Wer. I would like to share my observations on Har-Wer and ideas associated with him both in Egypt and in the occult milieu of the Twentieth Century.

Many Egyptian gods are named Horus. It means "the far-off one," the name belonging to the falcon. To the Egyptians it was a symbol of sovereignty. Picture yourself working in the hot fields; above you, floating with seldom even a wing flap, is a falcon. From time to time he darts down and catches a mouse that your eyes certainly didn't see. How like a ruler! He has magical powers of perception, he is above you, and he seems not to work hard. The second part of the name ,"Wer" or "Ur," means "the oldest." In Egyptian thinking, the older the better. The Egyptians (like most people with a shamanic mindset) saw the world as being in a constant state of decay. Older gods are better, bigger, stronger. The early pharaohs took the name Living Horus, with the exception of a Second Dynasty pharaoh, PerIbSen. He was a Living Set. A good deal of ink has been spilled to explain that early Egyptians were separated into two peoples – the Northern (more European) were followers of the solar Horus, and the Southern (more African) were followers of the darker Set. Civilization, therefore, was a gift that the lighter folks gave the darkies.

However, there are some problems with this notion. Firstly, the group of people that created Egyptian civilization as we know it – hieroglyphs, burial customs, god-kings, etc. – were Set-worshipers in Naqada. Secondly, the Palette of Narmer, the first pharaoh to unite the delta and the Nile Valley, says he came from the South. Thirdly, Set and Horus are worshiped in sites both North and South (and archeological evidence suggests that this has always been so). The early pharaohs maintained a cult of themselves during their lifetime focusing on the hidden rites of the Heb-Sed, a rejuvenation festival wherein the Pharaoh won a rebirth from Har-Wer and Set. The spells and ritual complex were reused to make his tomb. The post-death cult would die away, and much ink has focused on the "Pyramid Texts" as funeral only. A welcome correction to this is Jeremy Naydler's *Shamanic Wisdom in the Pyramid Texts.* Har-Wer and Set work as partners in the Heb-Sed ceremony. They hold up the ladder for the Pharoah's soul to ascend to Heaven (climbing a ladder to the stars is a common shamanic motif). Har-Wer and Set are also unified into a dual-headed god (occasionally named as the goddess Mehen or as the Lone Star (Venus). Utterance 245 says that the Pharaoh becomes the Lone Star (both during the shamanic initiation during his lifetime and as an afterlife state:

> Make your seat in heaven
>
> Among the Stars of heaven
>
> For you are the Lone Star, the comrade of Hu!

Newer research on the etymology of the name "Set" indicates that it may mean stability. Set's from as the North Star, a fixed point around which other stars wheel, is the visual metaphor. Animals do not rise from the immediacy of the cosmos to see themselves as separate from it. This is the Setian moment – seeing Self as an object distinct from the Cosmos. Many of the early determinatives for the hieroglyphs of Set are knives. It is His Tail that is used as the birthing knife and the object that Opens the Mouths of corpses and idols. This moment begins Duration, the subjective sense of time. It reflects the agony of the cutting off from the world and also the confusion humans feel in their alienation. "Hey, it's a bright, sunny day – why am I unhappy?" This is the true moment of self-creation – not conception, not some ritual that may be performed externally.

The following moment is the realization of the Cosmos as *object*. The Self realizes the Cosmos exists of its own. This is the true moment of world-creation – not the Big Bang or Genesis. The world and its parts acquire Time. An undifferentiated being cannot think about the sun that will follow the rain, and certainly not the winter that follows the summer. The god of the world that arises from human interactions is the Far-Off one, Horus. Horus is what most of the day-to-day life of leaders consist of. This is as true as a foreman of a truck dock who has plans for what happens if the number three semi is in the shop as it is for the general planning an assault. The leader may or may not have time or inclination for self-development, but he or she must be focused on analyzing, simulating, and ordering the world.

Many people have produced systems to explain time and change. The Greeks said it was getting worse (Age of Gold, Age of Silver, Age of Bronze, Age of Iron). Darwin said it was getting better (fish, reptiles, mammals, primates, Englishmen). Joachim of Fiore came up with a spiritual model of stuff getting better – God the (abusive) Father, God the (good-looking) Son, and finally the age of God the (friendly) Ghost. It was a useful model – it explained God's anger issues and tendency to hang out with Jews in the Old Testament, God's love of mankind and hanging out with people that read Greek and Latin in the New Testament, and a coming New Age where people will have special powers and realize how smart Joachim of Fiore was.

This is a great model for a magician working on the world. It gives hope (which empowers the magic of those who listen to you). It explains why the world has sucked – God is getting smarter, and you can, too. Finally, it deifies the prophet – if you want the better world, listen to me. He adopted a model that fulfilled his beliefs and provided a magical link with history and its processes. Crowley believed the history of the world must be written in the four letters of the Hebrew Divine Name "He Exists" --Yod He Vau He. It would make the God the Mom (Paganism and your room got cleaned up), God the Dead Dad (central authority but no child support), God the Crowned and Conquering Child (Bart Simpson is God), and finally God the Cheerleader, who will Put Out.

Crowley was at a turning point in his life. He could settle down, stop magic, and become a father to the little bun in the oven. He visited a really big heap of rocks called the Great Pyramid. He didn't know that this was Har-Wer at His best. The Pharaoh kept the world from falling apart during the floods by keeping people busy. He had built himself a great Initiation chamber, complete with escape route to the North Star. Crowley resonated with the resonating chamber, and soon his wife went into a trance. The trigger object was a burial stele for a Montu Priest of the 25th Dynasty. (If you have an old book, it will incorrectly list Ankh-f-n-Khonsu as 26th Dynasty). Now, if Crowley came along today, he would know that the Theban Set Priesthood had been absorbed into the Montu Priesthood and that Montu was often pained with Set's head. If he had come along today, he would have received a better translation of the Horus invoked on the stele. It was not the Child Horus, but the warlord Horus Behdety. Crowley hired the museum to translate the text, they were using a popular French dictionary and translated Behdety as Hadit. You can see Horus Behdety on a clear night, He's that reddish light we call Mars.

Crowley needed some way not to become a middle class, one-woman, no-men, father. So he got one. He Heard his revelation as the voice of Horus the Child. The problem is that there is no such animal. It would be equivalent to the Baby Jesus being something different than the guy on the cross. We might like pictures of the Baby Jesus on your Christmas cards, but we don't think his message is to stay in the manger at all costs. Horus the Crowned and Conquering Child is male adolescence writ large. Go for what you want! Screw around! Fighting is good, and we can all be friends afterward! The world is going to work out because I AM A GENIUS-GENIUS!

The Voice was the voice that objectifies the world. There is a break, and the world is seen as testing ground and pleasure garden. If someone gets hurt, it is because they must have wanted to. The higher end of this thought can be seen in Ayn Rand, Nietzsche, Robert Anton Wilson, Max Stirner, etc.

The lower end of this reasoning can be seen in shopping malls, usually wearing a holey T-shirt.

This leaves us with a few questions. What historical and psychological forces made this a powerful idea? What does Magick have to do with all this? Why did Set merge with Har-Wer – what was the Age of Satan all about? What practical things does this mean for me in my day-to-day practice?

Why it Worked. Jung wrote about this very well for his (in)famous Wotan essay. Christianity did a great job on splitting pagans into two parts. The "top" part is the willingness to work together, store food for the winter, care for the old. Every town in Europe was a map of this – the tallest structure was the church. "Good" people helped out (and the Church administered). Spiritual duties were never neglected because they came from the calendar and clock. The "bottom" part was suppressed – the joy of group ecstasy, the need for direct spiritual experience, the sacred nature of sex and drunkenness, the need to put the rules down as a reward. Just as a human deprived of half of his impulses will eventually crack, so to a society. Crowley was by no means the only

spiritual leader that reconnected the repressed – Jung slept with his patients, Steiner

banged everybody, Gurdjieff did the sex and drugs bit, and I won't even mention Timothy

Leary.

As Jung had predicted, the primal spirit would re-emerge. Most of the spiritual

thinkers of the time were fascists. Not because they were the mean Nazioids of movies,

but because they wanted group ecstasy. Julius Evola, Alain Danielou, Mircea Eliade,

Schwaller de Lubciz , and Guido Von List were all Fascists. All of them wanted to

rejuvenate society, and the Horian principle is to let out repressed energies with a strong

director/magician to control them. The Awakening that we call the "Aeon of Horus" was

a mass break with the immediacy of the world and seeing the world as object.   The

power of their force did things like turn a defeated WWI Germany into a world power.

How does "Magick" fit in with this? At first glance there seems to be no

connection. The expression of Will seems to need only a person who Wills and a Cosmos

to work upon. Yet the Aeon of Horus was filled with people driven to regain the secrets

of the past. There are several reasons for this. Firstly, for Horian consciousness to break

with the immediacy of the world, it needs to be reminded of Past and Future. Magick and

myth are great symbols of the past. Secondly, the magic of the past holds

codes/programs to realize the very energies that powered the Aeon of Horus. Thirdly,

Horian magic returns the group trance whether it is Thelemic mass, a rally at Nuremberg,

the Super Bowl, or a Wiccan bonfire. Group ecstasy breaks from the non-awareness of

the world into an awareness of power that might be brought to bear upon the world. Hail

the power of the posse! Advertising, mind controls, sports fandom, MKULTRA, and

Beatlemania are all examples of the return of group-trance.

Now, we looked at Set earlier as God of Self-Creation. It was easy to see why Self-Creation would precede World-Creation. But why would the god of Self-Creation merge with the God of World-Creation? Horian consciousness can do things on a heroic scale; it can cause millions of human to be inflamed and act (for good or ill). Since it based on Will – the experiencing of the world as a place of action – it makes people aware that they can do anything. Space program. Tear down the Berlin Wall. Give women the vote. Blow up the Twin Towers. This consciousness has come and gone in the history of mankind. We are amazed at its triumphs. The Great Wall. Stonehenge. The Roman road system. The Panama Canal. But Will without direction from an evolving source creates the Ukrainian starvation, the Holocaust, the Killing Fields. The willful child that builds a huge sandcastle can be the kid who destroys it in a few seconds. The more empowered mankind can be as a group, the more chances mankind can really fuck up.

Now, just as Horian consciousness is in part fueled by repression from viewpoints that claimed humans cannot make decisions about the Cosmos as object, Setian consciousness is repressed by group trance/ecstasy. You can look around a high school pep rally and see which kids are not energized by the group. They see no reason to give their attention to the defeating of the other team. Or you can see their sad faces at Mass while their parents are excited by getting a free cracker. They are unfed by group trance. Some of them may discover Apollonian trance – they may find yoga, or tokin' on marijuana, or made-up rites. But their growth is small. They see the universe as object – so what? And they see themselves as the Subject – the doer in the Cosmos. However, unless they find the arts or writing, their solitary pursuits can seldom amount to much.

The solution is to unite the forces. "I exist and my existing is Doing something about itself!" and "The world exists outside of me, and I can choose how to interact with some parts of it!" can merge into the "The world exists and I want it!" The possibility for small groups – Meso-Cosmos – to work on both increasing pleasure from the world and shaping themselves on their own principles – comes into being the moment the Setian and Horian consciousness merge. There has to be certain common factors – a hatred of the world that can be pleasurable. A distrust of the world's models of how-to-succeed but a frank desire to have some of the world's treasures. A belief in secret rules – this is a very important idea. Unless the Set-Har-Werian thinks there is some secret way to obtain goals, they would have the despair of realizing that they would have to do what everyone else does. So the follower/friend of Set-Har-Wer will have magic, materialism, a belief in self-driven self-development, and a desire to make fun of society. In Setian terminology we call this two-headed figure Satan. It has had other names, including Eris and Bob. "Lucifer" the Lone Star once again presaged the coming of Khephra, the dawn.

The end of the Age of Satan, and the separation of the Horian and Setian streams, is interesting. For Magister Aquino it ends with the "Ninth Solstice Message" – a document that annuls the Pact between Satan and LaVey. In this statement LaVey is encouraged to be his own self, a Daimon. In other words, his be-all and end-all were to see himself as Subject and Object, the receiver of all action. Although his actions may be aimed at the Cosmos as Object, they will affect him as Subject more profoundly. He is made into the first Setian. For Stephen Edred Flowers an audible voice says "Runa." He is given an Object to Seek, but the Object is one that can only sought by sacrificing the immediate self to Transcendent Self. His Word Runa becomes an imperative phrase "Reyn Til Runa!" – which he will later note adds up by rune-tally to 93, linking it with the Law of the Aeon of Horus. The Runes are the great symbol of Set-HarWer – they exist in the objective universe and in the Subjective one. Seeking them creates a break with the immediacy of the world that both furthers the Self's articulation and development and increases the effect of the Will upon the objective universe. At the end of year IX, a curious reception of a "Book" by Nema, proclaimed the speaking of a dual god – one part Horus and one unnamed that brought a word that is said to create change, IPSOS. The imagery of this "Book" is lovely – Black Flame as the form of the Mover of the dynamic universe. It can be read as the expression of consciousness (the Black Flame) naming the whole of the Cosmos as Object, IPSOS and the self as Doer, and suggesting that change brought about by repetition of the Word fulfills both Setian and Horian agendas. The Book is flawed by Setian standards in that it perceives the Black Flame as Ma'at, and holds to an older notion that consciousness is Order. However, its timing is suggestive.

Selves will seek other selves for the process of "Summoning." In the presence of a defined self, we respond from the depths of being by showing ourselves. If all we have is society to respond to, we usually work on the "I agree" or "I disagree" level. If we are in the presence of people that represent a different modeling of being, we can respond in simple ways (we copy), or more complex ways (we think), or very complex ways (we model our future selves thought behavior). If the core cell of Setian consciousness endures, the two-headed monster is not needed. Those who, on one hand, can perceive and reject the world as object and, on the other hand, see the response to this being the transcendental response will be magically drawn to us. If we wish to flourish we should up the flow with some sort of advertising – but even if we took down the website and forgot Set's admonition to wear the Pentagram proudly, some would continue to find us.

By the way, the transcendent function to the world is not to stare at your navel and chant something. It is the response to Transcend a problem. To mature, to gain knowledge or experience, to "think outside the box," to not view the world on its own terms. Each transcendental response the Setian makes, makes the Setian.

Timing

Here is another short article I wrote on magical training. Anton LaVey stressed timing as a part of Satanic magic. For example, if you are trying to influence someone, casting a spell on them near their last REM cycle before awakening is very effective. But there is more to timing than sorcery. One needs to know one's own inner seasons, what type of Work is best for your age. It is equally important to know when to launch projects in your corporation or your city. Ponder why Set moved on the world in Cairo in 1904, 1966, and 1975. If you study the world at these times, as well as Thelema, Indulgence, and Xeper, you can discover aspects of the macro-cosmos that gives you a picture of your own micro-cosmos.

Understanding timing is a big part of magic.

Here are six exercises that can help. You may share them with any Setian you feel may enjoy them.

1.   If you could only make one Wish in your magical life, it should be "O Higher Self, arrange my destiny that I always have the right work to do at the right time." To be truly adept would mean that just as you finish one task, you could take up another, being in the right space with the correct tools at hand. Try setting up occasions like this. Start focusing your days on transitions between work, rather than focusing on a series of unconnected tasks. When you feel yourself slipping from one job to another easily, thank your Higher Self.

2.   When trying to influence another magically, try the following. Find out when he

wakes in the morning. Then get up an hour beforehand and concentrate on him doing what you wish. Imagine that he is having a dream about it. That's the MBM part. Examine his day, when is he most likely to grant your request? (If you have worked with #1 above, you can figure this out). You give him the request on the day you sent the dream at the time it would be easiest for him to grant it. When such things work out in your favor, thank your Higher Self.

3.   Learn how to manipulate synchronicities. Pick a buddy, read a few books and articles on synchronicities at the same time (Such as 8-10 every Tuesday evening), send each other anecdotes from your lives about meaningful coincidences. Then pick a span of time (four days is good), write down anything that happens to you that you think of as odd. Compare lists afterward. See how many things you can stir up by simple Play. Write a brief letter to your Higher Self telling it that you like the power to alter time thusly and you Wish to use that more often for your pleasure, power, and Wisdom. Burn the letter to symbolically send it to another realm.

4.   Learn to wake up before the alarm. Look at the clock before you go to sleep, and imagine waking up five minutes before it goes off. Remember to thank yourself on days it works.

5.   Practice having thoughts. Try telling yourself "Today I will think about Xeper from 10:00 to 10:05" See when it happens by itself, see when it happens by your forcing it, see when strange things make it happen (e.g., someone walks into view wearing a scarab). Continue with the practice until it becomes easy to do.

6.   Once you have had some success in all of these games, Wish that you will know when it is the right time to celebrate your changing attitude toward time. (The right time

may come when a street vendor stops outside your office, an old friend calls up or "of the blue," etc.) It won't be by missing work and hurting your job, relationships, etc. Go and do the celebration, and as you Indulge tell yourself that you like time opening up for you. Then Wish that the Aeon could give you its Hidden Calendar . . .

Dominion

I wrote this essay as a gift to a Priestess on her 40th birthday. It focuses on the Utterance of John Dee, whose Word was probably "Dominion" cast in the form of "Ol sonuf vorsag." Dee's Word expressed itself in such concepts as his term "British Empire" and the creations of the idea of the modern corporation by his student Sir Phillip Sidney. The article focuses on the practical aspects of the Word.

The world is based on the idea of goals. At the end of the Made-for-TV movie we see the newly married couple embracing, we see the sailor sighting land, we know our hero has been elected President. We smile, we feel good, and the credits roll up the screen. Most of our practical magic, and almost all of impractical daydreaming, focuses on such happy tableaux.

What we don't focus is the rest of the story. What happens to the couple? What lies on the island? What are the challenges and struggles of the President?

These are questions of Dominion. The goal of the Left Hand Path is to prepare to rule wisely the very things that are the aims of most men and women. One may seize a throne by power or by cunning or by just inheriting it when your dad the king dies. But most people do not make good kings – once they are on the throne, they want to leave. They look for advisors to blame – or for new ways to amuse themselves. The original goal becomes hateful, but because of he strictures of society, it cannot be discarded. Others cannot try for new goals. For example, if the original goal was to make a lot of money, all they do is try to make more money. They are slaves to their goals because goals (once achieved) are distractors. Goals that have been met should be celebrated and put to sleep – before they put you to sleep.

The magician is always a trifle immature. (Alright, sometimes they are very immature.) This is because the capacity for magic is based on a certain dreaminess of character. The magician doesn't learn to get with the program early on, so they will always seem to be slow bloomers. So when their magic does work, they are in an odd spot. They are whiners, shirkers, complainers, and egotists. They aren't ready to rule, and their life goes downhill at the very point that it should begin its great movement forward.

The Initiate knows this secret. Now, probably he or she only knows this idea intellectually rather than truly Knowing it, but that is about the best you can hope for in your initiation. You looked around for people that overcame the same sort of struggles you have and asked them what they learned. (An Initiator that struggled through anything is worth a hundred times more than a success guru). The Initiate learns that in addition to seeking success, he or she must learn about themselves and what that success would mean along the way.

To exercise Dominion over something that one has gained (or found or inherited or created, etc.) there are four guiding principles.

Firstly, one must have a good idea of what the possibilities may be for having gained the target. If you want to be a king, you would think about waging war, building schools, commissioning artists, making wise laws, etc. The guide for this is looking at how you want the future to remember you for your kingdom.

Secondly, you must know what weaknesses in yourself that you now have an opportunity to overcome, having obtained the goal. For example, if you are scared of driving at night, winning that new car in the lottery is a great opportunity to overcome a weakness. This practice will keep you from either of the two magic-killers. You won't lie around thinking that you have obtained everything – gee, you're so keen. Nor will you discount your goal by saying with a shrug that it is not a big deal.

Thirdly, you must create pleasures for yourself out of the goal. If you wanted to get a new job with a window cubicle, you should stay late (or arrive early) to watch a sunset/sunrise through your window. This practice keeps you from minimizing the importance of your gain. This keeps the goal from fading as a source of pleasure – and motivates you to seek your next goal. This attitude, if entered into in an Awake fashion, is a Working in and of itself.

Fourthly, you must give yourself advice about your new kingdom as though you were advising a new king on the throne. This advice will help you out, and will make you realize the importance of letting go ("Sacrificing") whatever you create (or re-create). This is how force is built up in the world, and transmitted across time.

These four guiding principles are already known to us in some way. We probably found them in ourselves when we had our first job. But since these principles belong to consciousness, the world is opposed to them, so we lose them. We forget to take pleasure in our victories. We forget the power we have won. We forget that letting go at the right time and in the right way not only feels good, but actually sets up for immortality. We forget that we still have all the weaknesses we had before we started the quest for the goal.

Dominion is exercised in two ways. The first is a passive/receptive aware state of just taking in all that is going on your kingdom. The good king (or queen) knows a great deal more than anyone else about his or her kingdom. The good king learns to listen without judgment, to wake up and see what is really going on, to know the viewpoints of many. The good queen takes pleasure and pride in researching the elements of her kingdom. This is, sadly, often neglected by magicians, who feel that it is dull to know how plumbing works in their house but are really stoked to pick yet another book on the Kabala. The second way Dominion is exercised is action rather then re-action. The good queen, aware of what can be done with her kingdom, is ready to act to make it so. The king is starting projects, beginning initiatives, and seeing through changes – rather than making all of his decisions because he was forced to do so. The good king is proactive, to use the current corporate jargon.

Now, what does all of this advice mean to the magician/Initiate? It tells him or her how to gain Dominion. It tells him or her:

1. To look for other people (inside the Temple or not) that have overcome difficulties and risen to places of power. Find out how they did.

2. It tells them to invoke their Higher Selves often and ask that they see and learn the lessons they need as they make their rise to power.

3. It tells them to view the objects they get thought their magic as being as mysterious as themselves – and, like themselves, full of hidden resources.

4. It tells them to find pleasure into their victory so that happiness is always a part of their lives but contentment is not.

5. It tells them that seeking to rule wisely must be tied with a desire to pass their kingdom on to the correct heir.

These things can be sought by mundane means, but the wise magician also seeks them by esoteric means as much as he might try to bring about prosperity or health.

Once you have learned to rule things wisely, either inside of or outside of yourself, you will begin to have a deep feeling akin to happiness. You will develop a sense of sovereignty, which is the closest thing to a divine state that you can have as a human being. This state will calm those around you, cause them to listen to your words, and remove a good deal of the fear and anxiety of day-to-day life. It will also bring about great powers of concentration because you will have learned that struggle pays off – not with more struggle nor with rest but with a glimpse of godhood. Once you have had that glimpse of godhood from day-to-day life – and you know it is the same as the feeling you have touched on in the ritual chamber many times – then truly you are on the Left Hand Path and you will find that parts of your body-psyche-mind complex will be much more willing to help you out.

How to Make Gold

I wrote this for a short-lived British magazine called the Diabolicon, *which was a Setian-friendly LHP 'zine. The Renaissance was marked by taking the notion of Transmutation of base metals into gold as a working idea for public education. The fruits of this idea were the American and French Revolutions and the tradition of public education that rules the West. I wrote about the idea of educational alchemy to explain the Temple of Set and place it historically in a greater Tradition.*

Serious and objective students of the Temple of Set often have difficulty in classifying us as a "new religion" or an "occult society." The former is generally a marginalized group that seeks social power and respectability by increasing its numbers; the latter is a powerless elite, which gives its members an intellectual compensation for a lack they have in society. Although the Temple of Set has some features of each of these social phenomena, its emphasis on self- rather than collective-development places it in a unique category, which places the Temple as the leading School of the Left Hand Path in the West. I would like to discuss some of our uses of social phenomena as part of our initiatory practice. It is very fashionable and "occult" to say that one's interest is Alchemy. By using that word you touch a certain type of person at a certain stage in his or her development. It is a vague term, bringing to mind curious woodcuts and exotic phrases like "the Green Dragon" and "King's Bath." It is useful, in short, to turn down certain critical thinking apparatuses and open the mind to a dreamy world wherein self-change takes place. I will therefore describe the processes in this article as Alchemy, although from another perspective it would be called applied sociology and psychology. In this brief article I will reveal all the evil machinations of the Temple of Set, which have been the focus of the fears of so many conspiracy theorists.

The Temple of Set is dedicated to providing an environment that enables self-development to levels of being that would normally not be in the individual's potential realm of achievement. This sort of change requires two ingredients. Firstly, we need individuals who are seeking self-change and are not too immersed in the social matrix to be stuck in their roles. Secondly, we need an environment that provides challenges to those individuals while presenting a coherent model of change. Let's look at each of these ingredients and then at the reasons that the two things must be modified as the process continues.

Individuals in need of self-change, who are not immersed in the social matrix, means that we do not seek the rich, people at the end of their educational careers, or people that are totally happy in their job paths. These folk will receive too many signals from their environment telling them not to change. Satisfaction is not a motivator. We likewise do not seek the disheartened or the nihilist. Although such individuals may feel that they have thrown off the shackles of society, they are in reality within a tunnel of their own making from which they cannot escape. Such people join all sorts of social movements, only to "rebel" from them months later. Lastly, we do not seek those people under absolute social control – such as drug users or persons otherwise trapped in the domination of another. This is not to say that we feel no sympathy for these people; many Setians are as interested in social concerns as their neighbors. This merely means we do not try to make gold where gold cannot be made. The best Setian candidate is someone either in late college or early career, for reasons that will be explained below.

An environment that challenges individuals while providing a coherent model of change is the Temple's contribution to the formula. If we provided a model that suggested that change was not necessary – for example, if we taught that "You are God!" – this would be a stasis-producing signal. If we failed to provide a model for change, and merely emphasized success, we would be a booster club. In fact, we make people's lives harder by giving them intellectual challenges and testing their magical powers as they deal with their own determined life path. We are a school of light knocks, which, added to the harder knocks that everyone seeking to better him- or herself in the world receives, will produce better end-results than merely working one's way through the chaos of the world.

The individual who then succeeds in the Temple will have likewise needed to have an increase of wealth and status during the process. This is not because we charge higher fees at varying levels of Initiation – the fees are the same throughout. This is not because we throw out people for lack of success. It is because our philosophy works better with people who have decided to give up failure and despair but refuse to give up individuality. Only people going through this type of change of process can get the lessons; only they are helped out by our magical techniques.

This change in the body of Initiates produces a recognizable pattern wherever the Temple spreads. At first our idea/image arrives only as a curiosity on a slow news day in some marginalized 'zine about the occult. We will attract people who have tried everything and got no success. Most of them will not succeed at another, but there will be one or two people who will be awakened by our message. Their presence leads to their first challenge of attracting others with whom they can discuss the theory and practice of our philosophy. As marginalized individuals just beginning their path to power, their outlets are negative. Their articles don't show up in the proceedings of philosophical journals. The world learns of them (usually at a fairly great cost to the individual) through reporters wanting to have a colorful supplement in their rag. The challenge to deal with this negative publicity – which will teach tons of things about how the world works and make your defensive magic good – while at the same time making your way the world (and having enough time to read everything form Plato to Bateson), will make winners out of the first group.

The next step occurs when more serious journalists look you over and think it's time to tell the world that you are not baby-eating killers. Although this remains a largely negative signal, it does attract a greater crowd, who can look at the success of the first group and think they are making a less risky bet. So the next generation is a bit more cautious, usually with more to lose, and better educated. Meanwhile, the first group is retiring from the trenches, enjoying their status, and being able to develop and cultivate themselves. The second generation has been given some breathing room by the first, and they can take advantage of local meetings, traditions, and experiments. They begin creating a culture within, which means that it is easier for the third generation to come in and drink deeply awhile before having to produce.

The third generation will take up the task of communicating positively with the world. They will give talks at local occult shops, produce little magazines, and create web pages and so forth. At this point, the challenges of the Temple teach them things about publication, public speaking, video production, and so forth – while still presenting a coherent model of change.

The fourth generations comes in with the idea that they will make these outer world forms better. The journals look less amateurish, and the art tends to be produced by the fourth generation rather than public domain cut-and-paste art. These people begin producing material culture. Thus, from the lead rejected by the dominant culture, gold is made.

Now, the outer version of this is a standard path for any new religion, except for two major differences. Firstly, in addition to the growing status/respectability of the religion, there is a corresponding growth in the wealth and status of members. Secondly, the process takes years and not decades. This later dynamism is one of the earmarks of authenticity – of our relationship to the Prince of Darkness.

This differs from most "occult groups," which emphasize either tradition (i.e., "You must do what your elders did') or the acquisition of a model of the universe which requires no action (i.e., "You will get better – somehow – if you can just learn the Tree of Life.") We do resemble occult groups in that we do have esoteric teachings, and that, unlike new religions, we do not have a political agenda. We eschew group power because we don't think that giving power to a person just because they are a member of a group helps a person in his or her self-development. We prefer the smart few rather than the dumb many.

At its current level of development, the Temple seeks candidates who have four characteristics. One, they should have the ability to create a new culture; this means they have either educational or creative skills. Two, it means that they have a taste for real-world challenges as well as esoteric ones. Three, it means that they have to develop respect for the methods used before they arrived and a burning desire to create their own new methods. Four, it means, first and foremost, they have a desire to gain self-knowledge and Act on it.

From such as these we will make Gold, and the Gold we make will make Gold in the lives of many people – our Initiates, their friends, family, and the world.

Invisibility

The basic skills of the magician look very different to the practitioner in the trenches than they do to people who read about magicians. Another article for the newer magician.

One of the powers of the magician is invisibility, which is mainly an LBM skill. This brief essay will give you four exercises to play with. Like any skill you may really need at some point, learning by doing is a good idea.

I suspect you know the obvious – dress in muted tones, look like everyone else (or at least like a stereotype), speak quietly, don't make eye contact, etc. Here are a few things that can help.

I.   Make sure you see everyone before they see you. As you shop, walk down the street, enter a pub, and learn to see everyone first. You make the decision what face to show them. This has three great side benefits. Firstly, it gives you grace because you suddenly find that you can avoid tie-ups and crowds acting stupid. Secondly, it shuts off the internal dialogue so you have the chance of being brilliant. (You may have noticed this before – that when you are involved in movement, you suddenly have near-ecstatic flashes of brilliance). Thirdly, it helps with that important alchemy of changing "character armor" into "character awareness."

II.   If you are venturing into dangerous territory, know your routes. No one sees people that know their way to the elevator, back door, etc. The ability to "disappear" from a dull party can be part of your mystique.

III.   Learn a neutral visualization. One of the problems I had as I was learning magic years ago is that I "set off" vagrant insane people. These sad souls who have no buffers between them and other psyches – sort of dribble glasses of Self. I would walk by and they would want to talk to me or tell me that I was an Angel, etc. This was both gratifying to the worst part of my occultist's ego and scary to my rational self Now I think of a cinder block wall, and they go gaga over the local witch, who can then boast of her power.

IV.   Finally here is an MBM formula. Try it out. Don't "believe" it. As you go to sleep, say the following in your head a few times. The formula doesn't have to be word-for-word: "As my ba flies forth to interact with the bas of the sleeping men and women of my city, it casts invisibility in the eyes of those who would hinder me." After you have had a few solid-looking results – for example, your car is overlooked by a meter maid that nailed everyone else – try taking the practice up a notch and say, "As my ba flies forth from my body tonight to interact with the sleeping men and women of my city, it draws to itself those who will give it happiness, prosperity, and mystery."

The Earth

Since Setians say they focus on the "non-natural" part of themselves, the part that transcends the deterministic cosmos – many less-than-sharp critics of the Temple of Set think we hate nature. We adore and reverence the world of Life, which brings pleasure, peace, and teaches the psyche what it cannot learn in isolation. Setians have a great love of animal life, focused through Maga Aquino's Word of Arkte. I wanted to help some of our critics understand the place of Earth in our hearts and minds.

The place of Earth, like all the really big things (Being, Self, Becoming), is seldom defined in Setian philosophy. Partially this is because of the anti-Wiccan bias of Anton LaVey. Partially it is because of our own distrust of people on simple and happy-minded folk paths. I am going to sketch a few general ideas about the Earth and its meaning in our practice. Let us begin with a definition. The Earth is a planet, the planet we objectively experience. It is the source of perceptions that order and are Ordered by the Black Flame. It provides a common set of experiences that define human consciousness and therefore enable the possibility of human communication. It defines place. It is the holder of absolute predication from the absolute Subject.

Place is the most intimate of the human constraints. It focuses you. You are somewhere reading these words, you were born somewhere, and you will die somewhere. You share this constraint with seven billion other people. Where you are determines what you read, eat, screw, fear, and admire. Where you are is the matrix for action – authentic, inauthentic, or reactive.

Reactive actions are those things you share with animals. You seek food and pleasure; you avoid pain and starvation. Reactive actions may limit the range of your other actions. If finding drinkable water is an hours-long process (as it is in many parts of Africa), you will do little less. The driving force of the Black Flame causes humans to minimize reactive actions. It causes the questions that build and destroy civilizations. No one questions looking for or growing or trading for food. But the time you aren't doing those things leads to Questions: Is there life after death? Why did Oop get big muscles and I get small muscles? Wasn't it cold last year when that star vanished from the sky? If I could make this flint sharp, do you suppose I could wear the skin of animals?

Inauthentic actions are those things that you do because you are thrown into a human world with human consequence. This could be anything from attending a pep-rally to tipping a waiter to paying your taxes. Inauthentic actions create an inauthentic self. This is close to the postmodern idea that the self is a creation of social reality, but it neglects the authentic self, which is shapeless, imageless, and colorless. Inauthentic actions will often involve hurt to the Earth, ranging from pollution to sport hunting. People who live only in the human world are much less likely to receive the call of the Authentic Self, which, although it can manifest in many ways, often shows up when a person "opens" him- or herself to nature.

Authentic actions are those based on the intuition of the ultimate background of the Self, the Black Flame. The Black Flame is no-thing. It does not exist as "thing" in relation to any other; it can only be intuited. It lacks an opposite, and has the power to view opposites in their tension without negating them. It is not polarized by those things it perceives, for it alone is the absolute. It must act to discover how its presence acts upon the earth. The fact of its existence will cause a "Gap" – in the perception of the

Earth as a philosophically ordered world. For every being possessed of the Black Flame, there will be a moment of the Gap. (When a Wall becomes a Door). At that moment a person can learn the relationship between his or her Authentic and inauthentic selves. This moment transcends simple notions of Free Will. For Joe the plumber, it may mean that he is "meant" to be a plumber, or it may the moment that he discovers that he is meant to be an abstract painter. Once this Call (or Gap) is Heard, Joe has the choice of pursuing Authentic Actions (Xeper) or pursuing inauthentic actions (Wen). If one directly perceives the Earth – whether bathing in hot springs, or, like Magister S. leaping upon icebergs, there is a a greater chance of receiving the Call. For this reason most religions which are not ruled by a text worship Nature. This is not a faulty understanding, but it does not lead to more actions.

The Earth in its infinite richness does serve the same role as a Greater Black Magical Working. It can provide a place for the Call of the Authentic Self. Many overly intellectual folks disregard this. They become lost in the notion that the Authentic Self could be approached by pure reason, which, although excellent for deconstructing the. social "truths," does not lead to the absolute no-thing. Nor can mysticism lead there by finding things to meditate upon. The act of focus creates a prediction –"I am thinking about the Good." Any predication would be a mirroring of the transcendentals of being and of the one (*unum*), the true (*verum*), and the good (*bonum*). But those transcendentals, insofar as they themselves all elude predication, actually point to a more inclusive and undifferentiated topos, the Black Flame. A weekend in the wilds of the Earth will Open you more to your Authentic Self, than a dozen philosophy books.

The Earth as absolute Place is therefore sacred. It holds not only the ordering of all things, but also it holds Runa. It is the matrix whereby the Black Flame can intuit Itself and therefore bridge the gap between Authentic and inauthentic selves. In our symbols we see the Seal of Runa has the circle of the Earth, which magnetically holds the Seal at the Angles of Being and Understanding, which are the "angles" of the call of the Authentic Self.

Is the Earth, then, worthy of worship?

As the key to certain experiences, the Earth is sacred, but "worhsip" would further the gap between the Authentic and inauthentic selves. It would replace those intuitively derived actions with inauthentic actions – mere ritual or recitation. I suspect that any category of human action can be Authentic Action. It could include not only Art and Magic, but could even be operative in political-social action, or in scientific knowing, insofar as it grasps the world as including the selves.

Is the Earth conscious?

The Earth cannot have consciousness as we know it because it seems to have no ability for intuitive action. It would seem that it cannot Xeper – not because we in our human arrogance deny Xeper to others than humans, but because its existence as ultimate Place – as ultimate holder and reflector – is needed for Xeper.

Are the worshippers of the Earth our allies?

They can be, not simply because all alternative paths are in the same holding tank, but because their intention to seek social and political action on behalf of the Earth creates venues wherein our own Authentic Actions may occur.

On Perception

The magician is a practicing philosopher and vampire. He or she knows that perception is a willed act and subject to filters of the self as the philosopher knows, and he or she feeds on the sense data and impressions they gather. Normal humans may simply look at the world. The magician is deciding what to feed upon and then understand what leads they needs must make into which golds. I wrote this article for the newsletter of the Order of Xnum, which studies philosophy.

Changing Perception is the Great Work

BOOK OF THE HEB-SED

The problem of perception is central to philosophy. How do we know the "truth" of what we see? Do we have built in parts (Plato's Forms, Chomsky's innate grammar) that interpret the world? Or are we a blank slate that builds up a model of the Cosmos by representation? Common sense tells that we simply observe the world. Representative Realism suggests that we know the models in our heads only:

THE REAL world – is filtered – IDEAS OF THE WORLD – and adds to – MY KNOWING

(There is no direct path from world to knowing)

The model suggests that though the world is real, all I have are my representations of it – which are caused by this.

This is a pretty sort of philosophical idea and has backing from linguistic (Sapir/Whorf) and socially constructed theories of reality (Steven Pinker/John Searle). I wish to provide a different model based on the thoughts of Alfred North Whitehead (*Symbolism, Its Meaning and Effect)* and the work of Husserl. I feel my model is both an accurate description of how we navigate reality and a useful tool in dealing with Aquino's theory of magic. I am certainly not the first person to play with these ideas. Colin Wilson did an excellent job in his *Introduction to the New Existentialism*, 1966.

I propose that each act of perception has two parts or vectors, that when focused produce knowing in the subjective world. The first vector is *immediacy,* the non-filtered sense data. The house is on fire. My wife is crying. The curry is spicy. This level of perception does not call for a thinking self. Any mechanical simulation could do it. The event suggests an action. This is the world that we "live in." The perception may be valid or invalid. An illusion is as valid a set of signals if is acted upon. I see no *philosophical* justification in claiming that there is a filter (or a need for a filter) for this data.

I call the second vector *meaning perception.* Now, most thinkers would view this vector as an "effect" (David Hume's notion). That is to say, I experience something and then I think about it. I propose that *meaning perception* is a separate action and need not be seen as causally arising from sense perception. In other words, I don't think life happens and then we think about it. I am suggesting that the quest for meaning is ongoing and receives impressions and deals with them separately than our mechanical reaction. This vector is what I feel the phenomenologists call internationality. Perception is willed – you have to look for something and have some notion that you would find it. If I had never heard of a No Smoking sign, I would not look for it. It was said that Aztec shamans could not "see" the boats of Cortez. If one took the representative reality model, we would accept this – common sense refutes it. My model allows for both. In *immediacy* the sense data was there. In *meaning perception* there was no event because nothing had prepared an internal place for meaning.

Colin Wilson draws other conclusions from the existence of these vectors but gives us an insightful metaphor as to the relationship of the two vectors:

During the war, when it was the question of destroying certain dams in Germany, the R.A.F. was confronted with the problem of how an aircraft could be made to fly very low over a lake at a precisely determined height. It was obviously no solution to suggest trailing a long ruler from the underside of the aeroplane down to the surface of the water. Then someone suggested the obvious and simple solution: to install two spotlights, one in the nose and one in the tail, whose beams would converge at precisely the right distance under the plane. All the pilot had to do was to switch on both lights, and when both beams made a single circle on the water, keep the plane at exactly that height. (Pg. 72)

Much human disaster comes from the lack of focus of these beams of perception. Humans that are drawn to the magical life rely far too strongly on *meaning perception*. They live in their heads, basing their experience on pre-digested representations of reality often carving reality up into ten (Kabala), twelve (Zodiac) or twenty-four pieces (Runes). Simple parts of the human experience like keeping a job seem beyond them – and despite their vaunted Satanic ambitions of world conquest, they are baffled and stymied by the very aspects of the world that their "inferiors" negotiate with grace and ease. The opposite pole – people who are driven only by *immediacy* may excel in any endeavor that does not rely on matching current action to past deeds or future plans. They are great workers, consumers, and soldiers. They have no patience for symbolism – and are less likely to be duped by social engineering. They actually make up the stable matrix that allows human life to flourish. However, they cannot deal with events that are grounded in meaning. They have a hard time understanding difficult political issues, religious choices, or appreciations of the arts.

The Setian can use the two-vector theory of perception. She knows that *immediacy* provides a vast amount of data which she cannot process. It is important to note impressions beyond what would be logically deductible. This isn't mystic mumbo-jumbo – the well-known phenomenon of the "gift of fear" has saved the lives of many policemen and firefighters. The ability to derive insight (or as Magus Neilly would say Synesis) from raw sense data makes humans into great detectives, human resource personnel, psychologists, and con men. The Setian usually learns the need to try and keep sense data remembered as precisely as possible so that what is overlooked can be utilized. Aleister Crowley made a magical exercise of such remembering (in *Liber Thisarb)*.

A great deal of the Magus Polaris Law of "Reyn Til Runa!" is about the improvement of the contents of the psyche so that more accurate *meaning perception* can be obtained. Dr. Flowers told me the story once of a person asking him, "Who is Thorr?" At the moment she asked the question, a dramatic thunderbolt flashed outside. He gestured at the natural phenomenon, but his audience shrugged. Without having obtained the mythical information, *meaning perception* could not occur. Humans in leadership roles deal with *meaning perception* at all times. It allows them to make informed decisions about the cause of events and how to create a desired effect in a given situation. *Meaning perception* is the basis of law and government. If we can perceive events thusly, we can navigate toward an ideal. On less the noble front humans in leadership positions construct the *meaning perception* for humans who lack the ability (or more often are too lazy) to perceive thusly. The evening news, the editorial, the pep-rally are all examples of the leadership class creating *meaning perception* for their tribe. The apparent disconnect some people feel between Lesser Black Magic and Greater Black Magic is resolved in terms of *meaning perception* – both activities are about the enrichment and manipulation of *meaning perception*. In my model Medial Black Magic is more of an attunement between *meaning perception* and *immediacy*.

The magician trains her *meaning perception* through education and research. The better her efforts, the less she is bound by *meaning perceptions* of others. She can fly her plane further from the known airways without fear of flying too high or low. The magician becomes better at *immediacy* in both socially approved ways – for example, exercising as a method of staving off Alzheimer's – and in socially unproved ways – for example attempting to improve dreaming skills in the Order of the Wells of Wyrd or the para-senses with the MetaMind Element. Neither vector is sufficient for navigation, and the attitudes of Receptivity (to gain *immediacy* and data for meaning) and Will to focus the two vectors so that a new item can Come Into Being in the subjective universe must be cultivated, discussed, and experimented with.

SOME USEFUL LINKS

Social Construction of Reality

http://en.wikipedia.org/wiki/Social_constructionism

Phenomenology in Philosophy

http://plato.stanford.edu/entries/phenomenology/

http://en.wikipedia.org/wiki/Phenomenology_(philosophy)

Phenomenology in Psychology

http://en.wikipedia.org/wiki/Phenomenology_(psychology)

Phenomenology in Religion

http://en.wikipedia.org/wiki/Phenomenology_of_religion

Gift of Fear

http://www.uncommon-knowledge.co.uk/book_review/gift-of-fear.html

Liber Thisarb

http://hermetic.com/crowley/libers/lib913.html

Senses and Words

I am a Master of the Order of the Vampyre and make occasional contributions to its journal, Nightwing. *In this article I explain the Words of the Temple of Set in terms of their perception. This is a sensual example of the philosophical ideas in the last essay.*

When I first joined the Temple, the OV was said to Teach the Words Indulgence, Xeper, and Thelema as a guide to the Vampyric lifestyle. The OV sees the change it Works on its members as total change. You are as much a Vampyre while you are brushing your teeth in the morning as you are in the ritual chamber as you are in the club. I would like to offer the following meditation that allows the Vampyre to take in Words on a sacramental basis – in other words develop, methods to eat them when desired. The current constellation of Aeonic Words has sensory correspondences. If you feel that you need to take in one of their currents, you may do so in a physical way by turning into the sense and willing the inflow.

Indulgence is connected with the sense of Smell. Anton was fascinated with smell and sex, which is why he had *Odoratus Sexualis* on the COS reading List. LaVey's magical system works on Nostalgia. He had Erotic Crystallization Inertia as its method of Immortalization, and his Compassion Ritual sends the patient back to an earlier healthier time. Memory, as we know, is most strongly associated with Smell, and Smell is the key of Indulgence.

Runa is connected with Hearing. Flowers Heard "Roonah" in a trance state during a roadtrip/Quest in the Year IX. He immediately reworked his life to pursue what he had Heard. Fate had placed him in the University of Texas, where Edgar Polomé was working on the names of the Elder Futhark, and Flowers was soon to be one of the first humans to hear the reconstructed sounds in hundreds of years. The root word of Runa means something that is "whispered or yelled." Odhinn whispered the word "Runa" in his dead son Baldr's ear (see the *Vafthruthnismal*) so that he might Remember himself in the next life.

Xeper is connected with Sight. It came to Aquino by reading in Budge's *Easy Lessons in Egyptian Hieroglyphics*. Khepra is a sun god, the Dawn, described as an Eye. Eyes figure largely in Aquino's magical writings – he lists them in his Invocation to Set, in the Priesthood Ordination Ceremony and has described himself as an Eye. The initials of his name, "MAA" correspond to the Egyptian verb "to see" – Maa.

Remanifest is connected with Touch. It has the same root word as the English words "manual" or "manipulate." Remanifest is the Shaping of Essence by Will, Thought, and Feeling. If you work clay into a mug, you have Remanifested the clay. It is both still clay and yet individuated and made more beautiful. The imagery of Lewis' personal work that reflects the Serpent shedding its skin as a sign of growth reinforces the connection with Touch.

Arkte is connected with Taste. Taste is the sense that interfaces basic need with conscious desire. You don't need music or incense, but you do need food. In this we are most like our animal brothers. This is the sense that separates predator from prey, but also the sense that creates community – think of a Conclave buffet. Taste holds both the dark side of Arkte – it is an imaginal gateway for lycanthropy and Vampyrism – and its light side – picture Lady Lilith feeding birds.

You can work with this in many ways. You can choose a special perfume you wear for Indulgence, hang certain art for Xeper, paint or sculpt for Remanifest, have a special dinner for Arkte and so on. You are free to have the deepest religious and magical experiences of your life in front of anyone, using only one magical tool: your body.

Faith in Books (of the Month)

I wrote this for my friend Tiffany Brown's webzine Sugnum. *It discusses the imaginal – the eerie realms where the cognitive imagination illustrates the Cosmos to itself. Much of my practice as a fiction writer or reader happens in this realm, and I wanted to put down a few thoughts (albeit in somewhat tongue-in-cheek fashion).*

For Christianity, Islam, and Judaism there is the book, but for newer faiths there are novels, short stories, and movies. It is likely your own worldview is informed by these ideas.

Riding home from the University of Texas campus, I overheard two people discussing the merits of cable versus satellite TV. This was a vitally important discussion for me to hear since I had recently invested in the later and discontinued the former. "Brand X dish is better because they provide the SciFi Channel and I watch *Battlestar Galatica* religiously." Her friend gasped and told that it was "Blasphemous" to use the word "religion" for anything rather than Christianity. I started to point out to them that many religious moments in the late Nineteenth and Twentieth Centuries were based on fiction, but my stop was coming up and I never start a theological discussion unless I have forty-five blocks to finish it by.

For our ancestors' ancestors it was easier because they didn't have the tyranny of the Book. Fiction and religion were seen for the common activities they were. Both involved a trance state wherein certain images were presented in a certain order to produce a desired effect – bit by bit it was all laid out and in the end the soul was made better. Hopefully, the now-transformed soul would have both more knowledge and more strength/Inspiration to transform the world (in accordance with the model that had been presented). Storytellers have known this forever, and the first people to write down their myths certainly understood this very well. No one complained that Ovid restructured the myths into a good story. No one yelled at Plato when he created myths like Atlantis. Homer had few critics. Of course, Homer and Plato never rode the bus and Ovid did but seldom.

Let's look at a few modern faiths (and looser belief structures) that derive some of their philosophy and imagery from fiction and some fictional responses to these faiths. Since an average SIGNUM article can be read aloud in a forty-five-block bus journey, I should be safe. (If you read this article aloud, you will discover that it is an invocation full of hidden messages. (ffit ot yenom dneS).

Bulwer-Lytton, a popular novelist of the Nineteenth Century and that man who introduced the phrase "It was a dark and stormy night," wrote three novels about occult powers coming from secret societies, the future, or the mysterious and ancient East. Telepathy, remote viewing, healing by visualization, and other commonplaces of the New Age movement came from his occult romances, including certain occult techniques that he had heard of from friends that had visited India, such as the use of certain mandalas (tattvas) to invoke the power of elemental spirits. His novels, *Zannoi*, *The Coming Race*, and *A Strange Tale* paved the way and provided many ides for H. P. Blavatsky, who founded the Theosophical Society – which still has branched in every major world city. Lytton's novels also had a major shaping influence on the Golden Dawn and those groups which evolved from it, such as the Ordo Temple Orinetalis (OTO), the Fraternitas Saturni, and the Society of the Inner Light. His work also influenced a magical society with an American base, the Hermetic Brotherhood of Luxor, which was the world's first mail-order initiation society. The occultist who popularized these practices did so well with them that they are part and parcel of contemporary culture and can be read about anywhere from learned dissertations on parapsychology to the newspaper tabloids.

The OTO featured a reading list by Aleister Crowley that included fiction as part of magical training. But just as Crowley used fiction to teach Magick, fiction writers were quick enough to use Crowley as inspiration for their characters. He served as Oliver Haddo for Somerset Maugham in *The Magician*, as Christopher Carlton for E. M. Butler in *Silver Wings*, as "the Mahatma" for Arnold Bennett in *Paris Nights* and Dr. Trelawney for Anthony Powell in *The Kindly Ones*.

Crowley's' message about the importance of fiction was clear enough to one OTO initiate, Gerald Gardner, who decided that writing the weird tale could act as a kind of Wish, brings about a certain social and magical change. Gardner put forth his brand of witchcraft in his 1949 fantasy novel *High Magic's Aid*. This novel pretty much launched modern Wicca into the popular mind and was greatly responsible for its early growth in the United Kingdom. Wicca has reached out to both an historic past and a fictional one and cast forth new fictional visions in pop culture. It does not take a genius to see that the characters of Willow and Terra on *Buffy the Vampire Slayer* will attract a new generation of witches, perhaps even reaching entire language groups that had never heard of Gardner, through the miracle of international syndication.

As you can see, there is a strange loopiness in this. In 1922 a Theosophist named Talbot Mundy had a new novel of occult truths, *The Unknown Nine*, about a secret of society of nine wise men who ruled the world. This particular book inspired Howard

Stanton Levey to say the Unknown Nine ruled his Church of Satan, and the Church of Satan's successor the Temple of Set is really ruled by nine people called the Council of Nine. Fiction to religion to fiction to religion . . .

Howard Stanton Levey, who wrote under the name Anton LaVey, drew on several fictional sources. Church of Satan imagery can be traced to *Nightmare Alley* by William Lindsay Gresham, *The Devil on the XIXth Century* by Leo Taxil as well as Huysmans and De Sade. A stranger influence was LaVey's love of German expressionist films and the photography of William Mortensen, which lead to an "angular" aesthetic both in his artwork and ritual style. (Did I mention strange loops? German expressionists were interested in light and shadow effects because of occult research going on in the Fraternitas Saturni).

Early in the Church of Satan's development, LaVey realized the importance of using art to send his Vision into the world. He was the technical advisor to two films, *Rosemary's Baby* and *The Devil's Rain*. A young bishop of the Church of Satan who later went on to found the Temple of Set, Michael Aquino got a similar gig for the film *Satan's Asylum*.

LaVey had been avid reader of *Weird Tales* and a collector of Arkham House books. A non-Satanist acquaintance of his, the science fiction author Mike Resnick, once suggested to Anton that he could really spice things up by adding some of the images of H. P. Lovecraft, Frank Long, and Robert E. Howard into his rituals. LaVey did a few rituals on this theme, such as the "Die Elektrischen Vorspiele" and had his left-hand man Michael Aquino pen two as well – "The Ceremony of the Nine Angles" and the "Call to Cthulhu." These produced a big effect on the occult world, making other people try their hand at taking Lovecraft's fictional bogeys and making them into sources of power. Kenneth Grant, John Hay, and "Simon" all tried their hand at this, and it would be hard to walk into any occult store in the English-speaking world without finding one of their curious volumes, some slime spill from the trail of the serpent Cthulhu . . .

This, too, of course had its strange loop. When Aquino created "Yuggothic" for his Lovecraftian rituals, he certainly could not have predicted that Umberto Eco would use some of the same made-up language in his novel *Foucault's Pendulum*, which will no doubt create its own faith in the fullness of time.

The Temple of Set also features a good deal of fiction on its reading list from the *Her-Bak* novels of Isha Schwaller de Lubicz to *The Stars My Destination* of Alfred Bester. In the great tradition of strange loops, the Temple of Set is itself the object of an hilarious fictional parody by John Shirley called "Your Servants in Hell" (in his latest anthology "Darkness Divided") wherein the left hand path concerns with self-power are seen as comical mouthings of losers and the high priest of the group a lubricious fat man named Butterwick (who bears a strange resemblance to me – I discount that my friend John could have ever intended this).

The Devil's Rain was John Travolta's first film. He later became one of the best-known members of the Church of Scientology, a group whose belief structure some consider science fictional, perhaps because it was created by gifted Science Fiction writer L. Ron Hubbard – and, of course, Travolta went on to star in *Battlefield Earth*, based on a Hubbard novel. Hubbard himself had started out as a member of the OTO before embarking on a career of fiction-writing and religion-founding. Money from Hubbard's estate funds the biggest (and frankly best) contest for science fiction writers, so the beat goes on . . .

I had meant to cover the Church of All Worlds, which has roots in Heinlein's *Stranger in a Strange Land*, and the fiction of Ayn Rand, but I see the bus stop up ahead in the near future. There's a man waiting there. Is he reading a bible, or is *Year's Best Fantasy I* with my story "The Prophecies at Newfane Asylum" in it?

Only god knows.

On Runa and the Degree System

One of the most important magical evenst I have Witnessed in the Temple of Set was the Utterance of the Word Runa by Stephen Edred Flowers. The sense of the Unknown impels all human truth-processes: Science, Art, Love, Politics, and Magic. Flowers' Word made us acutely aware of our Desires and such awareness is the goal of Left Hand Path initiation. By more keenly feeling our desires we create the intent that not only guides our conscious action but, beckons the events from the "future" that happen to us. Flowers' Work, like the Work of all Magi, revitalizes the system it is in Uttered in. In order to facilitate such revitalization in the Temple, I wrote the short essay below in a letter to the Masters of the Temple. The Degrees of the Temple have a gem assigned to them and each grade has a manual we call collectively the Jeweled Tablets. These are Setian I° /Crystal, Adept II°/Ruby, Priest or Priestess III°/Onyx, Magister or Magistra IV°/Sapphire, Magus or Maga V°/Amethyst and Ipsissimus or Ipsissima VI°/Topaz.

Of late I have been thinking a great deal about Runa and the states of Being Recognized by the Temple of Set. We often perform our Recognitions based on the questions we ask of potential candidates, but it seems that their activity (i.e., what they want to know about themselves and the Cosmos) is what really reflects their Being.

On the Crystal Plain the candidate wants to know if anyone has ever created a way of knowledge. In other words, does this Setian stuff work? No one (that we want) comes to the Temple of Set for answers. They come for a way to ask questions. Most of what we offer is a rational approach, which itself is a rare thing – water in the desert of the irrational. But we offer a supra-rational way to ask, and once they prove to us and themselves that it is theirSelf they are asking, then they can play with the material that drives most humans mad in the "occult world."

In the Ruby Plain the candidate can explore those mysteries that others have fashioned, or create mysteries of their own to Play with. Here things are, for the most part, safe and fun. The deep mysteries of the Self do rise in symbolic form, but they need not have the searchlight of Self focused on them. Here is what most people that are interested in the occult world want. They can Play with magic, rather than have magic Play with them. The safe Playground has two borders – the divine and the other way of knowing.

In the Onyx Plain the two borders become obsessive. The candidate wants to know about two mysteries. She wants to know about the Divine, and as she Knows about a Wyrd thing happen to her, she starts to know about other people in a supra-rational way. Suddenly she knows things about Setian Q. She becomes almost addicted to Working with people for the strange moment of the Priesthood. Meanwhile, she begins to rationally figure out Set. She knows somehow the two activities are connected. Then she has the flash. Because the Prince of Darkness is Knowing her, she is filled with the way of Knowing others. She understands that just as her Essence directly works with others, it is being worked with. This is a staggering realization that will not come to all in the Onyx Plain, but there is a realization beyond it. One day she realizes that this Knowing/Being Known has been going on all her life.

In the Sapphire Plain the Master has a new Mystery. He knows that the interpretation all of his significant life events have been his work and that the reinterpretation of them is now a trans-personal Work. As he heals, explores, or Indulges in his history, people are drawn to him. Some come as people needing healing, some come (as Magistra C. pointed out to me) as living examples of the harm he has undergone, some come to Give the right Signs. Everything the profane world calls the "past" or the "unconscious" stops being either of those things to him. In searching these Wells he may have discovered a Secret rowned (= whispered) to him at an early age. This Secret is the organizing principle for the events of his life and explains all other Becoming he has Witnessed or is Witnessing.

In the Amethyst Plain the Maga has one Mystery. How did this great Principle remain Hidden to her for so long – and by the same magnetization principle for the Fourth Degree mentioned above – how is this Principle Hidden from enlightened beings now? Why don't people get it? This question burns with an intensity that is as strong as the Divine Knowing encountered in the Plain of Onyx. The period of the Fever is terrible and beautiful, easy and hard. If the candidate comes to Know the answer – that the principle was Hidden because it is one of many which must Work out their Wyrd, then she enters the Topaz Plain.

The Topaz Plain is the clarity that comes after the Fever dream. The great mystery has the same twofold seeming of the Sapphire Plain. On one hand the Ipsissimus wonders how each of the Mysteries have been linked in his own Becoming and why they are still there – why there are still questions in him from all of the Plains. On the other hand he wonders at how each of these fields of Mystery are linked both among living humans in the here-and-now and among those in the past and future.

At any time humans may fall away from these states, but the questions will find them wherever they are unless Self-destructive forces have been too well invoked.

Because of their magnetic power, the Fourth Degree by simply Being calls the saving power of mystery to the Earth.

The Last Word (on the First Beast)

This is a fictional/imaginal response to Crowley.

Do this, do that, they were always so full of things for little Alick. Just as soon as he would get father's boots polished, Mother's voice, "Edward Alexander, where are you, you little heathen?" She would have something else for him to *do*. The world of the Plymouth Brethren was a *Doing* world – all the time *doing*. There was no Be-ing at all. Just action. Actively reading the *Bible*, actively being birched by the teachers, actively missing father as he tramped around spreading the Word of God. He took aside a friend at school and whispered in his ear, "Be not Do." They threw him out for trying to corrupt another. But he still dreamed of it – a magical world where by simply Be-ing things around you changed. That would be god-like. Mother's yelling again. Yelling for "the little beast." Better run.

WHAT is this, Mr. Crowley? *Aceldama - A Place to Bury Strangers In*. Did you write this filth? Oh, very clever, by 'a gentleman of the University of Cambridge' you think people will think you're Shelley, don't you? What on earth makes you think anyone will think of you anytime? Your family's beer money? Or do you think that they'll remember you for climbing some mountain last year? Shelley was a poet, Mr. Crowley, what are you? I say, Mr. Crowley, that you are a nothing, and I am sad that this piece of doggerel was ever connected with our university.

THOU canst not pass by me, saith the Guardian of the West, unless thou canst tell me my name. "Darkness is thy Name, thou Great One of the Path of Shades." The Hegemon had pulled away the hoodwink for a moment, and the neophyte saw Osiris for the first time. Another damn dead man in his way. The Hegemon pulls the hoodwink over his eye and leads him to the North where purifications of water and fire await. The neophyte had already known water and fire; this was a waste of time.

WILT thou marry me? It will get thee out of thy troubles. Rose laughed. It was wonderful. They would piss off both of their families. From little risks and tiny sins came the little drops that will be the Nile. Drop by drop until the river comes into being that Re-shapes the land. And on the bank of the Nile, what did she tell him? "They are waiting for you."

SHALL I set them all free? If I tell them, really tell them, they will know freedom. Best I reveal bit by bit. It will take them three hundred years to awaken. Fortunately I will have heirs. That is all I can hope for. They will Understand. The others will have no idea that Joy is part of my Job. I cry for my heirs because of the Curse.

BE. I told him the truth in the way he would understand. *Being* is the state where your higher and lower selves are in harmony. It is the entrance to the City of the Pyramids. He went off to wander in the hills above the monastery. That either means he got it or he's gone crazy. If it's the former, maybe I'll be able to borrow a few pounds from him when success follows. If the latter, I hope there is no trouble with the bloody Italians.

THE Fourfold Horror of the Smoke. Unloose the Pit! By the dread Word that Set-Typhon has heard, "Zazas nasatanada Zazas Zazas!" Breaking the Veil was easy when you lived in both worlds. If he could just give a glimpse of that other world to the priest as the priest buggered him. It would Work here, Paris was the city of holy whores. Everyman dreams of Paris. If the priest would only fuck with courage, Hermes would come *verba* *nefanda ferens.*

WHOLE of the world is available to any man with four male disciples (who are deformed) and four women disciples (who come from the four corners of the world). Every movement starts with the very few. Nine is the number – if you could get twice that number. Eighteen conscious men and women you could create something that would last forever. If you can't get eighteen (including yourself) you'd best try for eighteen words. 11 + 4 -+3 will do.

OF the mechanism of heirs, he made a mistake. He thought that nine months of fucking Hilarion in Vancouver should a Childe make. You can't do the Work for another. Achad wasn't his son. Achad had the terrible innocence of Christ, an innocence that sees no distinctions. Achad was the Child of the Toad that he crucified. Death to the children of the Toads! Let them not walk with the shape of men. Let them not deceive the hopeful or mislead the true.

THE wizard Amalantrah explained to him about the Egg and the four elements, and he knew that he had crossed the desert at last. That was the most important lesson. That you must cross the desert. Cross difficult territories and be transformed thereby. The length of the journey is the power of Becoming. The visit with the wizard in the woods had taught him much. What he did not know was that the wizard changed his name to Gandalf and began visiting a man born in South Africa. He taught that guy the same lesson, too.

LAW that's mankind's problem, law. They're always looking for law and meaning from outside. What they need is a law to help them get at the *inside*. "Not to claw bark, is that not the Law? Are we not men?" No, that wasn't the answer. That wasn't the law that separated men from beasts. Twenty-two years after the death of the First Beast, theologian Harvey Cox was to deduce that the law was dreaming. Cox dubbed mankind *homo fantasia* and says, "...it was just as much his propensity to dream and fantasize as it was his augers and axes that first set man apart from the beasts." Harvey Cox, *The Feast of Fools* (Cambridge, MA: Harvard University Press, 1969), pg. 11. You Shall Dream And Make Dreams True, This Is The Law.

LOVE that's my problem. If I could find a love so perfect that it was Being — a love so perfect that it *made* me do things. I loved Rose. I loved the Monkey, I loved the Camel, the Spider, the Dog. I loved the Ape. I loved the Monster. I loved Victor. I loved Poppa. I loved Mother. I loved Jesus. I loved and I wanted. How I wanted. Who will love me, who will love little Alick?

IS the lissome lust of light

 And the riotous pipes of Pan

 Enough for the City of Dreadful Night?

 Shall excess light that dead soul land?

 Can I be caught up in scarlet snare

 And in Love by Leah eaten whole?

 Can I sacrifice myself on altar fair

 And be dissolved body and soul?

 Come with pipe and come with flute

 Come with trumpets sounding shrill

 Come play the devil's magick lute,

 And carry me to fire on yon Druid's Hill.

I will lay down gladly my one life

If I can cause the Fire to be my wife.

THE dawn came every day. Women came and went. Children were dropped. Men came and went. The dawn came every day. Here are the words, "Hail to Thee who are Khephra in thy rising, even unto Thee who are Re in they strength, Harmachis in Thy beauty, who travelest over the Heavens in Thy barque at the Uprising of the Sun." Say it every day. The dawn comes every day. Women come and go (talking of Michelangelo).

LAW that's the trouble with you Marxist chaps – your law is completely material – you're not going to transcend the world with a law *of* the world. Now if you would just adopt the Law of Thelema you could really get somewhere. I've already written Trotsky on the subject.

LOVE my poems please – three of them are in *The Oxford Book of English Mystical Verse 1917*. Love my mountaineering. Love my paintings. Love my *Book* more than anything. It was the one moment I knew Love. Love that moment and you love me. Do that in memory of me.

UNDER what lucky stars was I born that I might tramp up and down the whole of the world like Poppa spreading the word? Under what lucky stars was I born that I knew the love of hundreds of beautiful women and fierce-eyed men? Under what lucky stars was I born that I might see the death of the modern and usher in the Aeonic? Under what lucky stars was I born that I could say One Thing to all the worlds, and to all the Stars in their dance? Under what lucky stars was I born that I could utter

WILL

?

(for the Heir)

Why Bears?

I wrote this for a class in Indo-European linguistics I took at the University of Texas. The University of Texas has a strong connection with Indo-European linguistics because of the late Dr. Edgar Polomé. His connections to the Work of Mircea Eliade proved a crucial link when my mentor, Dr. Stephen Flowers, began exploring the Word "Runa." Amung the magical tools I gained from Dr. Flowers was an interest in linguistics as a way of Knowing how the intra-subjective universe changes over time. Magicians must be keenly aware of the Roots of the ideas they manipulate. Because of my Understanding of Bears, I was able to help Maga Aquino in her articulation of Arkte, which means she-bear and connects the Setian to the wild beauty of the animal world.

Speakers of Germanic, Slavic, and Baltic languages seem to react differently than other Indo-Europeans to the idea of "Bear." There seems to be a taboo, which they shared with Irish during the Viking Age. Most of the rest of the IE world seems to like *ɾkso-*, which can possibly rendered as "destroyer of beehives." When looking at the whole role of tabuization in language change, the lore theory of the *name* and its operative ("magical") function is key. The original Germanic word for "bear" would have been cognate to the Latin *ursus*. The only remnant of that etymon in Germanic is the feminine ON *yrsa*. I will look at the IE word; the Germanic, Slavic and Baltic variant forms; and finally propose that a pre-Indo-European bear cult encountered by migrating IE people lead to the tabuization. I will mention the last place I think we tend to see the bear cult in our day-to-day life.

The word for 'bear" in Greek is *arktos*, in Latin *ursus*, in the Celtic languages *arth* (Welsh) and *aruz* (Breton), in Avestan *arsa*, and in Sanskrit *rakshasas*. The later term comes to mean a variety of shape-shifting, flesh-eating demon encountered in popular tales to this day. The Romance languages copied Latin (It. *orso*, Sp. *oso*, Rum *urs*). Irish began with the form *ari*, but later adopted *mathgamain*, which means "good calf" – probably a euphemistic construction influenced by the same "Bear Cult." I will have more to say about this change later.

The Germanic peoples, the Baltic peoples, and the Slavic speakers euphemized the destroyer of beehives. The Germanic speakers (except for the exception I noted above) prefer words meaning "brown": ON *bjorn*, OHG *bero*, OE *brun*, and Du. *Beer*, etc. As I noted in my last paper, the OE hero "Beowulf" (bee-wolf)" is an interesting phrasing of the concept. Germanic people used the name of the bear in religious ways. Thorr's nickname was Bjorn. A few names attest a connection between "bears" and "holiness" in the Middle Ages, such as the ON name *Hallibjorn* (holy bear), or OHG *Halecbern* (holy bear). Grimm tells us that as late as the Nineteenth Century folk still regarded the bear as "holy" and "the king of beasts."

Baltic speakers avoided the original root as well. They preferred words meaning "hairy" or "shaggy": Lith. *lokys*, Lett. *lacis*, OPruss, *clokis* (all from **tlâkis* hairy). The Lithuanians were particularly reluctant to use the IE word, they also copied the Germanic speakers with *beras* and the Slavic speakers with *meška*.

All of the Slavic speakers used some variation of "honey-eater" composed of *medŭ* (honey) and *ed* (eat), such as the Russian *medved*, Polish *medźweidź*, and so forth.

It seems clear that these groups encountered some reason to lose the IE root during their migrations. They encountered the reasons before they had split into individual languages but after they had split into families of languages. They did not pick up loan words for bear, which suggest that they may have picked cultic technology but did not absorb the cultic practice. That is to say we are dealing with adoption not assimilation.

The bear-cult is well attested among Central Asians and among the Lapps. In fact, the marker of 'bear-cult" and shamanism almost exactly coincide. Many religionists agree that Odhinn's initiation by self-hanging is a direct copy of the tree-climbing initiation of Siberian shamans. The trance-magic of the ancient Germanic speakers was called *seidhr*, which belonged to the goddess Freyja. Although in later times two tomcats drew her chariot, in the earliest form it was drawn by two he-bears. The non-IE magical techniques not only seem to come from people that venerated bears, but have bears as guardians.

Old Norse literature is full of an idea of donning the skin of a bear (or occasionally wolf) to become that animal. This concept seems to arrive from exposure to a non-IE shamanic tradition, and lasted well into Christian times when the Viking wearers of bearskins gave us the word for *berserk* fury. Certain ethno-botanists suggest that the aid of certain mushrooms may have added to their bear-like fury, which would connect their practice to central Asian shamanism.

The 'bear-cult' seems to arrivamong the Germanic peoples from outside source and to make its mark felt in all divisions of German society. Thorr as *Bjorn* represented the warriors, Freya the third function, and the bear-names for highborn folk the first. The magic associated with bears, *seidhr*, is said to be "unmanly" and just plain bad. In the *Loksanna* Odhinn is made fun of for having mastered it, which may suggest a non-native origin.

Among the Slavs the bear was a symbol of rebirth because it slept through the winter. Until the coming of communism, the Slavic custom of having a man dressed as a bear leave a cave to terrorize a town and carry off a woman was part of spring festivities.

The next logical question is "When did these IE groups meet my hypothetical bear-cult?" It would have to be after 2300 B.C,E. or the adopted form would be the same. So it occurred after a commonality existed for Germanic/Celtic/Baltic/Slavic languages. It is likely the change in Irish, but not in Welsh, Breton, etc., indicates that the Irish got the magico-religious news after they had writing, likely during times of intense interaction with the Vikings, which was more trade and less raid than movies would tell us. The Baltic languages don't help us here because of their late attestation.

I would hypothesize that sometime during the intense Gothic-Slavic interaction of the Chernyakovo (Second to Fifth centuries A.D.) the active trade between so many groups brought the Germanic, Slavic, and Baltic speakers into contact with a shape-shifting bear-cult either from Asia or the extreme north of Europe, where such cults existed until the last century. This cultic process would have been attractive to IE peoples who had their own bear-cult connected with first-function power. The primal cult, which remains in people like Arthur = "son of bear" and Odysseus, who was the great-grandson of a bear (an actual she-bear), would be nicely complimented with a secret/taboo technology that lets you literally turn into a bear. One need not be descended from a bear anymore.

The original Slavic vampire was a bear-like undead, fat and covered in brown-fur, whose name was not to be mentioned. It has had a few centuries and a couple of notable literary creations to reshape its myth, but the shape-shifting creature whose nature is taboo and who can inspire fear is apt to be at your threshold as you read this. It is unlikely that it will say, "I am pre-Indo-European substratum!" but will utter other arcane phrases to obtain honey-sweet treats from you . . .

WORKS CONSULTED

Buck, Carl D. 1951 *A dictionary of selected synonyms in the principle Indo-European Languages*. Chicago: Univ. of Chicago Press

Campbell, Joseph. 1968 *The Masks of God: Primitive Mythology*. New York: Viking Press

Carpenter, Rhys. 1946 *Folk Tale, Fiction and Saga in the Homeric Epics*. Los Angeles: Univ. of California Press

Eliade, Mircea 1964 *Shamanism: Archaic Techniques of Ecstasy*. New York: Bollingen Foundation (Originally: *La Chamnisme et les techniques archaïques de l'extase*. Paris 1951

Grimm, Jacob. 1976 *Teutonic Mythology*. Gloucester, Mass: Dover Press (Originally: *Deutsche Mythology*. Berlin 1854 edition)

Mallory, J. P. 1989 *In Search of the Indo-Europeans*. London: Thames and Hudson

Our Unsung Hero

The Order of the Trapezoid uses the idea of the hero as role model. We are closer to heroes than we are to the gods. I have explored this idea in ritual, in essay, and I was motivated to take a course examining the hero cross-culturally from the late Dr. Mark Southern, one of Dr. Polomé's protégés. As a writer, I am interested in how and why humans tell tales. As magician, I am interested in the effects of stories on the psyches of others and myself. And as a cleric, I am interested in how mythology gives humans access to their psyches. I had written an earlier article on the Poetic Edda for the American Book Review, which I incorporate in this essay. A Setian is a Setian, whether doing college work, reviewing book,s or running a restaurant. Setianism isn't a costume for weekends.

In our quick course this summer, we have been reading texts and thinking about what the texts say. I've been wondering about why the texts are written. There is no need for texts – the Vedas have got along quite well without them. At first I thought I would write about some ideas about the future that I felt all of these texts contained, but I have realized that although I believe there to be some very similar reasons for the creation of these texts, there are certain differences as well. Therefore, I wish to address some of the similarities and some of the differences – but overall I want to start with the idea that "Deathless fame" is about more than being famous.

Books limit the interpretation a text can have. The "facts" of the narrative remain fixed, the hero's name doesn't change nor the god be replaced with one more currently in fashion. If the moral of the tale is written down, then each reader has to think about and evaluate that moral. Books represent an ending of traditional culture, where the memes and motifs belong to the organic evolving society as a whole – instead they fix in time one person's or group's ideas. Now, it takes hubris to be a spokesperson for a group. The idea of an honest human bridging the link between men and gods, and man and the ancestors, is ended with the coming of the book. Men may interpret the book, in which case they have become the link between not-so-literate man and the new artifact. Oral traditions are made by cultures, books by men.

The book has a different effect on its reader. He or she does not have to be in a sacred place or time to contact the text. People don't drop by the mead-hall to read. The book does require that the person consulting be trained in the art of reading. Anyone can listen, few could read. Books are the shaping of the world for a cultural elite. They shape the future by shaping the past.

Judaism, the great religion of the book, was shaped during the Persian conquest from a few sources eager to undo polytheism and introduce the idea of the historical manifestation of god in his interaction with his people. This text looks different than the others because it spends far less time with the archaic questions of creation and the nature of god and man, and much time with history. This is a great formula. It removes the cosmic focus and the personal one – and creates a focus on the learned group that can read and interpret the texts, and on the events of the day-to-day world. This powerful blend insures that tradition belongs to a learned elite that is continually repositioning themselves in history. This is the most successful use of the book Amung the groups we studied.

The Egyptians made two different uses of the book. The first was the great inscriptions that cover their stone temples and monuments. Here is a vast and impressive display, which also placed tradition in the hands of a learned caste. (Perhaps this is where the Hebrews got the idea.) The second use of the book was hiding papyri of magical and religious concern in Late Antiquity. This seems to me to reflect a desire to maintain a cultural secret – the religious and magical practices of the Egyptians that were unlike any other people's. This strategy worked. The Nineteenth and Twentieth Century is full of figures like Sir Wallis Budge, who published 150 books all chock full of spells and amulets – which were snapped up by occultists the world over. It is a very strange historical path that magical practices survive Christianity by waiting with a few mummies.

Augustus was less interested in cultural legacy than familial legacy. He wanted to legitimize the rein of the Julio-Claudians, so he hired the best poet he could find. This attempt didn't fare as well. There were many reasons, but the main was you just couldn't legitimize those guys. This use of heroic culture is closest to our own use of it – in other words, advertising. It wasn't written as a sacred text or a magical one. It wasn't performative.

The Greeks were performative. Their written texts were not about cultural identity. One doesn't become more Greek by listening to *Oedipus Rex*. One became a better, more purged Greek by watching a performance. This strategy worked fairly well, as well. Not only do we still discuss the moral, ethical, and emotional contexts of these plays today, but an entire school of psychoanalysis derives many of its notions from *Oedipus Rex*. This is a very peculiar form of survival by means of the book.

Snorri wanted to preserve. This is most like the traditional society's oral strategy.

He used the book, because paganism was dying out, even in the "Man's Halls." He sought to pass on lore, belief, and even poetic technique. (I have written about the passing on of the verse forms elsewhere, and I've attached the article as an appendix.) Snorri was successful – although the survival of only copy of the *Edda* by sheer luck reminds us of caches of papyri. His goal was to hide what was known with a conventional gloss and hope that someone would figure it out.

I am less sure of the motives behind the other texts we have studied and will think more about them. The two things that strike me are how the traditional society views the future and how the book both enabled and prevented this view from living on.

The traditional society sends itself into the deep future by telling what it is proud of in the deep past. The recitation of epic poems is not merely a link with past, it is a promise of the future. While you sit and drink your watered wine and think upon many-tricked Odysseus, you are not only dreaming back toward windy Troy, you are dreaming forwards to your great-grandson's hearing about the wooden horse. The traditional society had obligations to the descendants as well as to the ancestors.

The book fulfilled and destroyed that model. It was easy to send the words into the future. You didn't have to train people to recite; you just had to have faith that art of reading wouldn't die out. (Poor Linear A.) The book was not a communication of the folk to the folk, but of the intellectual to the intellectual. The book was also a terrible admission – it admitted that the culture might die.

The cultures that lived long enough to make the book had seen other cultures die. Often times at the hands of the book-makers. The writing – as the old saw goes – was on the wall. Learn this new technology, or you will vanish. You could cease to be a people.

The warm matrix that would listen to songs would be gone. Sure, the book serves other purposes than the oral tradition, but it does serve.

The book is the hero.

"Experimentation and Tradition: The Constraint of the Edda" in The American Book Review, January-February 1998

The creation of text is something we all have long since forgotten as an invention. Sure, somebody long ago started writing, then a long time after that people began writing stories and signing their name, and then experimental literature began by attacking the conventions. Experimental literature is loosely defined here as any prose whose intent is entirely to *subvert* an existing set of rules either explicit or just dimly perceived. One of the principle forms of experimental literature is that of the manifesto, where one or more writers create an entire poetics, a set of new grammar or other codification of stylistic form, so that the laws governing conventional literary/social/political reality can be overturned.

One of the single most subversive manifestoes of this sort is the *Snorra Edda* by Snorri Sturluson (1178-1241). Its intent was to counter the tide of Christian thinking that the new technology of the Latin alphabet had brought to Iceland around 1000 A.D.

The Icelanders had fled Norway to avoid the taxes and monarchical impulse of King Harald Fairhair. The settlers were intensely interested in preserving their traditions and culture. When Christianity came, it brought the art of writing in Latin, the language of letters and commerce. The existing Runic alphabet existed for wood and stone carving, , which were mainly used for magical purposes, had never bemused for either storytelling or literature. When Latin showed up, a worldview showed up as well, so the first documents reflected this worldview. What are appropriate things to write about? Historical tales, compendium of laws, and accounts of quaint lore. Snorri set out to do a subversive thing. He wanted his contemporaries to write in a vulgar tongue (predating Dante by a few centuries), but most importantly, he urged his contemporaries to write *new* poems in the pagan spirit. Now, this what marks Snorri as a subversive: he wasn't a mere antiquarian.

Snorri has a four-level approach in his *Edda*. Firstly, it suggested a forbidden subject matter -- the rapidly disappearing lore of Odhinn and his band. This is called the "Gylfaginning." Here a complete cosmology of the Teutonic tradition is written down, including not only the mythology, but also magical lore that the Church would rather have seen repressed, the knowledge of how to use writing, that is to say Rune-carving, to affect the world. Secondly, the Edda suggested a series of metaphors from existing skaldcraft. Some of the poems, such as the "Lay of Alvis," are almost nothing more than list of poetic kennings. This is the "Skáldskaparmál" or "Speech of Skaldship." Thirdly, he demonstrates all the verse forms he knows. This is the "Hattal" or the "Counting of the Meters" in which Snorri wrote his encomiastic poem of 102 stanzas, where he demonstrates the forms he has mastered, including such suspicious forms as the "magic meter" or *Galdralag*. Fourthly, he appended a section on the use of the letters themselves – not only in such obvious features as standardizing orthography, but subtle remarks on the esoteric properties on the letters. (Snorri's nephew Olafr Thordharson even wrote an essay on the meaning of the Runes which attached to certain editions of the *Snorra Edda*.)

The word "Edda" is of interest. It probably means "great-grandmother." Wisdom is a feminine entity. Now, we have no problem with the idea of old women as being repositories of wisdom, but this was aimed at the patriarchal Latin reader/thinkers. Later scholars have produced some interesting, but perhaps unsound, speculations on the word, which are a testimony to Snorri's successful subversion. Arni Magnusson suggested in the eighteenth century that the title was best rendered "poetics," and some recent scholars have attempted to link the word with "Odhr," the principal of Inspiration, pointing out not only the possible philological link, but also the idea which is echoed again and again in the poems – that the most precious aspect of poetry is not the technically difficult meter, but the inspiration the meter helps preserve as a mnemotechnic device.

If you doubt the subversive nature of Snorri's collection of poems, consider that it was done in the High Middle ages, a time not known for its free-thinking attitude. Five centuries later when the Italian Renaissance had begun to produce painter's manuals on classical themes, the Church, although weakened, still fought against these ideas. Consider Cardinal Paleotti's response to the painter's manuals that images of the pagan gods were "filthy and criminal" and should be kept out of sight, lest they corrupt the public. Paleotti published his discourse in Bologna in 1584 against the textbooks for artistic revolution that had led Michelangelo to create bas-reliefs of centaurs and other heinous crimes against establishment art.

The subversive nature of pagan iconography is difficult for us to appreciate. We tend to see Botticelli's figures as "pretty" rather than objects of intellectual war, and because of the lack of respect paid to the Northern traditions, Snorri's revolutionary

197

textbook may be entirely overlooked.

We too have the needs of Snorri. We look for the collection of subject matter, language, form, and even grammatical rules to set us free from an existing set of thought. Like Snorri, we wish not to merely play at the images of a forgotten past, but to learn or relearn ways of thinking for a lively future. The questions Snorri poses for us, through the mouth of Odhinn, are the questions that every writer who binds him- or herself with new rules needs to know. Odhinn cautioned those who would carve Runes, those blood-reddened mysterious characters said to effect the very coming into being of this and other worlds:

Do you know how to write? And how to read?

Do you know how to stain? And how to understand?

Do you know how to ask? And how to bless?

Do you know how to send? And how to sacrifice?

The Sumble and You

In the Year XXIV (1999) I experimented with making the hero-worship formula of the Order of the Trapezoid go viral, by writing up a description of the formula of the Sumble, which had been developed in the Hounds of Tindalos Lodge of the Order of the Trapezoid. I cast the essay upon the worldwide web in various places, and I have seen it quoted both with and without attribution in a couple of magical texts. The Sumble is not bound to Left Hand Path or Germanic practices and can be used with profitable results in places as diverse as modern business meetings and pagan gatherings.

It is truth universally acknowledged that we are programmed by our language. A ton of opportunistic therapies take advantage of this axiom. Lot of New Age occultniks sell seminars based on this simple principle. But very, very few people do what I'm about to do. I don't think people should sell water by the river, and if they are, I don't buy it. Here's how to do it. If you want to program your own wetware, find a study of the concepts that underlie the language, and then use the concepts. Step one means real research at seriously heavy libraries. Step two means try and try again until you get a formula that works and then use it. I've found (with the help of a few philologists, cultural historians, and health professionals) a formula that works. Or – like anything in life – it works for the dedicated self-programmer. It is never enough to just know the secret; you must practice it as well. Since I believe in human lib just as much I believe in computer lib, I'll give it to you free. I've passed it on to a software engineering group, and they're going great guns.

The technique is called the sumble. It is derived from a Viking custom of boasts and toasts made the night before an expedition was launched. I'll skip the mythic/philosophical underpinnings right now (although, as an amateur cultural historian, I not only can but sometimes do go on about them for hours). Suffice it to say that you don't have to wear a hat with horns while you do it, nor worship Odhinn, nor get into a longboat when you're done. It has nothing to do with racial ties, but with the language you speak.

Some will object that this is a practice of dead European white males. This is true. It is a practice of dead European white males who fought hard against the coming of Christianity and its practice of monolithic culture. If you're really interested in diversity, here's a test. See if you can actually listen to the goals of others and state your goals before them. With our society of lies, most of the readers of this article will lack the courage to proceed. The second object is that while many people claim to be interested in magic, the art of causing extraordinary events to come about through the use of the will, most people are actually afraid to try it. It's safer to read the tarot or, better still, sit on your butt and polish book after book as though the "feel-good" knowledge of the average occult text was in itself transformative. Magic, despite what you may have heard, is very hard to do – in fact, it is the hardest thing for humans to do well. It is indeed the royal of art of being more than you seem. Since the average level of ambition and willingness to try things is so low, I can leave a nuclear weapon like this laying around, knowing that only those who are bold enough to seek after the mysteries will give it a try.

The practice reflects the nature of time in Germanic languages – English, German, Norse, Dutch, etc. In these languages there are only true morphological verb forms for the present and the past. There are no verb forms for the future. "Future" events can only be described with "helper" verbs. The time notion of the Germanic languages (including the one we think with or try to think with everyday) isn't divided by past-present-future, but by Urdhr (everything that has happened), Verdhandi (everything that is in process now) and Skuld (that which *should* happen). In short, the Germanic languages focus on the past as a guide for the future, and the magical and religious practices of these peoples make use of the past rather than being doomed to repeat (i.e., What *should* happen rather than what must happen). If you want a quick handle on the nature of language as programmer, the works of Benjamin Whorf are good; if you want a book on time structure in the Germanic languages, try *The Well and the Tree* by Paul C. Bauschatz, Amherst University of Massachusetts Press, 1982.

This unusual and useful time structure is at the base of the sumble. I'll describe a sumble, and then I'll discuss its effects on the individuals who participate. A sumble consists of four rounds of toasts. Someone has brought apple juice, a pitcher, and cups. The sumble leader pours the apple juice into the cups at the beginning of each round of toasts. There is no passing, everyone must toast each round.

Before the toasts begin, everyone sits quietly for a few minutes to let all the goddamn Madison Avenue images be extinguished in their minds. Then the leader of the group, who can be either permanent because he or she is the natural leader of the group or rotating, begins the sumble with these (or similar) words:

"We gather to Honor excellence, the manifestations of the Principles here in the Middle World, and bind our wills to the process of Eternal Work. We forgive ourselves past failures, and we pledge ourselves to awareness of the manifestation of Mystery in our lives. We rise up to our greatest potential and invoke Honor as our guide."

The leader then fills the pitcher and makes his or her first toast.

The first round is to *Principles*, those things that each individual thinks are important. For example, the leader might say, "I raise my glass to the principle of Communication because through Communication our mental processes exceed the sum of their parts." Then she drinks her cup. The next person might say, "I raise my glass to the principle of Loyalty, because only through loyalty are we able to go that last mile." Then he empties his cup. And so on.

The second round is to *Heroes*, real men and women, living or dead, that particularly inspire us in our work. The leader might say," I raise this glass to Isaac Asimov because he showed that with clear and simple prose you could open the doors of others' minds." She drains her cup. The next person might say, "I raise my cup to Matthew Hanson, Admiral Perry's aide who carried him to the North Pole when the Admiral was sick, so that Perry might 'discover' it." And so on.

The third round is the round of *Boasts*. Here each participant tells something that he or she has accomplished and is proud of. For example, the leader might say, "I raise this glass to myself; I went to Dallas and presented a good paper on the de Bono method at the Association for Software Engineering Excellence."

The fourth round is the round of *Oaths*. Here each participant tells of something they are about to do. The leader might say, "With this cup I pledge to get release three out the door a week ahead of schedule with no defects." Note that the oath is something that the individual must have control over – you can't set goals for somebody else here. There is a meta-rule for the oaths. If it is possible for you to aid another in fulfilling his oath without harm to yourself or your goals, you are honor-bound to do so.

Each of these rounds of toasts has at least two distinct benefits each. In the first round, the participant has to figure out what principles are important to him or her. This isn't something we do in this country. We like to act as though money is the be-all and end-all of our existence. It is almost a taboo to say that we like any part of our jobs or think that they are important. Secondly, it lets you find out what other people think is important. I know of people that have sat at sumble who – even though they had worked on projects together for years – found the first session very revealing and transforming.

The second round produces effects similar to the first. It makes the participants see something heroic and meaningful in their own work, and it allows them to share that inspiration with their fellows. We know that our current difficulties can be solved because others have solved them in the past. We are choosing a heroic model from the well of Urdhr – if it worked before, it can work again. The discovery of transpersonal patterns that have Worked before is one of the safest and most effective source of tools for self-transformation. If we truly want to find out what we are and what we can become, one of the most important places to look for the structure of our consciousness is in the myths that shape the language – not only on a word level, but on a grammatical level as well.

This is one of the greatest hidden aspects of our lives, as mystery we should seek after if we are truly interested in self-transformation.

The third round is also taboo-breaking. We are never supposed to talk about our achievements – particularly if we are team players. However, this not only gives us a chance to brag, it integrates our achievements into the work of others. We achieve recognition for our own work, and we recognize the evolving stream of quality around us. Again, I have seen individuals walking away not only amazed at finding out what the guy sitting next to him did, but also amazed at the wonderful scope of achievement that he had to work with in his projects.

The fourth round is, of course, the kicker. This not only makes the individual come up with a reasonable goal to overcome, beyond the dead specs of a given project, but it also makes sure that each individual – now filled with the confidence that the toasts have produced – will apply his principle to give shape to the work that should come into being. It gives each individual a voice in what's taking place, confidence that his goals are both important and achievable, and a sense of commitment to the team.

In terms of the time model discussed above, the first three toasts come from the well of Urdhr and the last from the well of Skuld. It's programming that's deeply wired into us by our language. It makes an excellent use of wetware. Like any piece of linguistic programming, it works better if repeated. It's great if your goal is an individually determined freedom. Why not buy some apple juice and try one today?

A Mysterious Manifesto

I wrote the following article for the magazine SFEye *to express some of the effect the Word Runa had on me as a writer.*

Not long ago, a good writer named Wendy Wheeler interviewed me for *Gotta Write Network LitMag.* She asked, When did I think a story was successful? I started to - answer some flippant remark on the lines of, "I don't know what art is, but I know it when I see it." But whenever I can escape an easy answer and look for the Real answer, I try to do so. That seems to be the root of all true becoming. So this was my answer: "A good story makes us a little unsure of the world we exist in. It fills us with the sense of the unknown. Probably my guiding light here would be Russian critic Victor Shklovsky's remark, 'The technique of art is to make objects 'unfamiliar,' to make forms difficult, to increase the difficulty and length of perception because the process of perception is an aesthetic end in itself and must be prolonged. Art is a way of experiencing the artfulness of an object; the object itself is not important.' Real art creates the Unknown, not the Known. If I am stirred by the mystery of what I read (even if I have written it), then it is successful."

Although pompous, this answer gave my insight into things that I like and create that are always around the edges of the SF world but never in its center. I like writers who make the world mysterious – examples coming to mind are R. A. Lafferty and Ballard. I like those works which essentially violate the SF paradigm of plot revolution through cleverness and explanation of some obscure (or momentarily forgotten) physical law and replace it with a world of wonder that is essentially unknown. Hence, I've always been a big fan of Samuel Delany's *Dhalgren*. Now, I've noticed that if you champion those works that try for an opening up of the world over the implication of order upon it, you will invariably be confronted with a fan who not only pooh-poohs your taste, but *becomes angry* while doing so. If you doubt this, try championing Delany at the next con you go to. Now, this isn't a simple rejection of your taste, but an actual emotional disease of someone who cannot face an open world. This revelation startled me; like most people who have spent their years Amung the yellowing paperbacks of SF, I had always thought that there was an essential brotherhood of fandom. That our motives were more the less the same.

I have discovered that there are two sets of motives, which create two almost entirely different literatures. The consumer that seeks fantasy and science fiction merely as the drug of choice to end their focus on the workaday world and the individual who seeks it to increase his or her focus upon the possibilities of the world. I refer to these as the members of the "gray school" and of the "mysterious school." Now, this may not be a new observation. I am sure it doesn't take long to realize the difference between the reader of trilogies and dekalogies and the dedicated reader that spends a kazillion bucks in specialist catalogs. But for people who don't want to think and want instead the comfort of a an easily described world, SF is not nearly as efficient a drug as are videos, computer games, and the now arising possibilities of virtual reality. Since these drugs are already pulling in fatalistic youth, SF readership keeps declining. We must realize that it is in the interest of everyone not to lure kids away from video games, but instead to change the remaining print medium into a place where an ever higher level of energy can be made. It is time not to try to tone novels so that they sell better – in fact, they'll sell worse because the active reader will move more and more into a field where he or she finds the material that is needed. It is very important to not only to herald the new – such as the Black Ice series – but also to quietly do away with that type of critic which dismisses these books because they threaten him or her.

I'm not suggesting offing certain reviewers (well, I ain't against it, you understand), but instead rendering them helpless by giving them a new Nintendo game. Abraham Maslow in his *Toward a Psychology of Being* shows the conception between self-actualization and the mysterious:

'SA [Self Actualizing] people are relatively unfrightened by the unknown, the mysterious, the puzzling, and often are positively attracted to it... They do not neglect the unknown, or deny it, or run away from it, or try to make believe it is really known, nor do they organize, dichotomize, or rubicize it prematurely. They do not cling to the familiar, nor is their quest for the truth a catastrophic need for certainty, safety, definiteness, and order... They can be, when the total situation calls for it, comfortably disorderly, sloppy, anarchic, chaotic, vague, doubtful, uncertain, indefinite, approximate, inexact, or inaccurate..."

John Fowles, in his philosophical work *The Aristos*, makes this quite clear under the rubric of "Mystery" (p.28) he writes: "Mystery, or unknowing, is energy. As soon as a mystery is explained, it ceases to be a source of energy. If we question deep enough there comes a point where answers, if answers could be given, would kill. We may want to dam the river; but we dam the spring at our peril. In fact, since 'God' is knowable, we cannot dam the spring of basic existential mystery. 'God' is the energy of all questions and questing; and so the ultimate source of all action and volition."

Now, this distinction should not be thought of as in favor of the literary as opposed to the "nuts-'n-bolts" school of science fiction writing. The capacity for the mysterious can exist in any type of SF, including nonwritten material. It is the *function* of the writing that is the focus. Does the reader pursue the story for a sense of well-being that could probably be brought on better by a cup of Mexican hot chocolate? Or does she read for the moment of stretching the self? That instant when presented with a reality beyond the scope of the world she knows, she has to *create more of herself* in order to take it in. For those who seek the latter experience, a visit to an SF specialty shop is interesting – most everything is invisible in its grayness. There will be – if the seeker is incredibly lucky – one or two volumes promising the mysterious experience.

For those who shun the mysterious (out of an emotional disease), the visit to the SF shop is promising. Everything is there in its glorious commodity, except for the occasional weirdo book. And if they should have the unhappy experience of picking *Dhalgren* or *Nine Hundred Grandmothers* or *The Narrative of Arthur Gordon Pym*, they will go on a religious crusade against the book. Because the book stirred some of that mysterious darkness within, they will devote an astonishing amount of time against the book – if they are active fans, they will write LOC after Loc or flame on BBS. (Yes, I have seen modern cyberspace filled in a tirade against Poe). Poe is an interesting test. Ask people what they like. The seekers after the mysteries will go for "Ligea," "The Fall of the House of Usher," and will make a stab at reading *Eureka* because they wanted to get inside Poe's head and share the vision of the mysterious dark. The dwellers in grayness will love the detective stories – "The Raven," which they will explain to you as the suicidal poet meeting a trained bird by chance – and will say that Poe was completely crazy when he wrote *Eureka* (in fact they'll say it's a stain to his memory).

Now that I've put myself in the mysterious camp, what can I say about the good it brings besides enjoyment? It took me a long time to discover the good in those writers who exemplify the mysterious school. Who can claim there is good in the strained verbal style of an H.P. Lovecraft or the silly season stories of R.A. Lafferty? The great transformative good in these fictions is that they tell us that there is *so much we don't know.* Gray SF teaches us that we live in a world that is thoroughly determined by facts. If we can just get the facts, we either have power (optimistic "classical" SF) or we are absolutely screwed (New Wave SF such as *Oedipus Rex* by Sophocles). Gray SF teaches us that there is much, much more within and beyond us.

I suspect the love of the mysterious is hard-wired deep in Indo-European culture with its threefold division of producer, soldier, and king/priest/magician. All of us possess all three divisions in ourselves, but the last part – the king/priest/magician part – needs to be nourished by the unknown. Farmer-producer needs the known – when to plant, when to harvest, how to treat a cow with the staggers. The farmer-producer in us yearns for the cyclical fantasy tale – the hero that re-creates the sun's journey. The soldier wants the how-to of strategy – a mode based on "If I am smarter than my enemy." This section of ourselves yearns for the tale of deduction, cleverness, and strategy – this yearning being so powerful among us that it creates the strongly militaristic school of SF first most and the "hard" school second most. This also explains why the enthusiast of one is usually the enthusiast of the second. Neither of the first two functions, farmer-producer and soldier, have any taste for the unknown. It is the king/priest/magician who must face the world beyond the borders (whether beyond his kingdom or among the unseen powers) that hungers for the unknown. It becomes a necessity to cultivate a sense of awe in such individuals. Without consciously raising the love of the unknown in - themselves, they will turn from the hard job of facing the unknown and sleep with the peasants.

In the Germanic languages the words for advice and the mysterious are related. I chose Old Norse examples for this useful thought complex; since the modern English forms of these words, *rown*, "to whisper," is only used in the British army for passwords, and *rune* is regarded only as the written character because of Blum's terrible books on the subject (we may yet see a true runic revival in Modern English from the likes of Stephen Flowers and Edred Thorsson). Look at Old Norse mysterious school words:

run: "a secret, mystery, secret or occult lore; a magical character or formula."

reyna: "to try, experience, examine, search, pry, inquire into something." As a reflexive verb this means "to be proven, or turn out by experience"!

ryna: "to pry into."

raun: "a trial, experiment, experience"

Runi and *runa*: "secret adviser." The form in -i is masculine, the one in -a is feminine. These are valued and secret advisers – or inner advisers from the subjective universe – some of which may manifest in the objective universe from time to time.

The complex of thought I was trying to find in why I like certain modern (and postmodern) SF is there. It is secret (Run), it represents a methodical "prying into" – in other words, the characters want to know the answers rather than just accepting them as magic (Reyna), and ultimately it advises the soul (Runa). When I walk outside and look up at the stars after reading Olaf Stapledon, I have a spiritual experience. Not one based on faith or primitive emotions, but based on a love of the strange I have properly cultivated and purveyed.

Given the above that the mysterious school will interest the smallest section of readers, what does this do to the marketplace? The question of writing as commodity is seldom addressed in serious criticism, but I would like to discuss what effect the gray school has not only on the products we see, but the creators thereof – and then I would like to discuss certain strategies that we in our proper roles as kings/priests/magicians can use to ensure the production and availability of the substances we crave.

That the gray school rules is obvious to anyone who can count the number of sequels, "coauthored" books, and shared-world anthologies. These will no doubt always be with us – unless the promised five hundred TV channels of the future removes literacy altogether. But the dangerous phenomenon is that use of money to change the writer of the mysterious school into a gray school hack. The best example (I will limit myself to dead men because it breaks my heart to point out this slow death in the living – although two living authors came to mind as I wrote these words) is Frank Herbert, who produced two excellent mysterious school books – *Dune* and *Whipping* Star.

Dune has a high sense of the mysterious, but since the mysteries are incidental to - the plot, this high-energy book sold well. However, its energy, that is to say its mystery, irritated the comfortable gray school reader. So he demanded, and since demand = money, got a series of sequels, each worse than the preceding, explaining away the mysteries. Herbert sensed something was wrong and tried to pep up the books with sex and drugs, which along with violence are used as cheap substitutes for mysteries. An empty stomach is not a good political adviser; indeed that the mysterious school exists in SF is due to the fact that almost all SF writers have day jobs and it is essentially a literature produces by dilettantes. *Whipping Star* did not conceal its mysterious nature, and despite its excellence, not only went out of print, but produced no critical notice as well. The lure of money can't be denied. If you have to get medical treatment, fix your cheap clunker car, etc., it will be there whispering bad gray advice. So we have to change the lure.

So here are nine ways to promote the mysterious school. Only you can save the sense of wonder. If you let it fail, don't despair at all the gray people that surround you in your old age.

1. Read to your children. Do not let them listen to Barney, do not let your school system take care of this – the school system belongs to the grays. Get highly charged, mysterious books and read aloud. As the Runa-word complex illustrates, hearing the advice is important. Two books to begin with are *Half Magic* and *The Cat in the Hat*. Those who do not read to their children are accursed. Ultimately this leads to certain Freudian mysteries which connect infant sexuality with the wonder tale and the ability to find mates that give good story (and thus incarnate the mystery of Runi or Runa mentioned above).

2. Buy and donate mysterious hardbacks to your local library. Make damn sure that there's a copy of Edgar Rice Burroughs' *The Gods of Mars* for junior high school kids to read and a copy of *Naked Lunch* for that pervy high school senior. Fight the ban-the-books people toe-to-toe.

3. Never pass up an opportunity to use cultural prestige as a tool against the gray book. If you review books for the littlest fanzine, to your local BBS, to just your friends – you need to make a campaign of telling people that to be seen buying or reading X or Y gray book is to look stupid. Cultural pressure will take care of the rest. Better books will be printed (although not read), and the future grows more secure this way.

4. Write letters to publishers praising books for their mysterious content. If you happen to find a book that energizes your life through the sense of the unknown it gives you, you must write the letter of praise to the publisher. If by some miracle of miracles you find

the book in a chain store, mention that fact explicitly "At the B.Dalton's in Pinefart" and send a copy to the publisher and the head of the chain.

5. Write letters to publishers and chains complaining about any gray school book first appearance. If you can stop the reprinting of a gray school book, you have performed an important defensive action. It is particularly powerful to write when you see a good writer slipping. "Dear Publisher, whereas I loved D. B. Bowen's *The Cellophane Fawn*, because of its high sense of mystery, I feel his current *Cellophane Fawn Chronicles* is a boring book designed to fill in the "gaps" of the earlier classic. Why not let this one fade away, and encourage Bowen to return his creative roots. If not, I know he will lose me and thousands of others as a readers. The concept of the trilogy is, frankly, outdated in these new high-energy times." This also suggests creative pranksterism when you see such books displayed. Now, I would never advocate any illicit acts (yeah, right), but let those of you possessed of a trickster nature follow the dictates of your hearts.

6. Make sure that used copies of gray books go to the recycling bin instead of the used bookstore.

7. Write (and cause to be written) critical articles on mysterious school writers. The amount and direction of critical thinking both encourages young writers in certain directions as well as insuring the print status of certain works through the powerful force of cultural prestige (and if you are a king/priest/magician, determining cultural prestige is your job). Do not write that ten-thousandth essay on Ursula Le Guin; write about Lafferty, write about Cordwainder Smith. If you can't write (here is a secret everyone can write), then demand these essays from such critics and historians as you are apt to meet.

Better still, if you teach a class about SF, demand these essays from your students.

8. Tie the demand for mysterious writing with other demands in even the most unlikely places. Say you're writing your congress about the Thor Power Tool law, cast your thought in the form of preserving the imaginative mysterious wellspring of pour culture. Anytime you can push the idea, push it. This will have three benefits. Firstly, it will raise the love of the unknown in you. Secondly, it will awaken the occasional seeker who has looked for this articulation to explain her tastes. Thirdly, if you're a bit of a wordsmith, then it's likely that the congressman will plagiarize you – and you've released an important meme. Release enough and keep the pressure on the world, and the world will change. This is a great secret of magic.

9. Learn to use the word "weird" correctly and as a complement. This is actually a way of changing the word-map of the worlds through remanifestation. It is hard to shift a paradigm because it requires subtle, continuing work. Weird in the language of our ancestors' ancestors meant a mysterious Becoming – something happening in accordance with a hidden pattern. Nowadays we use the word merely to indicate something odd as in "Man that was weird!" One guy killing another guy with a sword is not weird. One guy happening to find his heroic grandfather's sword on the battlefield and killing twenty guys is weird. That pattern of the hidden becoming manifest was the source of wonder in ancient tales; it still powers modern folklore -- and it is the power, which in its most artful, refined form creates the writing of the mysterious school. It is a powerful feeling when you withhold certain parts of the message and meaning. It pulls the other in.

If you want to experience that hidden power as well as bring about more mysterious-school writing, here's your chance to shift some paradigms. Only use the word "weird" when it applies. Talk about those things which have a truly weird happening. Forsake the use of the word when talking about the odd. This is a very difficult exercise; don't berate yourself or others for failing. Merely try. And when you have reclaimed that word (through your hidden persistence), begin very sparingly to use it as a compliment for certain kinds of writing. Do this magic, my fellow kings/priests/magicians, and we can create that truly mysterious thing -- the Weird tale.

Why do Magicians Write Fiction?

This is a question I am frequently asked. This is a meditation on the imaginal world and the magician's bookshelf.

Many modern occult organizations either base their mission on, or at least have a great deal of supernatural literature in, their reading lists. It is not uncommon to see modern occultists perusing the works of Lovecraft, Chambers, Machen, or Blackwood. This practice leads us to two interesting and related questions. Why would a magician (Machen, Blackwood, Fortune) write fiction (beyond the obvious reasons of amusement and remuneration)? Why would other magicians find their inspiration in fictive works? A third question hidden in the first two is, How is magic similar to the acts of reading and writing? I would like to take a look at the nature of magic as a communication system, answer the first two questions, give a few references for where important magical writing may be found today, and sound a warning call for its protection. This is a tiny rivulet which I hope that others will take up as a new type of criticism. Like the dark streams that have never seen the light of the sun in the hills west of Arkham, I hope that this little rivulet may play an important role in the evolution of Life.

Mauss and other modernists attempted to reduce the power of magic to a sociological context – the power of magic is equivalent to how society feels about the magician. This dreary attitude is still largely present in popular culture; however, postmodern theorists such as van Baal, Grambo, Flowers, and Tambiah have provided us with a semiotic theory of magic which serves to illustrate both the practice of magic and its symbolic expression. Basically, the semiotic theory of magic is that man is able to effect communication with his universe and to think *ascriptively* (i.e., hidden meaning is ascribed to the phenomenon of the universe and it becomes a partner in communication).

The semiotic theory postulates three elements: the magician seeking either a

psychological change within him/herself or an environmental change, the message which

is cast in the form of cultural coded symbols, and the hidden "other side" of the universe.

This goes beyond Frazier's notions of "sympathy" by actually elaborating not only a

threefold process of sender-message-receiver but actually proposes a willed volition to

receive communication (in either the form of a revelation or an environmental change)

back from the universe. Summing up this model of magic (after Flowers' *Runes and*

Magic: Magical Formulaic Elements In the Older Runic Tradition, Lang, 1986 pg.17):

Subject --------> Direct Object ------->Indirect Object

(Man)   (Symbol-symbolized)   (Other reality)

$$|$$

$$|$$

$$V$$

Indirect Object <---- (Phenomenon) <------- subject

This model suggests that for the magician the great secret is finding the correct

mode of address – that method of communication which will produce the response from

the hidden realm. This has always been intuited in the Mediterranean school of magic, as

exemplified by choosing Hermes, god of communication, as its patron. For the magician

operating in a traditional society, the method of communication is generally heavily

determined – people know how to talk to the gods. But in modern and postmodern

societies the quest for the method of communication is ongoing. The book ranks high as a sufficiently mysterious form of communication (video, movies, and the computer network are waiting in the wings). Who among us has not had that mysterious phenomenon of having gleaned something from one's own writing long after it was written? And who among us has not had that mysterious process of "finding just the book we need" at a crucial time in our thought? So keeping in mind *your own* experiences of the mystery of the written word consider van Baal's description of the nature of a magical spell:

The formula takes its origin from the discourse between man and his universe, in the case of a particular formula a discourse concerning a certain object and the fulfillment of a desire. In this discourse man feels addressed or singled out by his universe and he endeavors to address it in turn trying to discover the kind of address to which his universe will be willing to answer, that is, willing to show itself communicable. The formulas he finally discovers in answer to his quest is not really man's discovery but a gift a revelation bestowed upon him by the universe. The formula is the outcome of an act of communication in which man's universe reveals to him the secret of how it should be addressed in this or that circumstance, a secret which is at the same time a revelation of its hidden essence in that particular field. . .
(J. van Baal, *Symbols for Communication: an introduction to the anthropological study of*

religion [Studies of developing Countries 11] Asen: Van Gorrcum 1971, pg. 263)

Given the above, why do magicians write fiction? Not as open communication of magic; it would be easier simply to write how-to books. The need to communicate with the *hidden* aspects of the universe of discourse is the magician's motive. Just as an Egyptian would stuff his letters to the dead in the crumbling tomb walls, the modern magician sends his or her message into the semiosphere. Dion Fortune didn't create her novels just as entertainment, but to actively Work the magic. By performing illustrative magic concerning the nature of initiation, of secret schools, etc., she actually received

219

(from the Hidden parts of her own psyche) such information.

The simple act of visualization (i.e., daydreaming) is known to produce effects both psychological and environmental; how much greater an effect can be obtained through the writing and publishing of magical work? The precision of writing, editing, and rewriting coupled with the aching wait for publication (with its inherent travails of lost MSS, marketing mistakes, fraudulent publishers) creates an unbeatable combination of passion and precision. These are the elements that effect any magical working. It is easy to get up passion for a particular end. We have all had that experience of having to get that job, make that meeting, etc., wherein our magical practice did pay off with the required miracle. But it is frankly hard to work up the passion required to get at certain desired spiritual states. However, the test of publication will place the magician in the desire-filled mode necessary to achieve his or her spiritual goals.

Of particular interest in this model is a man who would have been repelled at the - mere notion of placing him among magicians, H. P. Lovecraft. But he illustrates the case perfectly. Lovecraft, with his passions for astronomy and history, longed to be part of the vast forces of time. He longed to see the hidden essence of history/cosmology that he felt would dissolve the details of the present like an acid. With his entirely materialistic outlook, the practice of magic would've been absurd – but writing was another matter. His themes and topics were certainly not commercial (although there has been a good deal of money minted in his name). The desire to continue producing amateur fiction, or sticking with such fiction as could be only sold to the low-paying *Weird Tales*, show that his need was a purely magical one. And it produces results. The plots of his stories often came to him in dreams. Particularly noteworthy was the dream that led to the production of the prose-poem "Nyarlathotep" in which he found the Hermes of his pantheon. This particular communicator from the other side, with his swarthy Egyptian skin, resembles both the figure of Hermes-Thoth and the preternatural entity that Crowley contacted in - 1904.

Lovecraft knew his need for the cosmic feeling his stories brought him, and throughout his letters and critical writings we see that need to evoke a mood repeated time and time again. In fact, Lovecraft was sensitive enough to this process (despite the fact his materialist attitude kept him from ever consciously expressing it) that many of his stories are about the desired result of receiving communication from the other side. Cthulhu sends dreams. The Fungi from Yuggoth take the seeker away on a cosmic quest, or at the very least whisper all the secrets of the cosmos via certain human appendages. The primordial ones communicate through their vast murals found in hidden Antarctica. In the most revelatory of all his work, "The Shadow out of Time," the hero not only sends a message to the other side (by actually writing in the library of the Great Race), but actually receives a revelation of finding the message deep belowground (i.e., in the unconscious) written *in his own hand*.

Now, having seen why magicians have a need to use certain hidden or encoded communications such as fiction writing, we turn to the question of why magicians need to read fiction. The simple reason of "inspiration" suffices, but it is to be noted that it is not the same sort of inspiration that one may glean from, say, a straightforward biography. Very little occult fiction provides a step-by-step account of ritual procedure, and those that do are Amungst the most boring. One doesn't read "The White People" to find out the step-by-step ways of doing anything. Indeed, the operant material is generally described under only the broadest (and therefore most evocative) of terms. One may be tempted to invent the Aklo language or script out the Mao game, but the actual use of occult literature is to allow the magician to receive communication from the "Other side." By the use of imagination and mood, the nature of that hidden realm is disclosed to us; although most often in a mysterious way. It would be difficult to provide a description of the shudder that hearing the cauldron spell from *Macbeth* first gave us. Crowley choose *Macbeth*, *The Tempest*, and *Midsummer Night's Dream* for the reading list of the A.˙.A.˙. "as being interesting for the traditions treated." The objective reality of these traditions were very small, but Crowley (nobody's fool) knew that the effect they had on the soul allowed something of that mysterious realm to be communicated. In short, reading works that actually illustrate magic close the diagram above and enable the *discerning* magician to benefit from the others' illustrative work. This is not simply receiving a message from the author, that simple act of decoding which we all do as readers – this is receiving a *place of access* to the Unknown from the Unknown. The magician who manages both this feat and the act of fictional creation therefore achieves in this postmodern society a set of signs and symbols for communication with that unknown realm.

The question facing the modern occultist is where the unknown is most active or, to put it in literary terms, where are the new occult writers coming from, and in what arenas may they be found. As this quest has to be an intensely personal one, I can only give a few hints and recommendations. The works of Thomas Ligotti are universally praiseworthy and should be sought out. The works of Fritz Lieber and William S. Burroughs will make any magician's bookshelf richer, as well as the books of China Miéville and Alan Moore are good gateways to Otherness.

Love and Sex

I wrote this article for the Order of the Vampyre's newsletter Nightwing. All Tantric practices are based on Kama (Desire). In the West a great deal of ink has spilled on the idea of sex magic. Sometimes the ink is good, such as in Frater U.D.'s work. Sometimes it is simply silly. The deeper and more powerful aspect of Desire called Love is seldom dealt with.

There is nothing as compelling as sex. There are few things as disappointing as well. It can make you modify your body, empty your pocketbook, change your belief structure, restore/destroy your health, make you fall in (or out of) love, laugh, lose sleep, and put up with strange hairs in your shower. I would like to share some magical/Initiatory observations on sex and Sex, love and Love, and non-Self constraints.

Most of my Teachings on sex-magic are cast beyond the Temple to be shared with my lovers and their lovers – all that is ultimately magical in this realm can only be shared under certain conditions where Sex and Love are present. However, the following Truths can be shared. I choose to share them within the Order of the Vampyre because the Order's sex-magic formula makes it the most resonant place for such sharing.

The Formula of the Order is: The Self's Dreams-Made-Flesh feed Interchange of Desire.

This formula deals with two things. Firstly, it stresses that Magic is not fueled by Desire – it's not a group of horny people getting hornier, which was the Church of Satan formula. It deals with the feeling of self-love that comes from having already obtained one's sexual desires. The nature, frequency, and object of those wants is up to the individual. An orgy would actually ruin the formula. Secondly, it acknowledges the fact that a group of people who share their sexual confidence can create a special power to incarnate dreams.

When you have good sex, you feel good. (I hear many of you saying that you didn't need a Magus to point this out.) You feel confident, relaxed, and magical. If you live your life in such a manner that this is the feeling you have a good deal of, your life is better. If several people have this confident feeling and share it in a celebration of Desire, Desire becomes stronger in their lives. What they do with that Desire is their business, but it will automatically protect the place it is celebrated in.

Now here are some definitions that you won't find in most sex manuals.

*sex – anything that either excites your desire, or someone somewhere thinks should excite your desire. A social controlling force. Need not take place with love, cannot take place with Love.

*Sex – Sex (with an S) is a very rare kind of Working. Now, we've all had those Workings where all the externals go right. The flame suddenly shoots out of the candle at the right moment, the incense burns perfectly, in all ways the chamber is an EXACT, EXTERNAL map of the Mind. In Sex the partner or partners reacts thusly - and you react that way to them. It has physical, mental, emotional, and magical components. It makes you feel good for weeks afterward. You can Do anything. Need not take place with love or Love, but is rather enhancing with either.

Vampyres must have Sex.

*love -- anything that gives you the social inclination to do nice things for another human being. The creator of the social fabric.

*Love -- Love (with an L) is the impact of another upon your Psyche that sets you Free by suggesting possibility. It makes you Seek to Become better to please the Other, and it gives you a profound non-verbal magical "permission" to Be yourself at the same time. This is very rare.

It takes great strength and awareness to find Love; on the other hand love can merely lure you to sleep.

Now, I will talk about constraints. We are exposed to a false sexual dichotomy by society. There are quite a few human genders, from asexual males to pansexual females. This leads to various sorts of unhappiness. The most obvious is that of the homosexual who is caught in a heterosexual marriage because he has been made to feel ashamed of his desires. But there are other forms of sexual unhappiness that come about from social constraint. If you hang out with the "we eat anything" crowd and you are not a highly-sexed bisexual, you may often find yourself feeling that something's wrong with you for not being as aroused as everyone else.

There are even environmental constraints; for example if you are sensitive to melanin production, you will be horny as heck during the summer but would rather take up coin collecting in the winter – this may not sit well with your partner.

You may find that denying yourself sex is a great way to get things Done, or you may find the only way you get through life is with the occasional fling. If you enjoy D/S, you won't have a lot to say to someone who says, "But wouldn't that be uncomfortable?"

Above all, you will discover that you can only really understand others of your proclivities and activity level. Finding this World is part of the Vampyre's first job, and not being seduced into thinking that their Power comes from this world, her second.

Since the Order is only interested in the fact that you have 1) Fulfilled your Desire and 2) Wish to celebrate that Desire in a nonsexual way with us, it has no sex-magic teachings, or practices. We do, however, urge all who would seek the Vampyre to forget everything society has told them about their sex lives and to discover what Works for them. By our simple Being we urge people to put love and sex behind them, and to Quest for Love and Sex. (No one will be checking up on you, you will not be getting a call from Dr. Ruth late at night.)

Now, given these definitions, here are Nine Secrets of Sex Magic. They will not be found elsewhere, and I know some of you have Learned these in as painful ways, as I have.

1. Know your level of sexual activity. The person that needs sex a couple of times a year will not understand the person who needs it a couple of times a day. If you get too little or too much, you fall profoundly Asleep. Do not look at others' patterns for deciding your own (unless it is the Beloved's patterns).

2. To enter a world, an Aeon, is only possible through Love. Whether you Love animals, or a particular subculture – Love alone can take you to that world. You will never be able to Speak of a world you Love to someone who doesn't share that Love. Love can take you to worlds that you do not understand but immediately long to do so. Love is what brings people into the Inner Temple.

3. One is always made stronger by Love: inhibitions and fears disappear, deeply hidden resources appear.

4. In the presence of Love, Magic happens.

5. When Love and Sex coincide, sex and love become irritating. When Love and Sex coincide, there are as many new experiences as the magicians can Dream up. It is the land of a thousand virginities. (See #7 for hints.)

6. Bad Love leads people to bad worlds. The weaker or more hurt a person is, the more likely bad Love will occur. Thus religions like Christianity flourish because bad Love has trapped souls that could have gotten better but were trapped in life circumstances that were just too bad. Bad love can make an emergent Setian return to his or her slumber faster than 100 missionaries beating at his or her door.

7. For obtainment of material things like jobs and good real estate deals, natural sex is the best, if sex-magic is used. (Hump somebody and make a Wish.) For Initiatory magic, unnatural sex is the best. Art and Imagination are the biggest ingredients here.

8. Your body-mind complex will tell you that Sex and Love will save the world. They

227

won't. Many marriages fail because of this. If Love and Sex are harnessed into a desire to create a world of one's own choosing – connected with hard work, education, and so forth – the world will Come Into Being. This is *the* Secret of sexual creation, and it is practiced by successful partnerships everywhere.

9. For the successful sex-magician, libido is Willed to increase as the optimal level of challenge increases. *This is VERY antinomian.* The non-initiate uses sex like he or she uses food – something to comfort or distract from problems. The Initiate uses sex as a continuing celebration of his or her inevitable Victories.

Salem Witch Rite

Setian ritual has its roots in the personal. I had joined the Temple because of similarities between the Satanic Panic of the '80s and the Salem Witch trials, so my work reflected this root in certain ways. In the Year XXVII (1992) the 300th anniversary of the Salem Witch trials, I wrote the following ritual for the Bull of Ombos Pylon. Later that year the Temple had its Conclave in Danvers, Massachusetts – the site of old Salem Village – and performed another ritual I wrote, the Mass of Terrible Justice. With this we ended the Satanic Panic on a magical level. On the intellectual level we ended it with patiently responding to crazed and frightened souls who were caught up in the very human passion of scapegoating.

This ritual is an example of good group Work. Firstly, I passed the ritual out for people to read. Of course there is no blood-letting in Setian ritual, so people wondered about the drawing blood. This was accomplished by pressing a red Sharpie® firmly and quickly across the wrist – a very dramatic moment in a darkened room. The Pylon had expected me to play the part of the Black Man of the Woods. In fact, I had hidden away a visiting Priest, who wore a rather a gruesome mask. At the music cue he broke into the chamber and began seizing the witches to sign his Book. The rite addresses the twofold nature of America. On the one hand we are a fearful Puritan nation, and on the other we are the country of Magus Thomas Jefferson, whose magical law "Let an aristocracy of achievement arise from a democracy of opportunity!" is a basis for the Temple of Set. We are both an international group with Egyptian roots and a celebration of the American counterculture from Year I (1966) San Francisco. American Setians are active in various political movements from Libertarians to old school Liberal Democrats. All that is best in Jefferson's philosophy is manifest in our good deeds. The Lovecraftian window-dressing owes a great deal to "Dreams in the Witch-House."

* Prepare chamber

* Bell 9X

* Light Black Flame / Open Gate

* INVOCATION OF SET:

In the name of Set, the Prince of Darkness, we find our ways to the forest dark, where our magic overcomes the ways of the waking world. Hear us, look upon us, go with us upon this journey. Enfold us with the powers of darkness that they may Become one with us as we are Become one with the Eternal Set, whose seat is beyond the Constellation of the Thigh. As we send forth our most exalted and sublime selves, arm them with the Pentagram of Set and the scepter of Tcham that we may overcome all obstacles, dismay all challengers, and cast down all that is moved to appear against us. Let my eyes become the eyes of Set. Let my strength become the strength of Set. Let my will become the Will of Set.

As Fire in the Darkness we are Become, as Air in the Sky we are Become, as the Earth in Space we are Become, as Water in the desert we are Become. We are Lords of life and death – and life beyond death. Time and space bow before our will and all beings tremble at the Ka which Comes into Being through that art which is ours to command.

GRAAL:

This cup is brought into being by your most noble and evil deeds. This bread is the Power of the Promise of the Lord of this World. It is the red bread and red wine like blood.

ELEMENTAL SUMMONING:

Those who Work in Darkness beyond the village light have wrought the nightmares through which we walk serene. They cracked the symmetry of the Six and from the forest dark, we call them to life to ride with the gaunts and wreak revenge upon their slayers. Let those who introduced the fear of Darkness upon this nation come forth to fly free: John Proctor, Keziah Mason, Giles Corey, Bridget Bishop, Sarah Osburn, Septimus Bishop, George Burroughs, Rebecca Nurse, Job Tookey.

WORK:

The spawn of Set Works freely under the banner of the Five. We Rework the rites of this land to bring forth the Promise of the Lord of this World. We stand now as we have stood upon Sentinel Hill, in the Devil's hopyard, in the towns called Dagon and Salem. We speak the words of darkness, the words of pain, the words of hatred, and the Black Man of the Woods appears. We write our Names in His Book and we receive comfort, delight and wisdom. Hear the Words!

I'a Y'gs-Othoth!

I'a N'yra-l'yth-Otp!

I'a Sh'b- N'ygr'th!

P'rrt' Z' j-m'h v'-kh'yn v'-keu'-kh-i, kyr'wa phra goth-e rry'nrohze v'Sethek zes'm'!

(Rapid Strobe and eerie music begins, the Black Man of the Woods appears with his Book. He beckons each of the participants to the altar, draws blood from their wrists and lets them write their names in his Book. After they write their names, he warms the book in the Black Flame and says:)

The Pact is sealed. The Powers of the Sabbath are now yours.

(Individual Work and Recognitions, etc.)

(After Individual Work is done, the strobe is turned off and the Sentinel takes the American flag from the altar and holds it aloft, he says:)

Pledge allegiance to yourSelf!

(The Initiates rise, place their left hands over their hearts and say in Unison:)

I pledge allegiance to mySelf,

and to my influence in all lands –

all nations within the Aeon of Set –

with liberty, justice, and wisdom for mySelf,

unto the beginnings and endings of dimensions.

(The Sentinel returns the flag to the altar, a brief silent meditation on the Black Flame, and then the bell is struck.)

* Bell 9X

* "So it is done!"

When we met in Danvers in the Year XXVIII (1992), we stayed in the beautiful Tara Hotel. Dr. Aquino had intended to both lead and write this ritual, but circumstances changed the plans, so I both wrote the ritual and acted as High Priest. Setians spent the week doing the usual tourist things in Salem. Sometimes people responded warmly to our Pentagrams; some people said it was because of people like us that occultists are hated. One occult shop asked Setian clients not to touch anything lest we leave "bad vibrations." The night of the Mass a great deal of anger was let loose. Synchronistically, the hotel lost power about an hour afterward. Setians became very popular that night – in those pre-9/11 days we always traveled with candles. It was a strange and inspiring sight that October night; little groups sitting by candlelight – some just Setians, some groups sitting around one or two Setians telling us their scary stories about Ouija boards or dreams about dead uncles. The Invocation proves that my years in High School Latin were not wasted. The Statement of Belial is from the Diabolicon, which Satanist I* Michael A. Aquino penned on the battlefields of Vietnam. For the Black Magician, expressions of anger are as valid as expressions of love and healing. This is the angriest group I have ever seen in my decades in the Temple.

(solemn and dire music)

I. Bell x 9

II. Call to the Invisible Assemblage:

(The five Summons are to be read more or less at the same time. For historical reasons, the first summons needs to be read by the GM of the Order of the Trapezoid.)

"I call to all those who have minted money with the Dread Name. I call to the leaders of churches, to therapists, to journalists and hate-mongers of all stripes. Come and be part of our Work. I call you and bind you to this place by the Power of the Dread name, of which I am Master."

"I call all who have played with the Law of the Forbidden. All you little witches of the night, dabblers in the Art, poseurs of darkness, and posturers of grim powers. I call you by the Name you trade upon and bind you to this place for judgment."

"I call all those who truly seek the Aeon but have not found the Pylon Gate. Come and be with us that our Working of Ma'at may awaken you to the Mystery you seek after."

"I call all those Setians dead or as yet unborn, that they may witness our Working of justice and bear news of the terrible curse we pronounce this night. Fly free of the bonds of death and time, and join your brothers and sisters at this great coincidence of cycles."

"I call to all Setians who have become lost in the distracting shadows of the World of Horrors, that the clear black light of Ma'at may awaken them to the knowledge they once sought."

III. Light Black Flame and Open Gate:

"From the Hidden realm of Perfection comes forth Ma'at into the Realm of Being. In this place, terrible injustice was worked by daylight, by this Dark Light we Work terrible justice to persist throughout the coming Cycles. The Mass is begun!"

IV. The Invocation of Set:

"In nomine Seti, Principis Tenebrarum, abeo ad regnum facti adactum voluntatem meum universo. O Set-hen, audi me, specta me, et age cum me via ipsa. Tege me cum potestatibus Tenebris, possunt cum me idem, ut ego possum cum Seto aeterno idem, istum subsellium est ultra Kapesha. Ut mitto me meum supremum et sublimum maximum, arma me cum pentagramis Seti et sceptro Tchamo, posthac provocet omnino vis, perterrit omnino inimicos et substernit omnino actum contra idem.

"Oculi mei oculi Seti possunt, vis meus vis Seti possit, voluntasmea voluntas Seti possit. Tamquam flamma in tenebris possum, tamquam aether in caelo possum, tamquam terra in universo possum, tamquam aqua in deserta possum. Habito in flamma Ba. Tempuss

alutat volunte mea, et sum Dominus vitae et Dominus mortis, et Dominus vitae in morte.

Audite fatum, illum nunc dictito, et canite kam, illum nunc possit arte mea."

IV. RECOGNITIONS AND NAMINGS

V. THE PETITION FOR JUSTICE

(This is done by a Petitioner who approaches the altar, a Representative of the Temple,

and a Chorus of all).

Petitioner:

"I speak for the invisible assemblage demanding Darkness."

Representative:

"Their souls are weak and unprepared, the knowledge of the Darkness within would drive

them into a mad fury of self-torment. They would be consumed."

Petitioner:

"They have sought Darkness; shall they not receive what they seek?"

CHORUS:

"Let those who call upon the Devil find the Devil."

Representative:

"If they discover the Secret of Darkness Without, they will go mad with fear."

Petitioner:

"We in the Temple of Set seek Darkness; is it not fit and proper that we shall open them to the searing vision? Is not sharing and love the law of their Magus?"

CHORUS:

"It is their Law. Let us share with them that which we seek."

Representative:

"It will destroy them."

Petitioner:

"Let then the Mass of Ma'at proceed that we may find wisdom and that those who live by the lie may find destruction."

CHORUS:

"So it shall be done!"

Representative:

"So it shall be done even unto the ends of time!"

VI. MASS OF MA'AT

"In the Age of Satan, our mission became clear to us, through the Statement of Belial:"

* Reading of the Statement of Belial.

"To dare the Black magic, one must bring forth Ma'at from the Hidden realm and make it an absolute guiding force in the objective realm. To know the Good is to do the Good.

Within this black cup is the philter of Ma'at. When it is consumed, it is either the key to immortality, power, and knowledge – or it is the knowledge that absolutely consumes the drinker."

(Holds Graal aloft)

"He who knows not of Xeper and drinks of this cup is destroyed, because he will no longer be able to hide from his meanness. Some will be paralyzed, some will turn their hands against themselves, others shall run forth into the night to slay their own kind. I drink for all present, visible and invisible."

(Drinks Graal)

CHORUS:

"Hail the Cup of Rebirth, which brings Self-knowledge and consumes us not!"

Celebrant:

"The Doom is sealed. Henceforth all who appeal to the Dread Name to justify their own actions shall be smitten with the knowledge of truth and destroyed by the Power of Ma'at we have cast forth in the Name of Set!"

VII. WORDS OF THE HIGH PRIEST

VIII. THE PRONUNCIATION OF THE CURSE

"Hail to thee, Ra-En-Set! Thou art the mirror of all we have Become, Thou art the Word Xeper made Flesh, Thou art the repository of all our dreams! Even though we have and continue to perform feats of Becoming that stagger the mind of man, for the mere fact that we live in the time of the Second Beast and have Understood his Word – we shall be called the Blessed, yea unto the ends of Time. But to those who have not harkened to the Word, from this place of injustice I place a terrible curse. It repenteth me not that my words do ride upon the hot winds of Hell, which shall henceforth well up from this place. It repenteth me not that the Power of Ma'at shall drive the workers of the lie and the drinkers of kheft to terrible orgies of self-destruction and self-torment, the likes of which have never been seen. Henceforth this is the Law: Whenever one speaks the Dread Name, whenever Darkness is called to, the great obsidian mirror of self-knowledge shall be seen!"

IX. The Ninth Part of the Word of Set

X. Chorus:

"Our Xeper will Work through our deeds, and thus we gain the strength to live forever."

XI. Dismissal (By the High Priest)

"The Mass is ended, go in peace."

XII. Bell X9

XIII. Traditional Response:

"So it is done!"

The Unknown Nine

The Temple of Set has a check-and-balances system. The Chief Executive Officer is the High Priest. He reports to the Chairman of the Council of Nine. Our predecessor, the Church of Satan, was in principle ruled by nine men – modeled after The Unknown Nine *of Indian legend. The Theosophist "Talbot Mundy" had popularized their legend in his novel,* The Nine Unknown. *I wrote this short letter to the Council of Nine shortly before I stepped down as High Priest.*

In 1923, William Lancaster Gribbon, "Talbot Mundy," released an interesting spell on the world with his novel *The Nine Unknown.* Gribbon had traveled throughout Africa and India, sometimes working for British Intelligence but mainly making bad gambling debts and changing his name often.

In America he changed his name to Mundy, and his adventure novels began to involve Theosophy, the religion he took up after moving to San Diego. The first of these was swallowed hook, line, and sinker in *The Morning of the Magicians,* whose 1968 publication rather changed the Shape of who we Became. The Dream of a group of wise humans that possessed a super-science that ruled all religions, controlled all money, was more powerful than all governments is hard to pass up.

Both Robert Anton Wilson and Phillip José Farmer steal their Nine from this book, and it had huge influence on R. E. Howard (who gave us the phrase "Children of Set") and Sax Rohmer. Gribbon's Theosophy teacher was Katherine Tingley, a medium often accused of "black magic."

What do we make of this dream made Real?

I think the Unknown should have four characteristics:

1.   They should be shrewd judges of character, slow to act, and a balance of the ecstasy of the High Priest.

2.   They should be able to put practical concerns in motion (run Orders, etc.), and have their mundane work stir up parallel magical work at the same time. In other words, look for people who are changing the Aeon, not talking of doing so.

3.   They should know where the Temple has been, and have a passion for its unvarnished history.

4.   They need not have a vision for its future, but they must have integrity and a disdain for personal politics. Ideally, they should act as if their actions were written down and handed to future generations of Setians as the spiritual version of DNA – because it is.

Their words will have more power than the Dream that conjured them. We can be the wisest, who wield the greatest power.

Reyn Til Runa!

The Unknown Nine (Fiction)

I wanted to play with the idea of the Unknown Nine in my own fiction. This would be an example of an illustrative Working – an enactment of the phenomena in the intra-subjective universe. If you use your cognitive imagination to enact something, the playful and chance elements of your unfolding drama will reveal to you aspects of the Real. This story is set in the fictiobl universe of my nonSetain friend Uncle River.

The following tale – which is as true as history – may be read in three exoteric and one esoteric ways. One way is seeing the play *The Unknown Nine* as earnest John Fuentes' attempt to understand the mystery of the world through enactment of that mystery. The second way is seeing the play *The Unknown Nine* as ever-and-all-hungry Donna Fabreuax's attempt to eat the world. The third way is to see *The Unknown Nine* as a reflection of the world that slouched toward Nueva Bethlehem to be born. And the fourth way is known only to those priests of the god of borders, frontiers, and secret places whose yellow texts are covered by the lava...

The first problem was casting. John had expected the first problem to be a theater, because who would expect nowhere to have a stage. He had come here (to nowhere) because it was a stage. Nowhere is the best place to make magic.

But there was a stage connected with the rotting hotel. In the time of Queen Victoria, an enterprising miner named Yage Thomas took the fortune that he had made in Colorado silver and opened the first chain of theaters across the Southwest. This ill-fated attempt to bring Shakespeare to the great unwashed had the same effect here as everywhere, giving people new lines to misquote and mutate in slow language rot. The theater, however, currently named the Paramount, had managed various remanifestations over the years. It had brought silent films in the Twenties and Thirties (in fact, Clara Bow had spent a bored weekend there during the promotional tour of *Wings*). Like the mummy, it returned in the Forties to show some propaganda films. In the Fifties it had served for a few weeks as the office of a firm selling prefab bomb shelters, and in the Sixties a displaced hippie commune from Taos had made it into the Temple of Eros.

It was an ideal location for John's masterwork for two reasons. One, it was on the corner of Bandwidth and Ninth, opposite the Victor's Saloon, and two, nobody held clear title to the business. The first was important because of the Mystery of Opposites. The Victor's Saloon was loud, drunk, obvious, and connected with the ever-forgetting moment called the now. The Paramount was quiet, sober, hidden, and connected with the past – and John hoped the Is-To-Be as well. Since the property lacked clear title, it represented for John exactly those beings he was studying. The Masters of the World seemed to have an absolute control over what was seemingly free. It would be easy to see the Masters as, say, the two percent of Americans who own ninety-eight percent of the capital – but John had met the very rich and learned that they were no more in control of themselves than the junkies who shot up in the shadows of the Bandwidth Vortex. The Masters of the World owned things in a different way. They owned the rock that went into the slingshot that broke Fleming's window so penicillin spores could find their way into his agar trays. By invading the Paramount, he would be invading their sanctuary. Unless, as he sometimes thought in his most paranoid moments, it was their intent the play be performed at all.

Donna Fabreuax's first mission concerning the play was to seduce Gerhard Lopez, so that he would design the sets. Lopez would have done so anyway, but Donna wanted a double bond with all men. A bond on whatever level of interaction they might legitimately have, and the bond of sex. Thus, they fed her in two ways and were doubly beholden.

The sets had to be perfect, of course. If you wanted to change the world in a subtle way, you send out a subtle signal. If you wanted to change the world in a significant way, you sent out a significant signal.

So she put on her crotchless panties, her garter belt and black hose, her come-fuck-me high heels, her black and red striped dirndl skirt that swirled out when she spun on the dance floor, her black silk blouse that revealed her erect nipples so easily, and a string of carnelian beads bought from a bruja in Taos. She paused, watching herself in the mirror, tempted to masturbate at the sight of the goddess/material girl therein. Damn, she was hot. But she merely murmured her incantation for the evening. "Eat me now, paint me later."

It would prove to be the correct spell. She had already seen the set in her mind's eye, for as a woman she was a lot quicker to interact with the future than John. It would have a painting of her as the world, or at least as the whore of the world, hanging over a very pristine corporate boardroom. As the living altar, many fools might think she was lowering herself to the bosses of the world, but Those Who Know would realize that becoming the substance to be manipulated, the *prima material*, she could control the outcome.

Touching herself only briefly, she put some of her scent behind her ears and sashayed out of her house and toward the Victor's Saloon.

# # #

As Donna began her act of seduction, John began an act of concentration. If he could get enough of the picture of the Rulers of the World, he could write his play. He kept coming up with theories.

Who Rules the World?

1. The world is ruled by Chaos. At any given time, some people rise to the top of the heap. If you knew who these people were (and more importantly when they were at the top) you could change history. Working motto: "The beat of a butterfly's wings in Victor's Saloon causes a typhoon in Peking."

2. The world is ruled by Order. A long time ago, maybe in the Paleolithic, some small group of humans discovered the secret of rulership. They passed this on to others. This may or may not be connected with visible wealth. There is no way into (or out of) this secret society – its progress being completely mechanical. Working motto: "Welcome, my son, to the Machine."

3. The world is ruled by Understanding. People with great ideas rule the world.

Einstein, Plato, folks like that. Their memes are so strong that, once released upon the world, will drive it. When a better understanding comes along, it will kill off the weaker one. Working motto: "It's not who you know, it's what you know."

4. The world is ruled by Being. Some individuals through sheer force of will transform themselves into what are in effect superhuman entities. Hitler and Stalin on the negative side, Gandhi and Lao Tzu on the positive side. They have such presence that they deflect history – much as a stone changes the course of a stream. These individuals aren't unknown and don't need to meet in a conspiracy. History is just the story of the ripples and interference patterns they set up. Working motto: "Be all that you can be."

5. The world is ruled by the Cosmos. Some extraterrestrial entity rules through human agents. Magi, prophets, etc. This "god" sends concepts to people through its agent, and that concept rules the age. Working motto: "I am naught compared to He who sent me."

6. The world is ruled by Death. There is negative force in the world, probably controlled by a human conspiracy. They kill off anyone who would in potential disrupt the flow of things. They are responsible for all missing children, assassinations, fatal "accidents." They use death as a way of avoiding real change in the world. They may be wise and good rulers – or stupid and evil – but most likely they just represent that force in the human psyche that fears change. Working motto: "If it ain't broke, don't fix it."

7. The world is ruled by Birth. The rulers of the world are always trying to ruin the

cosmic inertia, to blow away the symmetry of events. They do this through long-term breeding programs that create Einstein or Nelson Mandela. Or they provide opportunities for learning and expansion. Maybe they have a long-term goal – or maybe, like Faust, they're just dissatisfied. Working motto: "It can't get any worse than this."

8. The world is ruled by Re-creation. The super-wealthy, the ultra-powerful merely spend their time trying to recapture the lost joy of their youth. Everything is a frenzied attempt to return to a golden age, an Eden that never was – save in the mind of the adult. Working motto: "Rosebud."

9. The world is ruled by Rebirth. A truly occult technology is used here. Certain Adepts of the Left Hand Path have mastered the art of rebirth. They return again and again, taking up where they left off. For them the world is either a plaything for their eternal desires – or a training ground for another dimension. Working motto: "Once is never enough."

Maybe it was all of these processes. Maybe from some higher perspective all of these forces could be combined – and made to start such disparate groups as the UN Security Council, Nissan Motors, and the Astronomical Observatory at Greenwich.

John pulled the hypothesis-covered sheet out of his typewriter, and started again. The best mix might be four and five and nine. People develop themselves to a certain level of being, then the Other sends word to them, and if they succeed in their task, they Other returns them to the world from time to time. Wasn't there something about that in the Yezidi holy books?

#   #   #

She got out of Lopez's van and the dark swallowed her. She was always happiest in the night, feeling a kinship with it. The night, as Those Who Know know, is a woman, and it has a woman's hungers. She watched a drunk cowboy stagger out of the Victor's Saloon and sized him up. The universe is almost entirely Female, which is why males are precious. They grew out of the female and the female will reclaim them.

#   #   #

John went to the Department of Institutional Adherence. His trip to the Goddess' hall was a well-arranged charade. Donna had told each and every thing to say. Which forms to fill out, who to compliment, who to snub. Which monsters to avoid. He got what he wanted. Some lights. Some drama students. Paint. Canvas. Xerox cards.

He did what no one in a decade had done. He threaded DIA's maze in a single day. He passed old men who had long since lost, long of beard with eyes blinking, toothless mouths gaping yet somehow smiling – happy that someone had made it. They hadn't known the secret of getting through the bureaucracy – you had to screw the king's daughter. They raised their frail cheer as John walked out with his permits.

He winked broadly at Donna shaking his green papers brightly.

He didn't intend to give any of the drama students lead roles in the play. He would make them understudies. They would paint flats and hang lights and take tickets.

But they would be influenced by the ideas; they would carry them out in their careers and throughout their lives. It was an essential part of the Work to insure its remanifestation. He began Xeroxing sheets for them to plaster around Nueva Bethlehem:

CAST CALL

FOR

"Rulers of the World"

A FIVE-ACT PLAY

BY

John Fuentes

Combining History, Comedy, Tragedy

and

FARCE

WHICH WILL RUN

AT

THE Paramount

THEATER

FOR A SUFFICIENTLY LONG TIME

Contact John Fuentes

at the Sands Motel

Room 7

\#   \#   \#

The casting was easy, far too easy. Nine men showed up. Each had almost no acting ability, but they were a natural for the formula that Fuentes had chosen. Eric Ratliff was perfect as Death, his voice slow and measured – it produced a mixture of sleeping boredom and chilly fear. Eric had wanted to be an undertaker, but his family had forced him into managing the local drive-in theater. He began reading for Birth and couldn't even pronounce the lines. John was about to have him leave when Donna suggested Death. It was perfect, too perfect.

The drama students were in awe. They began to feel that this was the most important play ever made. It just had to be. Look at Robert Robinson as "Being." Every time he spoke you knew exactly what he meant. Things couldn't be different, but the moment he shut up, you didn't have a clue to what he was talking about. He was the only psychotherapist in Nueva Bethlehem. Figured.

The students' awe became energy. If this was going to be the Most Important Play ever made, it was their privilege, hell, their honor – no, dammit, their DUTY – to do the best they could do. Gerhard Lopez painted flats – not just putting in long hours, above and beyond the call of duty – but with a flair of originality and design that would make the best designers in the world feel envious. Even little Mervin Ashwait, who designed the posters and tickets, found deep artistic resources that his eighteen summers and employment at a Taco Bell would not have revealed as hidden within him. The poster had an absolute command to look. As the kids hung them on every phone pole in the village, everyone gasped at their beauty and force. No one talked about anything except the play.

People read all they could about drama. People who had been to far-off places like Dallas or Shreveport talked about the wonders they had seen in Diner Theaters. It would be better than the movies, better than TV, better than church, better than the Fourth of July picnic.

Donna went wild. The money behind the play, plus her role in the play as the "World" – the mistress of the Nine Unknown Men – would give her this role in the real world. Everything she had done had prepared for this moment. She took to wearing red leather miniskirts and no panties, parading up and down the streets of Nueva Bethlehem, a sort of anti-Mary, Scarlet Woman. Her time was now. All was in readiness. She knew she would have to do something special for John. He after all thought it was his magic that was going on. Men always think that, and writers are the worst, they never grasp that it is the magic belong to those to who really makes things happen.

She would give him Australia or something.

He was busy with rehearsals. The Nine would seemingly get possessed by their roles. John had half hoped for/half feared this. All artists want control of their work. It is a big pain when your work begins to live and evolve. John guessed that some artists/magicians could handle that, even thrive on it – but he wasn't ready, at least not just yet.

But there was a payoff, an amazingly fucking big payoff. The things they would say. When they ad-libbed, they said all sorts of Secrets. John got a notebook with a purple cover and wrote down each Secret. He was writing down with a cheap pen the true Knowledge that all occult societies had always claimed to give out. Death would say, "Of course my other names are Sleep and Incubation." Birth would say, "Change leaves you weak like a butterfly. At first it takes a while to release you didn't go thorough that pain not to become a super caterpillar." They didn't do much talking about wars and the stock market and so forth, but sometimes the spirit took them there as well. John didn't care, but Donna was on the phone to her broker three and four times a day. John didn't pay much attention to the growing greed light in her eyes, but when she gave him the new black Mercedes-Benz, he guessed that the stock tips were great.

People began showing up from far away,. Everyone in town had told their relatives. They came from Polk City, Iowa, and Budapest; Osaka and Doublesign, Texas. Every hotel room, every house was full.

People were bowing to Donna in the streets.

Then Mervin Ashwait had a surprising thing to say. "Nobody has bought tickets for opening night."

It was true.

John and Donna rushed into the streets, asking everyone.

"Oh, I can't come opening night because I'm waiting on a phone call that night. I'll be the next night."

"*Survior* is on. I never miss *Survivor*. I'll come next week."

"I have to go to a wedding in Armonk, back on the weekend."

"Lodge Meeting. We're electing a new Grand Elk."

"My astrology book says don't go out that night."

The list was amazing and endless. No one seemed to be lying.

Then a few phone calls came in. One local, the others from far away. Nine people bought tickets for opening night.

John realized that they didn't have to buy the whole theater. In fact, they hadn't had to do anything. All John had done was want to know how things worked. All Donna had done was want to control things. All the others had done was want to do the Best Play Ever. That was all it took. They wanted, and the Nine showed up.

Then John began to wonder what they would want. What would the Nine feel after his farce. Happy? Mad? Sad? Or do they have feelings other than those John's life as a minor playwright and stagehand had prepared him for?

He thought about canceling the play, but maybe that was what they wanted to. So the night came. The rehearsals had been perfect. The curtain went up. John sat in the directors bow, running the cheap light board. He could see the ten actors onstage and the nine people in the dark hall.

And he waited.

Waited to see if they would laugh at the first joke.

On the Bus to Enlightenment

Initiation isn't just something that occurs in the ritual chamber. In fact, I would go so far to say that it happens the least there. Setians spend their time just like you – eating, sleeping, trying to earn an honest buck. But the Setian imperative is to transform such activities into things that stimulate the mind, body, heart, and soul. I wrote the following article for Austin Para-Times *to model this behavior. Try it yourself, pick any day-to-day activity and be Awake.*

Like most human beings, I spend a good deal of time trying to figure out how I'm wired into the Cosmos. The Cosmos is great for letting me know that I am connected, but only recently has it told me why I am. Fortunately, Capitol Metro Route 5 has helped. I am 41-year-old man that has returned to college in the middle part of his life to finish that degree-getting deal that most people do in their twenties. Parking near or at UT is an anomaly so rare that it isn't even mentioned in this worthy periodical, so I ride the bus.

I ride with three sorts of people: good working-class folk that are heading downtown to clean and run the buildings; fellow college students with their heads buried in books about statistics, physics, French, and math; and blind teachers on their early morning way to the Texas School for the Blind. None of these people notice me. I envy my fellow students; I cannot read from books in a moving vehicle. So I read the Tide ads, the "Poetry in Motion" placards, and the ads that warn us of undercover cops on the bus. I watch the cars go by and read their bumper stickers, and I look for the big liquor billboards that tell me I'm getting close to campus.

My wife is asleep when I leave. I always set my alarm, but I always wake up three minutes before it goes off. My house-leaving is very well choreographed so that I am grabbing my diet pop and out the door in 22.5 minutes.

Last semester, near Halloween, I had a dream. I dreamt that I got on the bus and checked the time according to the bus' lit clock. It read 5:30, a full three hours before I needed to be on my way to campus. I panicked in my dream. Not only had I lost three hours when I could be sleeping, there would be nothing to do on campus till 8:00. I woke from that dream early, checked my alarm. It was an hour before time for me to start getting ready, but I could not get back to sleep. I rose, wrote a quick poem, checked my e-mail, did the dishes from the night before, and left the house at my usual time. When I got on the bus, I checked the time as I always do. It read 5:30! Someone had set the bus clock wrong. An interesting co-incidence.

Last night, after reading my first issue of the *Austin Para-Times*, which SMiles had given me at the blowout launch party, I had the same dream. The result was the same I got up an hour after the dream did a little writing, a little household work, and I was out the door. When I caught the bus, the clock read 5:30! My October experience had repeated itself. I was amazed and dismayed at the same time. Was my consciousness simply connected with someone that can't set clocks right? Was the gift of having a soul only for such parlor tricks? I was contemplating asking the student next to me what she thought, but I decided that what she would think is that I am a bad person to ever sit next to again. What did it all mean?

About that time a powder blue LTD, the dream car of my youth, raced past the bus. Its bumper sticker read, "Reality: What a Concept!" I hadn't seen any of those in a while and certainly not any powder blue LTDs. The car, which appeared to be in mint condition, turned down North Loop and was seen no more.

It suddenly made sense to me. My soul had given me something. It had given me a sense of Wonder. For a very brief moment, I wasn't thinking about refinancing my house or worrying about that bump on my foot or stressing about job-hunting or papers for my senior seminar. I was totally engrossed in a cosmic drama. It might not seem as gripping as Stephen Hawking puzzling out the Big Bang, but it was much more wonderful because it was happening to me and it was weird. I had received (and given myself) a miracle. One of the signs of the miracle was its *strangeness*. It wasn't something that everyone has theories about. No Bigfoot, JFK assassination theories, no UFOs. It was me and the bus and a particular time. If I were to tell anyone else, all they would say is, "That is Weird!" Then they would forget the story before finishing their cup of tea. It was for me alone. It would change a simple piece of my landscape.

Now I don't expect that it will ever happen again. I suspect it may happen to some of you (I'll explain why below). It won't make me afraid to ride to the bus, nor will it make it seek omens about my life from the bus. It will simply remind me that there is more to life than papers, bumps, or refinancing. The "purpose" of the miracle was to stop the endless repetitions on my internal dialogue. It gives me a little moment of Otherness. A very wise man named Gurdjieff said that the problem with people is that they are asleep all of the time. He recommended various exercises to shake off the dull pseudo-thought trance that holds all of us. I recommend your moments of Wonder. Some people look toward synchronicities such as my dream-clock and the bus-clock as a source of Deeper Meanings. I think they miss the real opportunity. They have a chance to seize the magic and make some part of their lives magical.

Now, why do I think that some of you will now have some Wonderful moment on the bus? There are two reasons. One is that we actually have Wonderful moments all of the time, but we miss them. We have a preconceived notion of what reality is, and we don't see what doesn't fit. The second reason is that I have directed your attention to the bus as a source of such moments. This simple action is how we make both magic and religion: "Ladies and Gentlemen if you simply look over here, a great wonder will be revealed!" Unfortunately, simple explanations are used to diminish the wonder (it was the work of a saint, the devil, the space brothers), and money is collected. "If you give deeply you will see another wonder!" We don't have to put up with either of those forms of balderdash any more. We simply have to be receptive of such moments, and share them with others so that they are on the lookout for them too. We should avoid simple explanations of the Unknown, and we should avoid games of one-upmanship. Simply tell your miracles as they happen.

The net result? One, you and I will be Awake more often. Two, "reality" will become a little softer in our perceptions. Then we can pull a little more out of it than we do now. We can stop Operation Cover-Up that the sleeping parts of our minds have been pulling for many millennia. Heck – maybe we can see what's really out there.

Reality: What a Concept!

Yi-Jing: An Introduction to the Easy Book

In the Year XXXII (1997) a new entity Came Into Being in the Temple of Set, the Soa-Gild. Soa is one of the spellings of the Egyptian word for magical protection, Sa. In ancient Egypt the Soa Gilds worked spells the protection of travelers. The Soa sign is a knot and it usually associated with the goddess Taweret (you may know her from the TV series Lost). *One of the important Soa-sites was established by Ramses III, son of Setnakt. It is an idol of himself in the form of the Self-Created God Khepperer. The back of the idol is covered with the oldest example we have of the* Book of Felling Apep and Knowing the Spiral Force of Re, *which contains the formula Xepera Xeper Xeperu. The Soa-Gild began a book of their experiments with truth, which they called* The Book Of Changes. *They asked me to write a preface – here it is. I reflected that they had chosen the title of the ancient Chinese oracle. Later, with the aid of Allen Varney and Front Load, I created a modern phone app that takes the Yi-Ching and applies it to corporate life: Office Ching. I had signed my introduction with typical magical boastfulness: SetNakt Tian-Shi, or "the Celestial Master Set Is Mighty." I should point out that Allen is a Right Hand Path Buddhist, a great writer and game designer, and hosts some writing that he and I did together on his blog.*

You have chosen the Soa-Gild and therefore you have chosen this Book named after one of the great Confucian classics. The choice of a book is a significant one in Chinese Initiation. Until recently, Chinese parents used to place five objects in front of a son on his first birthday: money, silver, tortoise, a banana and a book. If the baby grabbed for the book, it was a sign that he would be studious. The idea of receiving a book from supernatural sources figures deeply in Chinese thought, "not only in the initiation but also as a harbinger of the new age; a concept that has struck particularly deep roots in the Dao-inspired secret societies." (Wolfgang Bauer in *China und die Hoffung auf Glück* , Munich 1971). The reception of this book, and your opening to it, places you in a tradition of such secret groups as the White Lotus and Triad societies. Like them, you have a mission. "Overthrow Ch'ing, Restore Ming!" Your job is quite simply to break free from the preconceived notions of mediocrity and confusion that bind you now, and begin to live in a world based on Quality. This begins with examining the lies you now hold as true – "I will always be poor! I will always be stupid! I will always be loveless!" and replacing them with other lies – "I am getting richer! I am getting smarter! I am finding my Beloved!" Proceed with these lies as if they were the truth. Tell them to others, tell them to yourself before the mirror each night when you write in your magical diary. Proceed with perfect sincerity, and all things may be attained.

Change in Chinese thought is said to be easy. In fact the words for Change (Yi) and Easy (Yi) have the same sound. The Chinese are right about this – the *moment* of Change is Easy; it is always our disbelief in this simple fact that keeps us from making self-change. Now, what is this – many of you are asking – does not the Temple Teach that self-change is hard Work? It is, but the moment the change occurs, the moment of Xeper itself is easy. Think of diving off the high board. Climbing the ladder is hard, walking to the end of the board is hard, looking down into the chlorine-scented water far below is very hard indeed. BUT the movement through the air is very easy. Once you have conquered yourself, you move into a new realm of pure exaltation – you have a moment of flying that plunges you into a new medium with its new rules and excitations. The moment of Xeper is like that, flowing into a new place of Being after the negative suffering that told you that you couldn't make the Change.

The other word in the Chinese *Book of Changes* (Yi-Jhing) is the word that is hard to translate. *Jhing* means "seriousness" or "calmness" or "focus." It refers to an inner-attitude. It is sometimes translated as "composure," "attentiveness," or "concentration." The oracular book called the *Ji-Jhing* (or, if you prefer Cantonese, *I-Ching*), means *Attentiveness to Change*. A good description of the attitude of a Setian is that she both notices her Evolution internally/externally and the changing state of the world around her. From these two forces she makes a series of places that she can Xeper in.

Just as the *Yi-Jing* described how a virtuous man could lead a harmonious life by balancing the forces of yin and yang and reception and caution, *The Book of Changes* describes how the Setian can lead a successful life by balancing the forces of internal progress and the randomness of the external world. It is easy to summarize both Teachings in an overly succinct form. For the first, "Xeper"; for the second, "If life gives you lemons, make lemonade." But such easy formulas tell you very little until years after you have mastered them.

The Way– the Dao – that arises out of this Book is as subtle as its counterpart in Chinese thought. For the Way, the Dao, will be for each Setian to find. The Secret is in the question of **Ease**. Sometimes we will have pushed ourselves as far as we can on an internal change – just like trying to force ourselves to remember a name, we have to distract ourselves so that our mind can come up with it. When we have pushed ourselves too hard in this way, we must then turn our attention to the external bettering of our circumstance – to money-magic, hard work, and careful shepherding of resources. When we have pushed as hard as we can in the outer world, we must turn our attention inward again with dialogue with our fellow Gilders, reading of new and interesting books on the Reading List, and Greater Black Magic – this gives our magic a chance to work in the world – to convince the boss to give us that extra week of vacation or whatever. This subtle interplay is guided by focus, by an ever-growing and defining Sense of Self that tells us when to be open and when to be closed to the influences we find both inside ourselves and in the outer world.

You are not alone in this struggle, but all of your gains come to you when you are Alone. There is a vast and powerful secret society called the Gild, each member of which works not only for his or her own betterment, but to change the world as a whole to reflect the virtues of Divine Selfishness. Learn how to use the Tool called the Gild. If you proceed in perfect sincerity, the Gild will Teach the subtle path called the Way, the Dao, both in exoteric means, such as this book you're holding now, and esoteric ways as your Will works in resonance with others to make this a place of Xeper, unique and as empowering as you allow it to be.

Put aside the cares of the workaday world for a space and read these pages. Open yourself to them, and then put them away for awhile as you apply yourself in very rational down-to-earth plans for your advancement. You have begun the ebb and flow of your Creation. Return – Learn – Teach. This is what the Gild asks of you, as your Higher Self has already asked of you when it caused you to grab this book.

Beating Fate

Like many occultists my age, I was entranced with the anthropological romances of Carlos Castaneda. My very first ritual I wrote for the Bull of Ombos Pylon has Aztec themes, and when the Smoking Mirror Pylon asked me for an article on Aztec fate concepts for their newsletter, I wrote them this.

The Azteca had a very pessimistic worldview. Elements of that worldview still dominate the politics of Mexico and show up in certain burial practices. Here's a preliminary look at Aztec soulcraft and afterlife. The usefulness of these ideas to the Aeonic Age Initiate must be weighed and investigated.

The average human had two bodies. One was the physical body we all see. Living inside of this body were two forces: the Life force and the Mind Force. The Life Force helped the dead along their journey and was to some extent conserved by the corpse. Even the cremated dead were given a jade stone to act as their "heart." The Mind Force existed before birth and will exist (at least for awhile) after death.

The second body was the Tonal or Fate body. It integrated the person into the unchangeable stream of time. It was fixed by the date of birth, and had a shape recorded in the "Calendar of Fate" or *tonalpohualli*. The Tonal had a shape, a totem animal, which caused it to relate to all other things in accordance with the wills of the gods. The person had to live out his or her life on Earth so that the gods' magic might be done. The Tonal with the Life Force and Mind Force was co-substantial with the physical body. The nature of one's Tonal was created by (and revealed to you by) Quetzalcoatl.

The average person went to a pretty dismal afterlife in the Underworld. They had to go on a long journey, cross a river, fight off snakes, flying blades, and other horrors suggestive of a Nintendo game. They died at their appointed hour, there was no way out of the sadness of this life, and they eventually got eaten in the Underworld. This belief is still held in central Mexico, where the effigy of a dog is buried with the dead to help them cross the river. There were some ways of avoiding fate. You could suffer an unnatural demise. Warriors who died in battle or sacrifice went to the paradise of the rising sun. - Children who died young went to the Tree of Breasts (from which they might be reincarnated). Women who died in childbirth went to the paradise of the setting sun, and people killed by lightning (or other odd natural phenomena) went to a paradise called Tlalcon.

There was another way to escape fate. You could cheat the gods by creating a Fate Body. The Created Fate Body was called the Nahual. It had a shape which represented a better fate. The word Nahual, which literally means "a thing interposed, a mask" comes from the root verb *nahua* – "to place something between the supernatural and the natural orders." You'll note the similarity to the Egyptian Ka. A professional sorcerer could create such an entity for you, but it was risky. If your Nahual died (or was wounded), you died (or were wounded). Better still, you could become a Nahual. This was the term for the professional sorcerer. Not only did the Nahual have a Nahual – they could enter that magical body at will and spy out others. The most common forms of Nahualli (the plural of Nahual) were jaguar, coyote, snake, eagle, and owl. Tezcatlipoca, who is himself a jaguar, has as a Nahual the coyote – placing the Aztec Set firmly in the Trickster role of American Indian culture.

This Self-Created form could survive death. It did not end the obligations of the manifestation that the Tonal gave one, but gave a special freedom to those who, having met their obligations, need not be crushed by the wheel of time. But it was hard work; you had to create another entire life in addition to your profane life – and that life could be snuffed out, leaving you dead in the profane world as well.

Bibliography

The Fifth Sun by Burr Cartwright Brundage 1979 University of Texas Press

American, African, and Old European Mythologies edited by Yves Bonnefoy 1991 University of Chicago Press

Setian Classic Revealed

The trail of the serpent leaves many strange traces. I had the delightful experience of seeing a Setian ceremony missed into great pulp writing when a fellow Adept gave me an old copy of Heavy Metal *for my birthday – April 30. I wrote about this in* Runes, *the newsletter of the Order of the Trapezoid. I was the third editor of* Runes, *following Dr. Stephen Edred Flowers and Dr. Michael A. Aquino. In the cYear XLIX I met the aithor of "The Alchemist's Notebook," Brian Clifton Hinds, who follows a different branch of the Left Hand Path.*

Every now and then I wonder at the effect of our Work on the populace at large. Sometimes I see it in the most unusual places. A few weeks ago, Sir Mimir, Adept J*** G***, gave me the *Heavy Metal: Special HPL* issue (October 1979). I placed it carefully in my bathroom for periodic reading. One story caught my eye, "The Alchemist's Notebook." I thought it had a very Setian sensibility. Its ritual sequence was derived from Magister Caverni Michael A. Aquino's *The Call to Cthulhu*, and its ritual technology – the strobe-like device – clearly came from *Die Elektrischen Vorspiele* . I queried Grand Master Emeritus Aquino to see if he knew of the film *The Cry of Cthulhu* from which this story was said to be a partial novelization. He suggested Sir R*** could be the hidden source, and after asking Sir R***, I got the story.

Magister L*** N*** and Sir R*** were in contact with Jerry Younkins, well-known author of survivalist philosophy and how-to books, as well as Donald Jackson. Younkins and Jackson had decided – perhaps with a little magical influencing by N*** and W**** – to do a series of Lovecraft-inspired films. The first film was made.

Entitled *The Demon Lover*, it contained ritual/invocation sequences designed by Sir R*** and L*** N**** (primarily the later). The film was made on the astonishingly low budget of $5,000! It apparently impressed the Paramount Studio heads enough to consider making the second in the series of films, which was to be *The Cry of Cthulhu*. Like many "sure" deals, it fell through. *The Demon Lover* was made in the Year XI (1976) Younkins and Jackson couldn't afford to have the film processed when it was done and had to sell all rights to pay off the bills. The original print was barely distributed, but if you went to the right grindhouse, you could have seen L*** N*** and R*** W**** listed as Ritual Consultants.   The film has been released on video cassette, but with a new and shorter credit sequence no longer listing Ritual Consultants.

An exciting film, according to the description that Sir R*** supplied me, "This particular film is about a Satanic sorcerer seeking revenge on his 'coven' after they bow out. There's a good demon in itand a good scene of a crossbow shot to the crotch. The sorcerer has very long red hair and doesn't act very well (not the right voice) – that's Younkins himself. According to *The Pyschotronic Encyclopaedia of Film* the film featured Younkins' friends and the breathtaking scenery of Jackson, Michigan. Other notables in the cast include Gunnar Hansen, Leatherface in *The Texas Chainsaw Massacre*, and"Howard the Duck" artist Val Meyerick. The characters are all named after fan personalities – Frazetta, Ackerman, Romero, etc. Jackson was able to go on to better-known pieces such as *Motorcycle Mamas from Hell* afterward.

I hope you enjoy "The Alchemist's Notebook," as a glimpse of what might have been (and may yet be).

Letter to an Adept

The Temple of Set is a neo-Platonic organization. We are influenced by Plato's scheme of the levels of thought – from received opinions and "faith" to reasoning and ultimately to direct perception of the Real. Here is a letter I wrote to an Adept who had become his Pylon's Sentinel wherein I discuss some of the aspects of the Temple's Platonism and how it affects our approach to the world. I also give some basic magical advice about running a group. The letter is in Setian jargon – for example, when I talk about the "God" of the human intra-subjective universe, I call him Har-Wer (the Elder Horus), and when I speak about Initiatory magic, I call it GBM (Greater Black Magic) and so forth.

Dear Adept Q.,

Don't worry that your opinions may have too much weight with I°s. The I° is a time of just Becoming aware that the psyche exists and deciding what to do with it. Some may already have that awareness when they enter the Temple. The I° period is one of learning certain technologies to direct the psyche to certain goals. In either event people may take your word as gospel for a while, but if they are truly seeking the LHP, they will have to come to their own realizations.

As far as what you need to do with your Pylon – think of it entirely as a tool for your own Xeper. If you want people to generate questions for you, have discussion groups; if you want to understand the Vampyric being, have an illustrative Working. The

II° represents a time of articulated desire as opposed to the unarticulated desire of the I°. This is the highest level of the reasonable human being. A clarity comes that enables you to see society, the Temple, and yourSelf in a new light. Sometimes this desire is strong enough for you to get a glimpse of the great secret hidden deeply within the objective universe – Set. This appearance of that secret drives us on in exactly the way the Graal does in Graal legend. In *Parzival*, Parzival encounters the Graal early on, but because his mother had told him never to ask questions, he didn't inquire about the significance of the moment. She represents an almost antiRuna force – the social norm that says don't ask questions. But we must live differently, asking questions all the time. What the force of - desire reveals, only Work obtains.

Group Work can be true Work and not only ceremony. But it takes a lot of talent and practice to make it so. One of the first things your pylon needs to do is create an egregore. Since we are Black Magicians, the first thing we do is reason the matter out as much as we can. Have a discussion with the group – what will this Pylon spirit do? It will enable us to have something Working on behalf of the Pylon at all times, attracting good members, increasing our influence, confusing our enemies. An egregore can also make the sum of the accumulated momentum of the Pylon available to new members. So that even though you're just starting out, you can directly benefit from the Work thus far. - The Bull of Ombos has a powerful egregore that has served its members well over the years. Of course, all these things begin as mental constructions in the mind of one individual, but as time goes on they achieve a life of their own. This fulfills the Setian mandate, Xepera Xeper Xeperu. The Self-Created God Creates Creations. After there has been a conceptualization of the egregore, the Pylon needs to Create it and put it to personal use. Find something that appeals to you as Sentinel and then transfer your excitement and thought to the group. One of the jobs of a Sentinel is to transfer his/her inspiration to the others in a precise language. In this way the Sentinel stands for the Pylon in regards the source of inspiration (Set) and provides formulas usable by the Pylon in the objective realm (Har-Wer). This process (the integration of precision and inspiration) is true of Black Magic as a whole, and that's why being a Sentinel of a Pylon can be a great aid to one's Xeper.

In answer to your question, our mutual acquaintance is an excellent magician of the Aeon of Horus. That Aeon, as you know, never resolved the paradox of the human condition of being opposed to and separate from the universe and yet at the same time being a part of that universe and functioning in it. As a consequence, he tends to equate the fitful manifestations of Har-Wer with genuine magical results. It's easy to get synchronicity. It's more important to control it. The problem with Thelema is that it does not separate the mental/subjective and physical/objective realms. Without that separation there is no true guideline for what to do. Natural processes are just as likely to get results as consciously sought paths. Now, don't get me wrong. You can certainly have magical interaction with the natural world – the important thing is knowing what you're aiming for. If you want to communicate to the natural order – and your communication is a valid one (i.e., "I want more tomatoes this year in my garden" rather than "I intend to dig up gold beneath my compost pile in a month") – the natural order might as well try and produce the effect. This is, surprisingly enough, not a violation of thermodynamics – since a valid request/order is within the realm of possible unfoldings inherent in the natural situation. The universe is prone to communication in a strange and fitful way.

This is a result of the action of Set on the universe creating a buffer zone called Har-Wer. Likewise, in your own life you can create an environment that – through the conscious projection of your psyche – may prove to be more interactive with you than mere chance may suggest. With the practice of this magic there are three great dangers.

1. You may not remember that this is an idiot system which is merely reacting to your presence. For example, if you use some physical method of divination (which of course reflects on what's coming into being at the instant – not the future, but that's another letter), you may be able to achieve better-than-random results. The danger lies in forgetting that this is an idiot system and basing your actions on its suggestions. At best such things provide another point of view and should have no more value than any particular newscast.

2. The second danger lies in mistaking material magic for Xeper. A lot of Setians are very good at sorcery of various types, but that expertise is only useful if it helps the magician control his/her environment in such a way as to make it maximally suited for his/her Xeper.

3. The third great danger is assuming that the external order mirrors your inner order. This is a very easy trap to fall in. A few things falling into place – such as that book you *really* needed dropping off the shelf as you walk by – and you begin to think that there are no accidents. The pathetic fallacy. This of course leads the magician to a simple Self-destroying formula: All good things that happen to me are the result of my power, all bad things – well, those are good somehow because they fulfill my destiny. This dissolving of the boundaries of the Self and the Universe is one of the most pernicious forms of the RHP – it doesn't clearly state a belief in a god – it just causes the

Initiate to wander off the track. If you're interested in the theory of this topic consult *The Game of Wizards*.

Although experience in such natural magic can be helpful to a Magician, (and in fact the word of RUNA presumes that a Magician will seek after such mysteries as well as those within), GBM is focused on either the world within the Self or in the subjective overlays that control mankind as a whole. It's easier, as Anton LaVey, remarked to change someone's mind than to levitate a teacup. It's easier because magic occurs in the mind. - The mental universe doesn't end at the limits of our skulls. There's a confused area in between created by the unconscious GBM of humanity. We may as well call this (after Jung) the Collective Unconscious. This collective basement is full of forms – *neters* – some of these *neters* may have a dim life of their own – their followers have given them power, *sekhem* (if you are familiar with tantra, these roughly equate with Shiva and Shakti). For example, a really big Baptist church may have generated an egregore. This dim entity may express itself by occasionally causing an errant member to feel that he should go back to church. Or it may provide some minor miracle for one of its flock. Or it may just be a "feeling" that some of the members get from time to time. In this, the members of the church are unconsciously fulfilling the Setian mandate, Xepera Xeper Xeperu. They have created a "thing" from their minds and wills (such as they are) that has an effect on the subjective and objective universes around them. Now, to do this they have to take what was in their hearts and put in a symbolic form into the real world. Church buildings are much more important symbolically than physically, which is one reason that Christianity is on the ropes – they can't build attractive buildings that dominate the landscape anymore. Now they accomplish all of this unconsciously.

As Black Magicians we can accomplish this consciously. We can build a form. It has to have a name, a symbol, and a purpose. The purpose is simple: represent the will of the Pylon to the Collective Unconsciousness of the geographical area. It keeps a continual pressure on the people around you, causing them to always be a little more willing to consider your ideas (in the long run this will aid in the Initiating of human consciousness, but in the short run it makes your lives easier), and it will help you find better members.) For those inside the Pylon it creates a sense of protection and trust that enables you to do your magic better. Ultimately the form of the egregore can be handed over to other Sentinels. I suggest that you conceptualize the egregore as a 24-hour Black Magician who is constantly Working on the mass of humanity around you in the same way that individual members of the Priesthood Work with each of you individually. Either stirring them up toward Initiation or doing protective or prosperity rites (for the membership).

A lot of magical things have to be experienced. Unfortunately the English language is very poor in terms for different kinds of understanding. Since we don't have a term like *noesis*, we don't really think in that category – or if we do, we think that noetic experience – such as some of your recent experiences – as somehow "irrational." Likewise, we lack a term for the kind of knowledge that comes from experience. The Greeks had a good one – *episteme* – the type of knowledge that only comes from doing. Poetry and cooking are two good examples of such knowledge. You can learn neither without practice. Observational science, such as learning to predict the weather or mineralogy, also fall under this category. Two other categories of the reasoning Self are necessary – the category of pure logic, *mathesis* (an example would be geometry), and the knowledge which comes from feeling, *pathesis*, need to be included as elements of *dianoia*. An example of *pathesis* leading to *dianoia* could be found in the answer to the question, "Why do I hate Mr. So-and-so?" When you analyze this feeling (rather than projecting something on Mr. So-and-so), you will first off remind your psyche of its existence (it's your feeling) and secondly give your psyche more access to itself.

Since ritual magic also comes under *episteme* it is necessary to **do** things like creating the egregore; discuss it first, but expect to discover more about it in the subsequent creation and use. The knowledge that comes through practical application (*episteme*) plus that which comes through pure logic and reason (*mathesis*) plus the knowledge that comes from a strongly felt experience – such as the death of a loved one or an intense romance – (*pathesis*) together add up to *dianoia*. *Dianoia* is the highest level that the non-noetic can function from. Note that all of these modes imply trust in the Self – my feelings are valid, my thinking is valid, and my observations are valid. But all of these things are to be tested in their own terms as well as in terms of the great*er* *synthesis*. The Second Degree is said to be a sense of the Self – essentially *dianoia* (and after all *dianoia* comes from *dia,* "through," and *nus,* "the mind" – thorough-mindedness). It is only from that point of reason that the Self is strong enough to experience *noesis*. Otherwise, the noetic experience merely unhinges or is interpreted outside the Self's Understanding ("...the texts of another are an affront...") as a *pistis*. Something we must believe in because it's the word of god.

Noesis is not necessarily repeatable. One can test it with the three facets of *dianoia*, but one of the true tests is through Remanifestation of the notion. One may never have the subjective experience again, but as you seek after its meaning and have incorporated it as well as you can, it will reoccur in a different set of subjective phenomena. It may just be that shiver that occurs when your psyche becomes aware of its own existence. Each time a little more of yourSelf is open to yourSelf.

Anyway, I hope this answered some of your questions. In the meantime, I'll leave you with a couple of questions to mull over.

1. One Egyptologist defines the *ka* as "what comes to mind when a person's name is mentioned." How does this relate to the *Ka* mentioned in the Invocation of Set (or, how does the way people think of us and remember us interact with our magic)?

2. What practices through life and at the moment of death are most likely to contribute to our conscious survival of bodily death?

Give my best to everybody. There is no need to hurry to reply to this. I hope this finds you well and happy as we,

Xeper and Remanifest,

Setnakt

REYN TIL RUNA!

My Spring Dromenon

One of the Orders of the Temple of Set, the Order of the Sepulcher of the Obsidian Masque worked with theatrical explorations of the ideas of Death, Fear, and Love. Order members were encouraged to find dramatic venues in the real world – in other words, on stages or before cameras rather than the ritual chamber. I was a member during my Fourth and Fifth Degrees. As a member we had to provide reports of these "Dromenoi" for the Order newsletter. Here is one of my reports.

My foreskin had been caught in a zipper in an airport bathroom. I put my painful member back, got on the long four-hour flight and had the scariest-looking infection by my arrival at home. My urologist sent to me to surgery the next day. My favorite moment was my anesthesiologist suggesting that he and I should write a post-nuclear holocaust novel together as he was putting me under. Most writers have had non-writers pitch an idea to them ("and we can split the money") but usually blood and anesthesia aren't involved.

Any Death is a loss of ego control. And if we identify entirely with our ego, not only our afterlife but our current life options are extremely limited. In the last part of July, I had ego-loss forced on me. I thought the fear I was confronting was pain, but

279

there was another fear – a true Unknown that reached out and grabbed me a couple of months after the operation.

One of my biggest fears is and has been loss of memory. Last year I had to undergo surgery – emergency circumcision. This is the physical ordeal by which one entered a training for a profession in Egypt, by the way. I had a bad reaction to the anesthetic, which resulted in my losing two or three weeks of memory. Now you don't know something's not in your head. About a month after my surgery, I went with an old and dear Buddhist friend to Dr. Chocolate, a store selling great, rich chocolate goodies. I thanked my friend for taking me "since I'd never been to the new store before." My friend looked very startled.

He said that we had visited the store about a month before. Normally if you've forgotten something, hearing about it wil lcause the memory to rise up. No, nothing. Then I was very, very scared. What had happened to those memories??? As best I can tell, they're gone. I even signed a contract on a short story, and then sold it again -- because I had forgotten that I had done so. (Fortunately, I'm a friend of everyone involved and they gracefully let me off the hook). I met some people at a party and didn't remember meeting them. Did I do or say or commit other things during this period??? Maybe. Just this week I was a party for SF professionals in Houston. Suddenly I felt very scared. What if I had met these people before? That section of my life has truly died to me. Yet I am here – I walk, I breathe, I have a sense of continuity.

Dunya, a local dancer, (MFA Julliard, Sufi Master), was asked to perform at the local poetry festival. She called me up and asked me to write some poems that she could dance to. I went over, and she began talking about how scary her surgery had been – and that she wanted some ritual to work out her concerns. The poems enclosed took me about 20 minutes to write. So I've begun some of my process, but much remains to do.

We were part of a poetry festival. The room was loud – people were walking around – some of the poets had been heckled. Then I began to read, and Dunya veiled herself for the first poem. It got real quiet. When we finished, there were several seconds of silence and then strong applause. Here are the poems . . .

The Cloth

I received a gift of black cloth

from a secret admirer,

a Hidden God that said he loved my art.

It came in the mail.

It was so black

so different that I unfolded it.

And it kept unfolding

And unfolding

And it covered up my room

It covered up my life.

I could not leave the cloth.

Then I heard the Voice say,

"He's ready. Take him now."

****

Ordeal

I knew that they were demons

but I couldn't see them in the dark.

I knew them by their knives.

I knew them by their rattles and bells.

I knew them by their laughter.

      I don't care what you say.

      It was not a little cut.

      It was not a standard procedure.

      It was death.

They cut each part of my body.

They scattered the bits.

And then I heard the strange and fitful god say,

"I want this, and that, and

Maybe the Heart or Mind if it

is sweet."

Then there was worse blackness

And Silence

And I missed even the rattles and bells.

I missed the knives.

They took me back to a normal place

Except the light wasn't real.

I was weak,

and I knew they had taken

real light away.

****

My New History

They put a new past in me.

I know they did.

The new past was unending weariness.

I had always been sick.

I had always been weak.

There was no life before.

I would always take long white pills.

I would always lie in bed.

My world was white linen.

It always had been.

I would always be sick.

There was no other life.

****

Bring Me the Elder's Staff

Bring me the elder's staff.

Bow before me.

I am an old man.

In a month I have become an old man.

Bring me my soup.

Bring me my hot tea.

It is late

I need a nap.

I am an old man

Initiated into the Mysteries of Life and Death.

Respect me.

Bow before me.

Bring me my chair

and I will tell you all.

****

I Have Come Forth

I have come forth,

I have walked out of the underworld,

where the savage god said,

"I may call you at any time.

Tremble and obey."

I have escaped for now

but I did not come forth by day.

My world is the starlit world.

And sometimes I see Him

      in the shadows

      in the corners and niches of my life.

I pit my fierce joy

against his sorcery.

I wager my happiness

and my loved ones

That I will finish my Work.

I have come forth!

The Doctrine of Effort

The Temple of Set, particularly the Order of the Trapezoid, believes that Self-Creation, which is the Temple's soteriological practice, is grounded in striving. Just as Set must work to know the universe, so must the Setian work to know the universe and herself. In Goethe's Faust, *Faust obtains his salvation by a mixture of endless striving and Gretchen's love. Setians see salvation not as escaping a nonexistent Hell, but creating themselves in such a way that the psyche does not have as deep a trauma when it is disconnected with the body. Endless striving to know and Love the mysteries of the worlds (both within and without) plus finding the Beloved is a very good formula. Here are some words I wrote about Striving taken from a letter to a new Priest.*

The Left Hand Path is grounded in, and tested by, the needs of human experience. It largely represents an extraction of the Principles of the Cosmos from human experience, just as the Right Hand Path generally extracts its Principles from the world of Chaos, or as the nonElect say, "nature."

One of the simplest ideas that mature human beings have is that Reward should be tied to Effort. Human beings that don't understand this spend their lives over their parents' garage. Most of the real frustration that permeates our world comes from the separating of reward and effort.

An Understanding of the Doctrine of Effort is an Understanding of commitment to action in the objective universe, which is a core principle of the Left Hand Path. I will point out the types of effort, the effect that Sorcery has on effort, and finally the application of the doctrine to society and employment.

Types of Effort. There are four types of effort – animal, human, heroic, and semidivine. Each is chartered by the source of guidance, the limits of freedom, the voluntarism required, and the type of reward obtained.

Animal effort is the effort required of humans to perform thoughtless tasks under close supervision. The mantra associated with animal effort is "Would you like fries with that?" The job is totally defined; creativity is discouraged; if performance isn't up to a low objective standard, people are dismissed; and there are no rewards for excelling in your performance. The job would be done by a trained monkey, except that trained monkeys are too expensive.

Human effort is the effort that most people hope to achieve, and almost half the population does so. It is the sphere of effort in a closely supervised environment where excellence pays off. Here are the jobs where, if you work hard, you will be rewarded by greater opportunities of freedom (i.e., your superiors leave you alone), Recognition for your creativity, and increased monetary benefits. Within broad parameters, you are rewarded for voluntarism.

Heroic effort is the effort required when you place yourself in a difficult situation for the self-transformation obtained. This is the type of effort that begins to set man's rulers apart from the herd. It requires freedom of action, followed by submission. A perfect example would be someone volunteering to join the Marines. Voluntarism ends after that. The drill sergeant doesn't ask you to volunteer to get up at 4:30 in the morning. The rewards for heroic effort are the acquisition of human virtues like Bravery, Determination, Patience, and so forth.

Semi-divine effort is, of course, the most difficult. It requires constant voluntarism. You put yourself in a difficult situation to transform yourself that is not supervised but suggested. This is in an environment where an Ideal is held before you, but the achievement of the Ideal is up to your own actions. The Temple of Set is an arena for such activity. Our Priests don't call you up and say, "It's Tuesday, are you Xepering?" or "I want to see some serious Xeper by the end of the month; you're off on your Xeper quota." Here a type of Effort is exalted, but there is no direct supervision. For most people such types of activity are truly impossible. The rewards for semi-divine effort are the acquisition of magical power. People who can set up and keep a grueling schedule of personally directed work simply become "lucky" or "powerful" or "wise" or "charismatic." Now, each type of effort remains part of the picture as you advance. You will need to keep your animal effort well in hand to do human-level work. You will need to do human-level work when going though the Ordeal of heroic effort. You will need the discipline of heroic effort to strive in the semi-divine.

Effects of Sorcery. Now, as magicians we are lazy and greedy, so we want to get reward without effort. If we are any good at all at this, we usually give up effort altogether. However, if we decide to put our Sorcery in the service of our Xeper, we can accomplish a miracle in the above schema. Sorcery has the power to transmute the arena to the next higher notch. We may be working at a burger place, but with magic we can cause human opportunities to open up. (This doesn't mean we are smart enough/tough enough to take such opportunities.) We may have a simple human job, but with magic we can manifest a heroic job (for example, we go from being a desk jockey to having a globe-traveling job that requires much and rewards with both money and self-transformation). We can even change an heroic job, like being a PSYOP in Vietnam, to a semi-divne job, like starting an Aeon. Properly Understood and applied, Sorcery can change the playing field. This is the "break" that Black Arts give us.

But the opposite is sadly true as well. We can use our magical powers simply to make our lives easier, and then fill that ease with more time to pursue the mind-numbing amusements of our neighbors. We can change a heroic job into a human career. We can turn a human career into an animal job. The possibility for de-evolution is always around us. Our fellow humans are too stupid and weak to know this, or they would have dragged the world down a long time ago. But we, the Elect, Know. We can make things so easy on ourselves that we merely sleep.

Application of the Doctrine. As an Initiate proceeds down the Left Hand Path, he or she develops the Need to remake the objective universe more and more in the image of his or her values. This means that we have to modify what we do for a living, since that is where we spend the most of our time. The first modification that we have to bring about, is to be sure that the environment provides Reward for Effort. One cannot pursue an LHP life in a system that either ignores or penalizes effort. The second task is more subtle. We must modify the environment so that it allows us to gain personal reward for our efforts. For example, it isn't that hard to get raises for jobs well done (millions of non-magicians manage this), but it is hard to get our companies to provide places for our Selfish development. Learning to train your company to think it's a good idea to help you get your law degree, or your engineer's certification, and so forth is the Great Work. Your efforts, which will be hard, benefit yourself, and you will have changed your employer into your tool.

We also realize that any force outside ourselves that draws rewards from our efforts is a Right Hand Path force. The primary examples are governments, who take our moneys for their ends. The game that these forces play is to make us debate which of their ends is the better one – do we spend this money on government might (military) or government co-dependence (social programs)? As long as we debate this, they draw in the shekels. The Left Hand Path Initiate must oppose (in well thought-out, legal means) these forces on the one hand. This is much, much tougher than the easy antinomianism of making fun of the church. But a second, more subtle task exists – we must Do the action that the government has hooked us with. If we are really concerned about social injustice, we have to act in the trenches by feeding the poor. If it's an environmental issue that pulls our strings, we must be in the front line. It is not enough to oppose injustice; we must Work to produce justice. The lessons learned in changing the world, are the lessons that will work in changing ourSelves.

My First Rite

As I wrote earlier, my first ritual within the Bull of Ombos Pylon was a

Castaneda-esque Invocation of Tezcatlipoca. I occasionally boast that I

wrote the first Working in the Temple that has hot choclate in the Graal. I

wrote up an account of the Rite for the newsletter of the Bull of Ombos

Pylon. This Working was rewritten and performed by the Smoking Mirror

Pylon at Las Vegas Conclave in the Year XXX. I met my wife wearing

lovely quetzal feathers in her hair while she did the Graal Work of that

Working. The following version was performed in April of XXIV (1989)

about a month after I joined the Temple. The god Ah Balan Dzocab was

the one supposed to return on December 21, 2012.

In *The Fire Within* Carlos Castenada (Arhena) posits the existence age-old sorcerers living a vampiric existence. They prey upon the fear of normals (fear in C.C.'s system being a manifestation of the life-force – probably a valid equation since fear often releases previously hidden aspects of ourselves for our self-preservation). They also accept small gifts of life energy from living sorcerers to whom they give sorcerous techniques in return. This image holds the past-present-future image of sorcery very well. In ritual we are attempting to emulate parahuman entities. All ritual is, of course, white magic ("vain repetitions"), but it can prepare us for GBM.

This ritual calls to Tezcatlipoca, a complex Aztec-Toltec god similar to Set. We awaken Tezcatlipoca and allow him to walk again in the world of men. Tezcatlipoca teaches us – in the shamanistic sense, he places things inside our bodies – certain mysteries as he taught his priests of old.

The fourfold god Tezcatlipoca resembles Set in many particulars. He is identified with the constellation of the Big Dipper. He causes droughts. He teaches black witchcraft. He is a patron of princes. He is mighty in war. He teaches magic. He is worshipped at night – particularly in his aspect as Black Tezcatlipoca. He is apparently equivalent to the Mayan god Ah Balan Dzocab (otherwise known as God K) whose sacred number is 9.

Tezcatlipoca has many titles and attributes and I have chosen those which I feel appropriate. I have also often used English titles due to the difficulty in pronouncing Nahuatl. Aztec deities are strange and horrific – nearly complete in their otherness. Even the gigantic demons in East Asian temples look almost insipid when compared to the famous Coatlique, whose effigy has caused thousands to turn away shuddering.
An *ixiptla* is the living representative of the god. Generally, these were sacrificed at the end of the ceremony. I have decided to omit the human sacrifice as the ritual chamber is carpeted rather than tiled.

Inspirational Reading

The Fifth Sun , Burr Cartwright Brundage, 1983. University of Texas Press. Excellent

overview of Aztec thought – particularly useful in understanding the god Tezcatlipoca.

Echoes of the Ancient Skies, Edwin C. Krupp, Harper and Row, 1983. A good non-crazy

guide to archeoastronomy with emphasis on the history of astronomy, star lore, and

ancient calendars, mythology, megaliths, ice age artists, Celts and Druids, California

Indians, Mesoamerica (extensive), Peru, other South and North American Indians, Egypt

(extensive), Mesopotamia, China, and Japan. A very useful bibliography is attached.

Comments

1. I played the part of the *ixiptla*, the living idol. When

    the drum was struck after the First Call, I really did

    convulse – even though I was expecting it.

2. I lay on the floor rather than slumped.

3. Adept R*** suggested placing a mirror on the North Wall

with smoking pine resin cones to stand for the Smoking

Mirror. I think that would be great.

4. If we perform this again, we should lengthen it. Everyone

in the pylon concurs.

5. If I could obtain a Mexican demon mask, it would make the

drama more effective.

6. This was my first group ritual, and I want to thank the

members of the Bull of Ombos pylon for not only dispelling

"stage night jitters," but making this a full WORKING.

7. Although no doubt a framing effect, since this ritual

Aztecana seems to be everywhere and I've got a few more

paperbacks wedged into my overfilled library.

8. Priestess F*** had hung Priestess R****'s

Anubis on the eastern wall. I was very aware of its

watchful eyes during the ceremony. This was the first

time I felt magical contact from someone in the Temple

that I hadn't met personally. Since this was my first

ritual, I found this to be a very good omen. I have sent

my thanks to Priestess R***** in a letter.

9. I would very much like to receive anyone's comments,

criticisms, or questions.

Night of the Ixiptla

Special preparations:

The North Wall of the Ritual Chamber is draped in black.

A strong chocolate drink is in the Graal. Mexican hot chocolate is preferred!

A drum replaces the bell (Tezcatlipoca introduced drumming and dancing to men).

The Ixiptla is provided with a shard of obsidian for the Smoking Mirror.

Haunting flute music is preferred.

The chamber is prepared normally; however, the Black Flame is not yet lit. (Materials for lighting the Flame should be on hand.) Copal and candles are lit.

THE WORKING

(The Ixiptla slumps against the South Wall. His head is down, covered. He is lifeless.)

* Drum 9X

* Invocation of Set

* Reading from the Words of Set

Fourth Part (Enochian)

The Four Calls

(As each call is read, the caller faces the indicated direction. The other celebrants face the Ixiptla watching for signs of life.)

First Caller

From the Yellow East I call Moquequeloa, the Mocker who created men for his endless amusement. Come, Moquequeloa, teach us how to laugh at the lower orderings of men. You place men upon thrones or fasten the slave collars upon them, and we would do so. Come and we will teach you to feel the breath in your lungs again.

(The Drum is struck. The Ixiptla twitches as through struck with electric current, but he does not rise.)

Second Caller

From the Black North I call Cetl who controls all that is dark, dangerous, and Cold. Come, Cetl, and teach us how to blight our enemies. You blight your enemies with frost and cut them down with the sharp obsidian knife, and we would do so. Come and we will teach you what it is to walk with your feet upon the rich ground.(The Drum is struck. The Ixiptla stands. His head remains bowed.)

Third Caller

From the Blue West I call Huemac, ancient god of Tula who is the double or phantom. Come, Huemac, and teach us the art of the double and its projection. You may move in two places at once and in many forms, and we would also. Come, Huemac, and we will teach you what it is to feel blood coursing through your veins again.

(The Drum is struck. The Ixiptla raises his head but it remains hooded.)

Fourth Caller

From the Red South I call Tezcatlipoca, God of the Smoking Mirror, who may see into all things. Gods and men fear thee, for you know their innermost hearts and may act accordingly. We would have such perception. Come, Tezcatlipoca, and remember thejoy of lighting the Black Flame.

(The Drum is struck, and Tezcatlipoca reveals his face. He holds up the smoking mirror in his left hand. He walks to the altar with the fourth caller to observe the kindling of the Black Flame.)

Fourth Caller

I kindle the Black Flame, symbol of Set-Tezcatlipoca's gift to us. This is the Flame that quickened the human race's development, burns brightly in all civilizations. It reminds us to strengthen our mind and refine our will.

(The Fourth Caller retreats and joins the semicircle of celebrants behind the altar. The god quietly works his will and then takes up the cup.)

Tezcatlipoca

Yes, I am Moquequeloa, and into this cup I put laughter that your spirits may be always glad and I put the power of upset that you may change the stations of men as you will. Yes, I am Cetl, and into this cup I put the power of the Night Ax that you may be able to assume terrifying forms and live off the fear of mortals, far beyond your normal span of years. Yes, I am Huemac, and into this cup I put the power of the double that you may send forth yourself into other worlds or into the many corners of this world. Yes, I am Tezcatlipoca, and into this cup I put seership that you may know the innermost secrets of gods and men. These mysteries are here for those who would drink.

(Tezcatlipoca sets the cup on the altar. He turns to address the celebrants.)

Tezcatlipoca

I have left an image of myself in your cup. It is good to feel air again, to stand on earth again, to feel blood course again, to kindle the Black Flame again. I go now revitalized to work my magic in the world of men.

(The god walks toward the East or West as convenient. His spirit passes beyond, and the Ixipatla joins the celebrants. The Priestess takes up the Graal and faces the celebrants.)

Priestess

Behold, the god has left. We have never needed the gods save for friendship and advice.

We too will offer friendship and advice when our time comes. This is chocolate, sacred

drink of the Aztecs. If you would be as the gods, drink this. If you tremble and hesitate,

it will surely kill you.

(Priestess offers the Graal.)

(At this time the assembled may approach the altar to work their will in silence or no.

After a suitable interval the drum is struck four times.)

        ALL

It is done!

Some Numbers

From time to time I will encounter an interesting number or word or bit of history. I may someday write a short encyclopedia of the Left Hand Path. For the time being, I will share some of my numbers with you, for some these may attract synchronicities. For others this section will be nonsense – as sorcery always is for most people.

118 the number by Hebrew Kabbalah of the Word Xeper. Other words of the 118 current:

To pass, renew, change

To ferment

The High Priest

The Goddess Nu

To pierce, to sprout; sharp knife (This is related to the Greek for a cutting – TOME (*Liber Al* "To Me")

Also, the 118th Psalm:

"The stone the builders rejected

    has become the capstone."

A symbol of a human or idea that has come into being and, although it does not register to the existing scanning patterns of the dominant paradigm, is destined to reshape the world in accordance with its inner patterns.

18 the number by Hebrew Kabbalah for *Ratzon* (Hebrew *Will*). This is always linked with Eretz (Hebrew *Land)* because both derive from the same root (*R-tz*). In Jewish tradition it is the Will of the Creator for His people to take over land. Anton LaVey chose this number as the number of years in a Working Year. The magician permanently gains anything gained after 18 years of effort. Also it is the sum of 6+6+6; the sum of its parts 1+8 =9

1872 The Year Richard Dedekind divided the real number line, thus beginning Modernism in mathematics. Victoria Woodhull runs for President of the United States – the first female candidate – she believed in magnetic healing, spiritualism, civil rights, abortion rights and eugenics. The *Marie Celeste* is found crewless in open water. The great fire of Boston destroyed everything that Paschal Beverly Randolph owned and forced to him to begin to sell his self-discovered sex magic techniques that later show up in Adonism, the Ordo Templi Orientis (OTO), the Fraternitas Saturni, and modern sex magic in general.

1895 The Year Carl Kellner founded the Ordo Templi Orientis (OTO). John Uri Lloyd published *Etidorpha* (read it backwards), a novel of Initations that featured a journey through Mammoth Cave and ended with an allegory of sex magic and the use of psychotropic mushrooms. Konstantin Tsiolkovsky proposes a space elevator. J. P. Morgan and the Rothschilds loan sixty-five million (in gold) to the United States so that it doesn't go out of business. Japan whipped China's butt in the Sino-Chinese war – this scared Europeans so much they divided up China before the Japanese could get it. Charles W. Leadbeater and Annie Besant began studying atomic structure with the third eye.

1902 The Year Guido von List began to Receive esoteric insight into the Runes. Aleister Crowley scarified a goat to Bhairava. Father Alfred Firmin Loisy began the Modernist crisis by suggesting that the first five books of the Bible were not literal history and that reason could be applied to scripture. Valerios Stais discovered the Antikythera mechanism. The OTO published the first issue of the *Oriflame*. George Ivanovich Gurdjieff reached Tibet. William James published *Varieties of Religious Experience*.

1904 The Year Aleister Crowley received *The Book of the Law*; Herero Wars begin – first genocide and first concentrations camps; Leopold Bloom walks through Dublin; Joseph Campbell born; Salvador Dali born; Poincaré made his conjecture. Dr. Iwan Bloch discovered the lost manuscript of *120 Days of Sodom* and published it under his pseudonym of Eugène Dühren.

1948 The Year Herbert Sloan founded the Lady of Endor Coven of the Ophite Cultus Satanas ; M.C. Escher's *Drawing Hands;* Claude E. Shannon creates Information Theory; Mahatma Gandhi murdered; Hideki Tojo executed; Alice Cooper born; Harry Price (ghost hunter) died; Kenneth Grant recognized as IX° by Karl Germer. Grant meets Austin Osman Spare; Frater Achad Utters MAnifestatION; and a month later James Lewis is born (who later Utters Remanifestation), Henry Wallace runs for President of the United States but is disgraced because of connection with Nicholas Roerich.

1955 The Year Kenneth Grant publishes his manifesto on the Set/Sirius current and named Eugen Grosche as an associate, Grant founds the Nu-Isis Lodge, Grosche publishes the manifesto in German; The Reverend Sun Myung Moon is released from prison in South Korea; President Eisenhower sends "advisors" to Vietnam; Rosa Parks refuses to give her bus seat; Jean Cocteau (said to be the 26th Grandmaster of the Priory of Sion) was elected to both the Royal Academy of Belgium and the Académie française. Kenneth Anger films *Thelema Abbey.*

1966 The Year Anton LaVey founded the Church of Satan, Ronald Keith Barrett received the I AM papers, Mothman appeared in West Virginia, *Dark Shadows* and *Star Trek* premiere, Ken Kesey does the first public LSD "acid test" at the Fillmore, Black Panthers founded, and John Lennon says the Beatles are more popular than Jesus. *The Comet* photographed Alex Sanders' coven naked, and world-wide interest in Wicca began.

1968 The Year Michael Aquino joined the Church of Satan, debut of *Rosemary's Baby*, Apollo 8 astronauts read from *Genesis* in space (including the BRAShITh – which esoterically symbolizes the Hidden and the Manifest); Margaret Murray O'Hare (of the American Atheist) tries to sue the government over this. *Time* published an article on Hippie religion equating occultism, the Neo-American Church, and Satanism – "Doctrines of the Dropouts," Jan. 5; *Hair* told us the "Age of Aquarius" had begun, "May 68" – the student revolution in Paris was the high tide of Horus the Crowned and Conquering Child. *L'ennui est contre-révolutionnaire!*

1970 The Year Michael Aquino received the *Diabolocon,* My Lai Massacre, First Earth Day, *Love Story* and *Equinox* released, Jimi Hendrix dies, World Trade Center becomes world's tallest building. In an episode of *Dark Shadows*, the witch Angelique invoked Set (and I was thrilled watching on ABC after school – my first glimpse of Set – at least that I can recall).

1974 The Year Michael Aquino received *The Ninth Solstice Message,* Stephen Edred Flowers Hears "RUNA," Maggie Ingalls (Nema) receives *Liber Pennae Praenumbra:*

The Book of the Foreshadowing of the Feather, Symbionese Libeartion Army kidnaps Patty Hearst (their symbol is a seven headed Serpent), Ronald DeFeo Jr. kills his parents in siblings in Amityville, and Chögyam Trungpa founds Naropa University, bringing "crazy wisdom" to the West (Tibetan Left Hand Path). Julius Evola dies.

1975 The Year Micheal Aquino received *The Book of Coming Forth by Night* and the founding of the Temple of Set, "Carla Moran" claims that she is raped by an invisible entity, the Altair 8800 is made and thus begins the era of microcomputers – Bill Gates forms Microsoft, Pol Pot seizes power in Cambodia, the term "fractal" is first used, several Jehovah's Witnesses believing it to be the end of time sell all their possessions. Gurdjieff's *Life is Real Only When "I Am"* is published for the first time.

1983 The Year Michael Aquino Uttered the Word "Walhalla!" in the *Valhöll* of Himmler's Castle in Wewelsberg and refounded the Order of the Trapezoid. President Reagan called the U.S.S.R. an "evil empire." *Pioneer 10* left the solar system carrying a plaque to contact extraterrestrial life. Sam Rami released *The Evil Dead.* Arthur Koestler died.

1984 The Year Stephen Flowers joined the Temple of Set and its Order of the Trapezoid. Stephen Flowers published his dissertation *Runes and Magic* and (as Edred Thorsson) *Futhark.* First Working Year of the Church of Satan ended. Haunted Castle at Six Flags Great Adventure burned down.

24 The number of Order in the Indo-European Cosmos. It signifies that Mystery can be Hidden in observable objects and experiences by immanent means, but that the Cosmos itself Hides a Mystery only for those who seek it with Transcendental means. It is the number of Runes in the Elder Futhark, the number of Trumps in the Magian Tarok, the number of letters in the Greek Alphabet, the number of syllables in the gayatri meter which begin the *Rig Veda* and comprise one fourth of it. The Gayatri Mantra, which is the mantra of enlightenment (second only to Aum in power), has 24 syllables (and as always with 24 organized in three groups of 8):

tát savitúr váren$_i$ya

bhárgo devásya dhīmahi

dhíyo yó na pracodáyāt

May we obtain the excellent glory

Of He-Who-Inspires

So that he may impel our thought

Rig Veda 3.62.10

In Iranian religion both the good god Ahura Mazda and the bad god Ahriman Remanifest themselves into 24 forms.

31 In the Tree of Life Path 31. It is the first of the left leading paths and symbolizes "Ageless Intelligence." Its element is fire, and its letter is Shin – the special letter of 666. The number 666 in Hebrew is Mem, Samekh, Vau – these letters becomes the Tarot trumps 17, 3, and 11 – 17+3+11=31.

It is the number of Set by way of the Tarot. Shin (Sh) is Trump 20 = Fire and Teth(T) is Trump 11 = Force. Fracter Achad discovered that 31 was the Key of the *Book of the Law* indicating its authorship. Thirty-one is a prime with the interesting property that no number in base ten adds up to 31 by sum of its digits (i.e., it is a self number). Pradjapati created the universe by speaking the odd numbers from 1 to 31, (*Vajasaneya Samhita*)

37 Nmber by English Kabbalahh of the Word Xeper.

According to English Kabbalahh it is 111/3—number of the manifestation of the Magickal current of Set.

Other words of the 37 Current:

Amrita

Bride

Cakes

Dance

Dark

Double

Eros

Frog

I Am A God

I Am Life

I Am Nuit

Is A Key

Naked

Night

Prana

Rose

Sevek

The Gate

The number of the demon "Phoneix"

418 The line in *Paradise Lost*, Book III, that begins the description of

Satan's flight to Earth:

(*Milton: Paradise Lost*, iii., 418 to the end). He starts from Hell, and wanders a long time

about the confines of the Universe, where he sees Chaos and Limbo. The Universe is a vast extended plain, fortified by part of the ethereal quintessence out of which the stars were created. There is a gap in the fortification, through which angels pass when they visit our earth. Being weary, Satan rests awhile at this gap and contemplates the vast Universe. He then transforms himself into an angel of light and visits Uriel, whom he finds in the Sun. He asks Uriel the way to Paradise, and Uriel points out to him our earth. Then, plunging through the starry vault, the waters above the firmament, and the firmament itself, he alights safely on Mount Niphates, in Armenia.

Source: *Dictionary of Phrase and Fable*, E. Cobham Brewer, 1894

In Thelemism 418 signifies the Great Work unifying the Universal Perspective (signified by the Hexgram) with the Individual Perspective, summarized in the Word Abrahadabra.
BVLShKIN (Boleskine, House of the Beast), the power of owning land
RPSTOVAL (Ropstoval, the Solar Logos. Read AL,II:76) Notarikon for: "Rightful Priesthood Set True Origin Volume AL" in the Book of Coming Forth by Night.
AIWASS in Greek
BITH HA (the House of He', the Pentagram

In English Kabbalahh:

ABRAHADABRA, THE GREAT ORACLE THAT ISSUES FROM

SPACE BY THE GATEWAY AT THE BACK OF THE TREE

666 The Number of the Beast of Revelation. This magic number has

many interesting properties. It is 18 X 37. In Roman numerals it is

DCLXVI, the six numerals equal or less than a 1000 in descending order. In Greek numerals it is κξϛ' – symbolizing the Creator K and Man ϛ' with the Serpent between them ξ.

In Judaism 666 is the Cabalistic value of "Ata yigdal na koach Ado-nai -- Now, I pray, let the Power of my Lord be great." (Numbers 14:17) "And now, I beseech thee, let the power of my Lord be great, according as thou hast spoken, saying. . ." This is Moses prayer for divine mercy when the Jews were wanting to go back to Egypt and god was pissed off that his Will (ratzon) was not being done. In Rabbi Eliyahu of Vilna's commentary on the Zohar, there is the idea that 666 contains hidden within it an exalted and lofty messianic potential. Six is the number of the physical universe – the six directions in Hebrew North, South, East, West, Up, and Down. Repeating the number three times reveals that when the Messiah comes he will be able to fully transform the world into a perfect form for those upon it to experience the Creator. This doctrine (of the reuniting the material world with the divine through the figure of a deified human) had been lifted straight from Zoroastrianism. The messianic idea (in Zoroastrianism the story of Zoroaster's lake of sperm causing virgin births) passed not only into Judaism, but also was the root of the Islamic notion of the Occult Imam and Buddhism's Maitreya.

The idea that a human will come along and save the world is a powerful one, and has been the root of both rebellions (under 666 figures) and repressions (claiming that a 666 figure had emerged. When John of Patmos wrote his best-selling *Book of Revelation* he had already foreseen the threat a future self-deified leader would be to the existing faith, much as Jesus had done about sixty years before John wrote his book. John's naming of the Antichrist as κξς', it became a past time of the followers of the Resurrected God to name the Antichrist. Candidates have ranged from Nero to Ronald Wilson Reagan. This is an example of one of the powers of White Magic, forming a *communitas* by creating a scapegoat.

This number has a doleful effect on mentally unstable Christians who view its appearance (say, for example, in a bill they are paying at McDonald's) as a bad Omen. The reverse form of Magical Thinking is true of weak-minded Satanists.

Aleister Crowley identified with the idea of the Antichrist from childhood due to his overly strict Plymouth Brethren upbringing. Predictably, the Number Worked its magic – like a good Zoroastrian Messiah, he mythologized his birth, and in Egypt, having married his Scarlet Woman, received the call to create a new Aeon. His wife Rose led him to the "Stele of Revealing," an Egyptian painted wooden tablet from the 26th Dynasty, depicting Horus Behedit receiving a sacrifice from the deceased, a priest named Ankh-f-n-khonsu. The tablet belonged to a Montu Priest, whose priesthood used such objects in place of the heart scarab. It contained a formula of allowing the dead one to return to earth to work his

Will Amung the living. This idea that the afterlife was not the restful hypostasis of the Resurrected God (i.e., unmanifest Being) but active Becoming opened Crowley to receiving the Book of the Law. He changed his name to Aleister Crowley from Edward Alexander Crowley, because of its number. His use of 666 is an example of both Greater and Lesser Black Magic. It is a Solar number, and on that basis Crowley once said his name was "Little Sunshine." He preferred, however, To Μεγα Θηριον (The Great Beast) whose number in Greek isopherey is 666 and is a reference to the First Beast in Revelation (Revelation 13:1).

The magic number likewise Worked over Michael Aquino. In its predictably Solar fashion on the Northern Solstice of 1975, it helped him gain awareness of his own mission to renew the material and divine worlds by creating an even stronger and clearer understanding that the world of action was the place toward which Life now and spiritual rebirth were aimed. His Word of Xeper is the absolute renunciation of both the de-centering of the Right Hand Path and the notion of divine hypostasis. He adopted the number 666 based on the circumstances of his birth and his decipherment of the numeric code in the Book of the Law. The magical Order he created inside the Temple of Set, the Order of the Trapezoid, has an angular 666 design in its seal. The Second Beast brings down the Fire From Heaven (Revelation 13:13), which reveals Aquino's connection with the Black Flame.

The number 666 is considered by Agrippa to be the number of the sun. Here is the magic square of the sun, each row, column and diagonal adds up to 111 – any six of them 666:

6	32	3	34	35	1
7	11	27	28	8	30
19	14	16	15	23	24
18	20	22	21	17	13
25	29	10	9	26	12
36	5	33	4	2	31

Here is Agrippa's description. Note how the 666 number makes some men Princes, but others tyrants:

"The fourth tablet is of the sun, and is made of a square of 6, and contains 36 numbers, whereof 6 on every side and diameter, produce 111, and the sum of all is 666. . . . This being engraven on a golden plate, renders him who wears it renowned and amiable, and equals a man to kings and princes . . . but with an unfortunate sun it makes a tyrant".

A few other associations (in Hebrew):

BRAShITh: Berashith; in the Beginning

In Greek

H phren: the mind, reason, understanding.

o niketes: the conqueror (Comprea NIKE = 93)

Lastly, I posses as a magical talisman a license plate with S8N 666 signed by the members of Deicide, which I won in a church raffle.

77 by English Kabbalah the number of the Word Remanifest. Other words of the 77 current:

Beast Gods

Black Pearl

Chorazin (Choronzon)

Crescent

Female Cleft

Great Mother

God Of Night

Honey of the Dead

Mother of Fish (Iyemoja)

Path Of Ipsos

Space-Double

The Dark Aeon

The Dark Moon

The Empress

Some Hebrew Correspondences:

NUBTI = Nun (50) + Vau (6) +Beth (2) + Teth (9) + Yod 10) = 77 Set,

Lord of Ombos (Nubti his oldest cult site)

Also, Magician Aion 131 points out on his website that this encodes the

Magician (Beth) within Nuit:

N U - B - T I

---> <---

OZ (Ayin-Zayin Strength or Stability)

Also, the number of the aphorisms in the Shiva Sutras of Vasugupta

9   The Number of Control. Anton LaVey took as source material A History of

Magic, Witchcraft and Occultism by W.B. Crow that the number nine (that in base ten

math) the digits of multiples always add up to nine or another multiple of nine was sign

that Nine Ruled the Cosmos. (Crow, by the way, was consecrated as Head of the Ecclesia

Gnostica Catholica.) LaVey married this idea to that of The Unknown Nine, a novel by

Theosophist Talbot Mundy that nine unknown men rule the world by magic power. From

this he created the idea that Church of Satan would be ruled by a Council of Nine, an idea

that was actually put in practice by the Temple of Set. Setians and Satanists begin their

rituals with ringing a bell nine times. Some modern Indians believe in the Nine sighting

such marvels as the Delhi Iron Pillar or the super science of Jagadish Chandra Bose. Nine has a huge fascination for the spiritual part of the human mind – it shows up as the Nine Worlds of Germanic Mythology, the Nine Muses of the Greeks, the Nine Heavens and Hell of Dante, the Nine Layers of Xilbalba of the Mayas,. Certain powerful magical seals that show the process of Becoming in all the planes of existence are nine-angled, such as the Valknutr, the Ennegram, and the Seal of Runa.

The number 9 is at the upper limit of our ability to process short term memory, as George Miller showed in The Magical Number Seven, Plus or Minus Two: Some Limits on our Capacity for Processing Information. When we hear or see nine versions of a stimulus we "trance out" – an effect the self-transcendence of the God gene kicks in and we feel religious ecstasy.

93 The number of the Words: NIKE, THELEMA, and the phrase "Reyn Til Runa"

Thelema: Θ (Theta) 9 + ε (Epsilon) 5 + λ (Lambda) 30 + η (Eta) =8 + μ (Mu) 40 + α (Alpha) 1 = 93

The word begins with a Theta, whose number Nine signifies control and separation from the Universe – Tarot Trump IX The Hermit. It ends with Alpha, which signifies control of all things under the Moon/Khonsu – power over the Becoming World. This word is New Testament Greek for "Will" or "Intention."

Agapé: A (Alpha) 1 + γ (Gamma η (Eta) 8) 3 + α (Alpha) 1 + π (Pi) 80 + η (Eta) 8

=93

It begins with Alpha showing that controls all things in the Becoming World, and ends with Eta showing that it is the domination of Aphrodite. It is the Word of Jesus Christ and means "Love."

Crowley equated these two Words to rework the maxim of Paschal Beverly Randolph," Will reigns Omnipotent; Love lieth at the Foundation," as part of his world mission as an Antichrist.

REYN TIL RUNA– the law of Stephen Flowers is an 11-letter expression of 93. In Crowley's system 11 is the Number of Magic, and this phrase "Seek the Mysteries!" shows how Magic is Worked both on the self and the objective universe by seeking after the Unknown. In many ways it could have been carved on Crowley's tombstone – if he had one – since it summed up his life.

A few other correspondences:

Aiwaz, the name of the entity that dictated *The Book of the Law* in 1904

TzBa –Will; star, host. This is the Hebrew cognate of the Egpytian S'Ba = to Teach. It shows another path of the Will, which is to initiate others after one has received

Initation. It is the magical application of the truism that one "does not really know something until one has taught it."

MBNA – the Word of the Third Degree in the OTO, which symbolizes birth and death of Mansur el-Hallaj, a Sufi Left Hand Path mystic, who was crucified in Baghdad for saying "I am the Truth" and identifying himself with Allah. MBNA derives from the Notarikon of "Mortis Beatus Nunc Apparet" – "Now the Blessing of Death is at Hand." The Hebrew letters are Mem (40) + Bet (2) + Nun (50) + Aleph (1). The Initiate becomes a Master Builder with the knowledge that if Self-deification is practiced while he or she lives as active afterlife is possible

Here are a few choice entries from the English Kabbalah:

THE LEFT-HAND PATH

A FEAST FOR LIFE

ALL POWER GIVEN

THE AURA OF THE ADEPT

On Death, Darkness, and the Heb-Sed

***The following article I wrote for the Scroll of Set** deals with forces that can either empower us or distract us when we seek Self-renewal. Both Darkness and death can either be obstacles or forces that empower the psyche. As the **Book of the Heb-Sed** says, "Changing Perception is the Great Work."*

What is darkness? For many in the Temple, there is a simple understanding that Darkness is our friend. Nothing could be further from the truth. Darkness is our adviser and tester. Darkness is whatever comes from the Unmanifested into the non-natural world.

All new things come from the Unmanifested. If you didn't have love last night or gold yesterday, and have it today, then it has come from the Unmanifested. And such things are always tests, resistors. Think of your first car. At first all you could think of was that you got it. Then you thought that you'd never be able to master it. Then you could drive it, and the only thing was the driving of it. Then at last you mastered it, and the real possibilities opened.

That car had come out of the darkness, and for a while it held you in its thrall, then you overcame it. This is a small eddy of darkness – a small piece of the non-natural world which, like all things created by the action of the Black Flame on this world, has the capacity of being our tester and adviser.

Now, what of the darkness within? Here, too, new things appear out of the Unmanifested. When you have a new idea – never mind that you may have read it or heard it somewhere – when you have the idea and it shakes your world, it is come from the Unmanifest within. The Idea blots out all else for a while. It becomes a god by insisting that this is the only Door to the LHP; and because of the power of our creations, of our Remanifestations, we are held by the idea, and not by its possibilities. Only if we learn to seize each new insight by putting it into practice do we learn to Xeper. Many people in their development only go as far as their last really great idea. It may be a really great idea – but just like the most ornate and impressive Door, it remains a Wall if we don't go through.

Now, what of Death? Death is, of course, the great Unmanifested in our lives. It changes every day; it informs and tests. There is no natural event that has the force it has on our psyche. Like Darkness, it is not our friend. Like Darkness, it is not our enemy. And of those Creations of Darkness, it supremely takes on the power of the Unmanifest. In fact, death is the supreme magic that mankind has wrought on itself. Every other construct in man's subjective universe, whether it is religion, alcoholism, medicine, psychotherapy, art, etc., comes from the knowledge of the inevitability of death. This also shows how much bad GBM man can do. Unfortunately, most of mankind turns to a worship of their ideas of death, which are, of course, their own creation. We can consider this mysterious thing intellectually or emotionally, but the real experience is going to be different. We do have one clue in that, in the Egyptian pantheon, it was Set who created death – by killing Osiris, the god of Stasis. The Magus Gurdjieff once said that if mankind could be gifted with an organ that made him aware of his death at every instant, there would be hope for mankind. We who live freely within the LHP know that there is no hope for mankind, but for us there is a hope that we can learn to see our death. Let it instill in us a sense of urgency, an Understanding of the Unmanifest, of Darkness Herself. Then we will cease to view darkness as our friend and see her for what she really is – an absolutely necessary element for our Initiation. If Death wasn't of Darkness, if we could freely speak with the Dead, if we KNEW – then we wouldn't have the possibility for Becoming, none of the urgency, none of the many-layeredness of Xeper.

But if Darkness is not our friend, and Death is certainly not our friend, are we friendless? No, for the first of our kind is our friend for creating these things. The Prince of Darkness created the Unmanifest with His first Thought, "Xepera Xeper Xeperu." We, with each use of that formula, good or bad, Create the darkness around us and beckon to us manifestations of the Darkness. In this we are even the Creators of time, in all of time's manifestations beyond the wheeling of the stars.

Mankind's relationship with the Unmanifested has changed because of our Aeon. The rate that the new – which to say the dark – manifests is much, much faster now. This type of change has occurred in other times in human history, generally with the visible appearance with the friends of the Prince of Darkness. The filtering mechanisms such as Church, State, Party (or whatever), are falling into disrepair since they cannot deal with the level of manifestation. These structures of the Age of Dependence will, in their death spasms, be dangerous, but much more so the average individual who has depended on these structures for his or her identity. The sudden exposure of self will leave them raw and violent. The very darkness that we must have is, in their lives, a source of confusion and fear. In this we see Set as the Ruler of the Aeon. Under these conditions, more will awaken, but since human nature, which has not fundamentally changed, opposes this force of non-naturalization, they will become either violent (one way humans become more natural) or learn to pacify themselves with illusions of consciousness, already clear in the great herds of pseudo-intellectuals roaming the plains of the Internet. Indeed, although this is a good time for sudden awakening because the forces of naturalization are at their strongest, it is a bad time for us. We are surrounded by those forces of naturalization – either hatred (naturalization through violence) or ignorance (naturalization through sleep). We must guard ourselves against this.

The Infernal Choir

The Temple abounds in professional musicians. In fact, one of the largest study groups – the Black Muse Element – is devoted to their studies. One might expect that a group like ours would be strongly into Heavy Metal. Although we have a few metal-heads and Goths, we also have classical harpists, jazz pianists, Southern Rock, industrial, electronica – you name it. Because of very scant credentials (I co-wrote a song for French rocker Alexandra Roos), I hang out with these guys and gals some times. Here are some thoughts I had about music:

The human mind has several nice modules, according to recent evolutionary theory. Most of these help us out by helping us to recognize animals, to have religious joy, to be shy, and to have music. Music showed up some time ago – let's say 60,000 years ago – when mankind started using Symbolic behavior. It had been a rough time for mankind. Oh, he's looked the same, but there was a little problem with a volcano and some dust, and an Ice Age, where all the rules changed. Mankind Needed something more than his inbred smarts. A little something called the Gift of Set. It provided the 10,000 or so members of the population of the time with flexibility and learning so they didn't go the way of other mammals surprised that it got cold.

One of the things that showed up was music.

Now, at first that doesn't seem like much of a survival skill. You can't kill a mammoth with music. You can't warm yourself with music.

But you can do something very interesting. You can alter your brainwaves with it. You can alter the brainwaves of others with it. Altering brainwaves is good way to do a couple of things. Firstly, it provides access to memory. How many of you can recite your alphabet without singing the "Alphabet Song"? Did you know that by the time you have finished with it, your brain is nicely firing at the same rate it did when you learned the song? Most people feel something very warm and childlike at this moment, even though the circumstances under which they are accessing the memory (such as looking for a file) are distinctly unappealing. Secondly, it provides a medium for emotional sharing. Get a group of people and get them listening (or performing) the same piece of music, and the mood fills the room – happy, nostalgic, romantic, martial, you name it.

Now, these are basic survival skills. You can teach useful information (where the cave is), and you can motivate the group (which no doubt got our ancestors' ancestors through many a tough winter). Music is one of the first activities that mankind picked up as he developed his symbolic capacity. Unlike most of the Gift of Set, it is deeply hardwired in your brain. Moreover, it's there for you to use. Now, most of us discover how using a certain piece of music in ritual can create a permanent anchor for the mood of the ritual. A few of us play around with influencing others with music. However, we remain in the very infancy of a musical-magical system.

It is time for one of the oldest "Secrets of Perfection" to be explored more fully by the Children of Set. I will offer four short experiments to Open you up to certain possibilities.

I.   Perform a ritual to regain lost memories. The format is simple – standard *Crystal Tablet* rubrics. When you get to the Graal, sing a song from an earlier period in your life. The "Alphabet Song" is a good start. When you've sung it until you feel different, simply say aloud, "I want the memories from this time in my life to show themselves to me so that I can integrate them into what I am Becoming." Close the Rite in the normal way. The memories won't come all at once, but take notice as to when they show up. How was your present activity like the memory? How had that memory been unconsciously shaping the current activity? Is this a good shaping or one you would like to change?

II.   Pick a piece of Classical/Romantic music. Preferably one you haven't heard before. Listen to it with eyes closed and let whatever pictures or moods come to mind to have full play. Try later to remember them. Can you make a story out of them? After you have given the music to someone else, ask him or her to try the same process. How similar are your stories? If there were such things as telepathy or mental communion how could you use the music?

III.   Go to some place that a good deal of music has been played but that is currently silent. Be very still yourself – still your breath and your thoughts, and try to hear the music played there days, weeks, and months ago. Is there something different about the air of such places? How do they compare to the feel of a natural "power place," a church, or a library? What effect does music have on a space? Is this an entirely subjective effect? Is it cultural?

IV.   Play musical tag. When you are around a group of people, try humming or

singing a catchy little tune. Do this until someone else says something like "Great, now

I've got that in my head." Just observe during the day how many people can be caught.

You "win" the game of musical tag if when you leave you can pick up the tune form

someone else. Now there you've experienced placing something directly in the

subjective universe of another and then picking it up from such a universe. How is this

like/unlike magic? Is it magic?

These are very simple games, but they can lead to a good deal of interesting thought

if played sincerely.

Walhalla

One of the most notorious divisions of the Temple of Set is the Order of the Trapezoid, a Knighthood dedicated to the Honor of the Two Beasts – Aleister Crowley and Michael Aquino. Its primary expression is Germanic occultism, and its secondary language is the myths of Lovecraft. The Order was founded in the darkest of the places, the Hall of the Dead in Himmler's Castle. There are few symbols of wrongful empowerment of the psyche as telling the Nazis. They practiced a simple and effective self-deification magic but did not couple it with virtue-ethics. They are forever the Sign in history that you cannot give the Powers of Darkness to humans that do not place these powers around a core that believes freedom and diversity are not only part and parcel of the Gift of the Prince of Darkness, but that fighting for freedom actually makes the Black Flame burn more brightly on this Earth. During my stay in the Temple I have seen both Jewish and Black Grandmasters of the Order. All races of mankind take their turns as victims and tormentors – yet all humans cannot only be better humans, they can be semi-divine. But woe unto any whose schemes to destroy mankind's freedom of joy. If you do not realize that making yourself into a God also means that you are making yourself into a Demon, then you must flee the dark path.   I wrote this essay for Runes:

Persons of a certain level of being can utter words of power – words that can cause others to do and feel things – words that can open into worlds.

One such word is Walhalla, the watchword of the current manifestation of the

Order of the Trapezoid.   Heard and Uttered by Sir Michael Aquino on October 17, 1984, in the Hall of the Fallen of Himler's Castle, this Word Remainfested an Order of Knighthood that protects the liberating effect of human desire on Earth.

On the surface it would seem to be an unlikely word for a group of men and women pursuing real world change in a Left Hand Path faith. It comes out of a super-Right-Hand-Path environment (the Nazis weren't big on individuality). It refers to an afterlife state (sounds more like Christianity than Satanism). It does not seem to promote life worship. Yet the Order of the Trapezoid is the largest order of the Temple of Set, a vanguard for the Left Hand Path in the West – and has cast its sinister shadow into the occult community, the illusion-filled land of conspiracy theory, and even into academia and the military.

At times the face of the serpent is seen. This is one such time. Let's look at the implications of the Word and a few preludes to its Utterance.

Here is the bedrock magical principal: changing the past is subjective; changing the future is objective.

Most humans struggle daily with changing the past. The limitations on their lives were placed there in the past. Someone may have told them that they were stupid, lazy, or ugly; and they wear and resent these labels everyday of their lives. We can sympathize with the young woman who was told in her early life that math wasn't for girls and didn't discover her gifts until age 30. She can't change the bad grades and wasted time of her youth – those things are objective – but she can change her attitude every day.

The future, however, is malleable. If you and I agree to meet for coffee tomorrow, we have created an event if we are both true to our word and the world doesn't overcome this plan. The further we cast our vision into the future, the easier it is to cast that vision. You may have tomorrow scheduled and can't meet for coffee, but if we make a date for next week, you may be freer, and certainly next month has nothing staining the fair pages of its calendar.

Walhalla is the future. It is an enclosure built to hold warriors who are not enjoying the divine hypostasis of the Christian heaven, but who by merit have won a place to train for the next evolution of the cosmos. It is not the final goal, which would be Unknown, but a target. It is a target that requires objective action in the world now and magical action of assuming/creating a fraternal bond in the future.

Here are the Secrets of the Order:

Just as the Temple of Set is the creation of the light side of Michael Aquino, the Order of the Trapezoid is a creation of his dark side.

Just as the Temple of Set is about Being, the Order of the Trapezoid is about Doing.

The Temple gives people the tools to discover what they really are; the Order gives people the tools to shape what the world may yet become.

One Lives in this world and the next by seeking after the unmanifest and bringing into being, or by making the Unknown Known.

The Order of the Trapezoid has roots in the work of Aleister Crowley, Twentieth Century German occultism, and other sources. I wanted to share a few of the electrifying preludes of this stone of precious water.

When the Hyskos ruled Egypt, they brought ideas of horse-culture and honor. Although the Hyskos were not Indo-Europeans, they did bring the Indo-European notion of rule by cavalry elite to the Nile valley. This lead to changes in Egyptian thinking in the XVIII-XX Dynasties. It saw the emergence of a military elite, the *mari'annu*, who considered honor as a key to personal immortality, a method of thinking that Egyptologist Jan Assmann has described as a "theology of will." The *mari'annu* took over the higher positions of the Egyptian priesthood to end economic corruptions of offices. They instituted the fortified temple with its large trapezoidal pylon gates, and they revived an ancient and near-forgotten god, Set. The meeting of Odhinn and Set along the southern road had all of the markings of the Order: the use of deep past as a key to the future, the emphasis on personal and clannish honor as a mechanism of personal immortality, the safe-guarding against temple corruption, and the use of the symbols of power to communicate these goals too all realms of being. During *mari'annu* times the Empire spread both southward and eastward, archeology and library-keeping began, and the word for an individual first appeared in hieroglyphs.

I.   The first use of the Sacred Trapezoid in Western Magic was the Freemasons' Apron. Proportioned at 6, 5, 10, 6 it reflected the values of the name of Jehovah. The Yod (=10) is the base, the two Hehs (6) are the sides and the Vau (=6) is on the top. Sir Albert Pike traced the apron somewhat fancifully to the white sheepskin worn by the priests of Jupiter-Amun, who provided the oracle legitimizing Alexander the Great's rule. The Freemasons, whose network of secret and belief in equality and brotherhood brought about the American and French revolutions, are a prototype of our Order. We likewise believe in the equality of members, the use of fraternal bonds to achieve worldly power, and the long-term importance of secular human freedom.

II. Young Howard Stanton Levy caught a flick in 1943 that was to change his life. *The Seventh Victim,* a Val Lewton production, featured a group of Palladium Masons, devil worshippers, who possessed the power to alter their members fates. Their magical focus is a parallelogram. The screenwriter David Bodeen claimed to have visited an actual Satanic group in New York. The eeriest and (perhaps) most magical part of the film is composer Roy Webb's score. This little film I ntroduced Howard to four important magical ideas: the power of music as spell-casting, the use of geometrical symbol as group focus/inspiration, the power of people that are devoted yet "hidden" in the roles of prosperous, hard-working men and women, and most importantly, the idea that popular images of magic can be used as gateways to magical states with as much validity as (for example) Hindu Tattwas. All of these principles not only shaped the magical career of Howard Levy, but became his magical legacy that lives on the Order of the Trapezoid of the Temple of Set.

The film also hooked him on Val Lewton, and when 1957 brought *The Curse of the Demon,* Val Lewton's version of the classic M.R. James story "Casting the Runes," Howard was quick to pick up on the magical references. In his later life Howard dated the foundation of the Order of the Trapezoid to 1957; although in reality the Order and its rune-casting were more of a creature of ink than reality during the Church of Satan's heyday.

IV.   In March 1929 *Weird Tales* magazine brought out Frank Belknap Long's short story "The Hounds of Tindalos." This story, inspired by the works of

H. P. Lovecraft, featured an odd sort of magical being – the hound-like stalkers of "angular time." Long had created a new paradigm Unlike linear time, the progressive time of history, or circular time, the mythic/religious time that mirrors the seasons, Long had created a time for the creatures that had truly fallen by eating the apple of knowledge. Angular time is partially based on will and partially based on unseen obstacles. It could be likened to the processes that the mind goes through when solving a problem. One vector may move quickly, then direction has to be changed when encountering an obstacle. Things may leap ahead, crawl ahead, or backtrack. Long's description was a perfect model for the human thought process and showed its "evil" nature – since it was out of sync with the orderly processes of nature. Long's bogeys, which are described as immortal, became the model for Magus LaVey's Rite of the Is-To-Be, which used the notion that the wants of the magician could enter into the minds of mankind via angular gateways. This notion is hidden in the word "tindalos." In Melanesian folklore a *tindalo* is the spirit of a man who had possessed great mana in his life and now could control fate. A *tindalo* can enter the body of a snake or shark or, in rarer instances, a human.

From these Roots, you can gain insight into Walhalla. The knight who gets a name for him- or herself and wills to exist in a post-mortem state that continues to influence the world through magical technologies, while awaiting a final battle that represents the next leap in consciousness, is the knight of the Order. He or she will generally look like any hard-working pillar of society, yet he or she is willing to battle (even die) for human freedom. He or she is in magical contact with others that are of the same current, and his or her magical weapons can come from the distant past, the imaginary present, and most importantly from contemplating their future state of being. Their deeds manifest that future. Like a new idea popping into one's head, they disturb – even shatter – realities, but their position in society not only helps new knights with jobs and advice, but makes sure that the forces of stupidity can't shut down the process. In one sense they are battling Ragnarok today, having already been in Walhalla; in another sense they are the inheritors of all those who have used magic and secrecy as part of the battle of human freedom.

Play

Setians are seriously questing for their own power and immortality. However, no one enters the realm of the gods who does not become lighter than an ostrich feather. The central part of the path of the Left is Play. For the human that does not want to play with his fellows, and laugh at himself and universe, no amount of Will shall lift him into the starry night. Set desires companions, companions to Play with, in the long years of Allternity . . .

I'd like to put forth a model of Play that may be useful to the playful magician. This is personal and subjective and, like all things from the Heart, it must be tested and adapted but not simply adopted. Many people have the silly idea that things of passion are for everybody but that things of precision are for the Elite. It is actually the other way around. Everyone can be taught to do precise things. The teaching may take awhile. It took me a long time to teach my IQ 75 yardman to do my yard. If you hang out on the Internet, you'll discover quickly how people can learn to do whatever they need to do to post on a newsgroup but still be without a clue. Passion requires the most education and self-training. It can't be proven or demonstrated or given to those not Elected by both your Heart and theirs to receive its transmission.

Play is not necessarily easy. Play is ongoing in all aspects of your life, if you Will it to be so, but on the level of a particular Game, it has both rough and easy parts. A

Game is any manifestation of one's Xeper whose primary purpose is the fulfillment of the Self's Will-to-Pleasure. Games involve other people and generate their own rules in interactions with existing forces in the objective universe. Games can be anything from getting someone in bed to planning a birthday party for your 80-year-old father to having people over to your house to watch a video.

We play Games in order to glimpse and direct the Process of Play. Games have four parts: the plan, the setup, the payoff, and the end. Each of these is characterized by the *level of interaction* with the outside world.

The Plan. Here is where you shut off the objective world as much as possible and dream up what you're going to do. Most of a magician's Games die in this phase. You think about quitting your job in some flamboyant way, or you engage in a fantasy about your fellow airline passenger. Almost *all* of non-magicians' games die here. They lack the Knowledge that you can, in fact, make what you want happen in the world. In this stage the Game is at its most perfect. In a fantasy, the birthday cake is never accidentally dropped on the floor.

The Setup. This is the phase of making you Game real. Here the most important thing is opening yourself to information. While you're running around to buy flowers and candles, you need to pay attention to stores' hours and to traffic reports. If you hear someone telling a horror story about a bakery, you stop and ask "Where was this?" so you can avoid it. You must persist and improvise. In this stage you must immerse yourself in the world. The bigger the Game, the greater the immersion. This phase maybe fun or terrible, boring or fascinating – but it requires the greatest open contact to the objective universe. Most people's plans end here because this phase is so opposite than the first.

Sometimes the forces of the world will end your Game here. Because of the danger of things not working out, most people don't even try. During the setup the GBM occurs, reconditioning both your consciousness and the world.

The Payoff. Here the desired result is Seen and Heard and Felt. This is the stage where you have safely setup for *positive feedback-loops* only. You have turned on the answering machine or unplugged the phone. You've put out the "DO NOT DISTURB SIGN" on the hotel door. You've made sure that the moment unfolding before you is not going to be interrupted or marred. The seduction, the birthday party, the first drive in your new car dominates and eclipses all other things. This moment of external, objective pleasure is the moment of Xeper. You are experiencing the Coming Into Being of something whose Coming Into Being was patterned on your won Coming Into Being. These moments are Essential to your Xeper – the images, sensations, and moods are the Source of all your Power. They prove to the psyche its own existence and affirm its decision to continue. These moments are missed by two types of so-called magicians. Self-denying mystics miss these because these build up the Self. Such pleasure, made by actualizing your dreams, is the greatest blasphemy on the Right Hand Path. These are moments sacred to Victory. The other type that misses these moments is the vast army of wannabe magicians who keep the amulet and incense trade going. They hope that somehow – if they keep those candles burning – a good thing will happen to them.

The End. Here is what separates the Setian from the hedonist. The Setian, knowing that such moments of payoff are part of a bigger process, will unhurriedly end the glowing moment. This is because the period of perfection ends of its own because anything in contact with the objective universe is subject to the laws of decay that rule that universe. The Setian ends things on a high note, in the sure and certain self-trust that he or she will create another payoff. This period is characterized by selectively interacting with those aspects of the objective universe that have nothing to do with the Game. The seduction is over and you call for your dry-cleaning. The birthday party is done and you mow your lawn. You're finished cave-diving, so you start fixing your pickup.

Now the glow of the payoff radiates out into your life for many days. Even non-magicians know that after a good party they're smiling all week. So what separates play and Play? Two things – two ideas held in the minds of the magician change pleasurable actions into Transformative ones. One, he or she knows what the different phases of Play feel like and can *pit these against* life circumstance. They can arrange to have the afterglow of endgame the day of a trying presentation at work, or they can have the busy fun of doing setup to distract them from the boring part of their work cycle. In fact, when they learn to have a few different Games going at once, they begin to actually *Sense* their Essence as it is ebbing and flowing in and through them. Two, the magician can begin to realize that all these steps they are consciously going through as they work on a particular game are being done by their Higher Self in the Game called Life. The Magician slowly comes to the self-transforming knowledge that Life is a Game. When this is Known at the deepest level of consciousness you have access to – as opposed to merely intellectual knowledge – you will have obtained Being. The experience of Xeper as Being will cause a certain blessing and perfecting of things around you, and you will bring a certain otherworldly grace into any situation you enter. Things can still go wrong, which is true of anything happening in the objective universe, but the energy to improvise will become yours abundantly.

This Magic can be taught to non-magicians, but it takes years of example to do so. Make it your job to teach it to those few who have truly helped you along the path. These Works of magic mark the passage of those with being in this world and, on a cosmic scale, fight against the decay of this world.

APPENDIX

I wish to thank the High Priest of the Temple of Set for the permission to reprint this document:

General Information and Admissions Policies

Updated: 30 April 2011 CE

The Temple of Set is an institution unlike any you have previously encountered. It has been designed as a tool for personal empowerment and self-cultivation. To decide if you can benefit from affiliation with the Temple of Set, carefully consider the philosophy of the Temple, the concept of Set, and the obligations and responsibilities that a Setian assumes.

SETIAN PHILOSOPHY

All schools of introspective inquiry [as opposed to those of faith] address the one difference that distinguishes mankind from the rest of the cosmos: the feature of being, of conscious willful existence. This self-awareness makes possible all of our arts, our sciences, our notions of "good" and "evil" as well as free will and the ability to assign meaning to thoughts, statements, and actions.

Religions confront this phenomenon of individual consciousness in various ways. Some—for example, the Buddhist quest for nirvana—endeavor to extinguish it outright. Others, such as the Abrahamic religions, label it "the soul" and posit that somebody else will rescue it. Still others deny it altogether, relegating man to the same status as an animal. Nevertheless there have also been consciousness-worshiping (or –respecting) religions throughout all historical civilizations and cultures.

Historically consciousness-worshiping religions have been more intellectually demanding than their nature-worshiping counterparts, since it is more difficult to reason a path through one's span of conscious existence than it is to be swept along by a current of semi-rational stimulus and response. Such schools were admired in certain societies, such as ancient Egypt and Greece, but generally their elitism and "supernatural" activities made them objects of resentment and persecution.

The Temple of Set seeks above all to honor and enshrine consciousness. We wish to apprehend what makes us each individually unique and use this gift to make ourselves stronger in all facets of our being. To do this we preserve and improve the tradition of spiritual distinction from the cultural universe, which in the Judeo-Christian West has been called Satanism, but which is more generally known as the Left-Hand Path.

The Left-Hand Path is a process for creating an individual, powerful essence that exists above and beyond animal life. It is thus the true vehicle for personal immortality. It has several components:

ANTINOMIANISM

The values of the masses, whether inculcated by conventional religion or by mass media, must be recognized as an obstacle to individual spiritual development. Human society values predictability, stability, or stasis above all things. The Initiate, by contrast, seeks continuous, positive self-evolution.

Objective understanding and evaluation of the host society's values are necessary in order to intelligently formulate one's own. In Western conventional religions such independence is frequently condemned as "Satanic". But the Initiate is rebelling against more than the idea of an external "god": he also seeks freedom in his secular life from such external controlling forces as propaganda, custom, and habit.
To work magic that evolves the self, the magician's will must prevail in the subjective universe as the massed wills of others do in the objective one. Once such strength of individual will is obtained, it can be extended into objective environments as well. But as long as an individual allows himself to be governed by animal emotions such as shame, fear, or the desire for social acceptance, he cannot become an Adept of Black Magic.

Conventional society instinctively fears and often hates what it cannot easily understand. If you seek out the Temple, you may find yourself accused of all manner of popular evils of the day: racism, sexism, anti-this or pro-that. When you can look around with your own eyes and see that the Temple embodies and promotes none of these things, you will have learned much about the suspicion and antipathy that greets any manifestation of intellectual independence of consciousness.

INDIVIDUALITY

No one else can do the work of self-change for you. The intensity and pace of your own initiation will be up to you, not the Temple of Set. Nor can the Temple dictate your personal goals. You yourself must do so, again with wisdom rather than emotion or impulse.

CONTROL

The world is a chaotic environment characterized by the masses' lack of both intelligent goals and the discipline necessary for their attainment. The Initiate must have a strong sense of personal discipline before embarking on any adventure. The ability to recognize, start, and complete great quests distinguishes the Initiate from the 'occultnik'.

BLACK MAGIC

Followers of the Left-Hand Path practice what, in a specific and technical sense, we term *Black Magic*. Black Magic focuses on self-determined goals. Its formula is "my will be done", as opposed to the White Magic of the Right-Hand Path, whose formula is "thy will be done".

Black Magic is shunned and feared because to do Black Magic is to take full responsibility for one's actions, evolution, and effectiveness.
Since magic enables you to influence or change events in ways neither understood nor anticipated by society, you must develop a sound and sophisticated appreciation for the ethics governing your own motives, decisions, and actions before you put it to use. To use magic for impulsive, trivial, or egoistic desires is not Setian. It must become second-nature to you to carefully pre-evaluate the consequences of what you wish to do, then choose the course of wisdom, justice, and creative improvement.

The Temple of Set utilizes a wide cultural and conceptual spectrum of magical tools, far beyond just the "Egyptian", and is always seeking new approaches and techniques.

Magic may either be operative—to cure your mother's illness, get a better job, strengthen your memory, etc.—or illustrative/initiatory. Illustrative/initiatory magical workings seek to enable and enact the lifetime process of Initiation. They are are comparable to "rites of passage" of many primitive cultures and conventional religions, but are distinguished from these in that they represent individually-crafted rather than socially-prescribed change. Initiatory workings thus represent the actualization of self-deification, while social "rites of passage" integrate an individual into society. A "rite of passage" communicating passage into adulthood establishes that the individual involved is now possessed of certain dignity and responsibilities. An initiatory working awakens one to certain individual powers [and responsibilities], which may or may not be used in a social context. Initiation does not occur within a ritual chamber, but it is illustrated there.

Black Magic is the means by which Initiates of the Left-Hand Path experience being gods, rather than praying to imaginary images of gods.

SET

The oldest known form of the Prince of Darkness, the archetype of isolate self-consciousness, is the Egyptian god Set, whose Priesthood can be traced to Predynastic times. Images of Set have been dated to ca. 3200 BCE, with astronomically-based estimates of inscriptions dating to 5000 BCE.

Set is a more complex figure than that of the Judeo-Christian Satan. Satan, the archetype of rebellion against cosmic order and stasis, may be the symbol for many people's initial commitment to initiation, but this symbol is too closely linked to conventional religions and their moral codes to be an effective representation of the richness, subtlety, and complexity of the Left-Hand Path.

In ancient Egypt Set went through periods of immense popularity alternating with total denunciation. Set in the Predynastic and Archaic periods was an essentially positive deity introduced from the east as a god of the extension of existence. As such he was god of expanding borders and radical changes of being—particularly birth, circumcision/initiation, death in battle, and rebirth through the Opening of the Mouth ceremony. As early as the Second Dynasty he appears in royal iconography, on the *serekh* of Peribsen ("Hope of All Hearts") and Khasekhemwy ("The Two Powers Appear").
Popular among easterners—his first cult site being Pelusium in the eastern Nile Delta—Set's worship spread west and south to border regions, where he was identified with local gods of initiation. Examples of such cult sites are the oasis of Dakhleh where Set shared with the local god Igai the title "Lord of the Desert", and the Libyan settlement of Ombos, wherein Set was identified with the local god Ash in the Second Dynasty.

Set's worship as a circumpolar/stellar deity suffered a decline with the rise of solar worship in the Fourth Dynasty. The Great Pyramid of Giza is one of the last early monuments connected with the idea of a Setian afterlife as well as a solar one. The Great Pyramid had a special air shaft for the king's *akh* to fly to the star alpha Draconis, the pole star of Old Kingdom Egypt. Unlike the sun and the stars that appear to rise and set (mythologized as birth and death) the *Pyramid Texts* assert that the *Ikhemw-sek*, the "imperishable ones" or circumpolar stars, are the realm of the royal soul.

During the Middle Kingdom Set was reduced to a symbol of Upper Egypt in the iconography of the *sema tawy* and the Heb-Sed festival. It was around this time that Set was first blamed for the murder of Osiris, a Semitic god of agriculture whose cult arrived in the Third Dynasty.

No matter how "evil" Osirians might portray Set as being, his essential function—of going out and expanding the borders of existence and then returning that Chaotic energy to the center—persisted in Egyptian thought. It is the darkness that binds together the Egyptian light. The murder of Osiris is the destruction of the fetters of society, of accepting self-change and cultivation over the forces that lead to self-stagnation.

The Hyksos, foreigners who invaded and ruled Egypt during the Second Intermediate Period (Dynasties XIII-XVII, roughly 1785-1580 BCE) actively identified themselves with Set and established their capital at an ancient Setian site, Avaris. The Hyksos were great horsemen, and the horse (like the ass) was identified with Set. Indeed not until the Hyksos dynasties was the horse, which had been known in Egypt for at least the prior two centuries, portrayed in Egyptian art.

The second native blooming of Setian thinking may have begun in the Eighteenth Dynasty, but certainly it reached its peak in the Nineteenth and Twentieth Dynasties, when a family of Setian Priests from Tanis became the pharaonic line. During this time of expanding borders, Set was extraordinarily popular, as can be seen from pharaohs' names such as Seti ("Set's man") and Setnakt ("Set is Mighty"). The cult of the stellar afterlife re-emerged: complex "astronomical ceilings" adorn the tombs of the pharaohs of this period—and of no other.

Two Setian texts survive from this period. First, the *Tale of Two Brothers* tells how Set (identified with the god Bata) undergoes a series of metamorphoses (*Xeperu*) that change him from a farmhand to a star in the Constellation of the Thigh (our "Big Dipper"). Thus Set represents the individual who through his own hard work, magical skill, and the use of the resistance of the world Becomes divine.

The second text is the *Book of Knowing the Spiral Force of Ra and the Felling of Apep*. This protective formula, which Rameses III, son of Setnakt, inscribed on certain border monuments, shows two Setian particularities. First, it recounts how an unnamed god comes into being in the psychic (subjective) realm as the god Xepera. Second, the spell gives the magician one of the powers of Set: the ability to slay Apep, the dragon of delusion. Set again serves as a role model, in that each Setian seeks to end delusions in life.

With the coming of the Twenty-Second Dynasty, Egypt entered its long decline. Set became a tremendously unpopular deity. His worship ceased everywhere except the oases and the city of Thebes. His cult was absorbed into others, primarily that of Montu, warlord of Thebes. The negative aspects of isolation and destruction were emphasized. Set-heh, the god of the void called the future, became a scapegoat in rites of execration—foreshadowing the role of the Satan in the Judeo-Christian West.

The third blooming came with the arrival of the Greeks in Egypt. It is in this period that Hellenic notions of independence and self-worth began to revive operant and initiatory aspects of the New Kingdom Set cult. The success of Graeco-Egyptian magic, despite Roman persecution, saw an expansion of both the philosophical and magical aspects of this tradition as far north as Britain.

The Third Century of the Common Era marked the height of Setian Hermeticism. But with the imposition of Christianity as the Roman imperial religion, individualism was again despised. Egyptian (Coptic) Christianity identified Set with Satan, and he almost disappeared as a figure in Egyptian magic.

The fourth blooming of Setian thought began in the nineteenth century with certain archaeological discoveries, but became explicit in 1975 with the reconsecration and founding of the modern Temple of Set and proclamation of the Word of the AEon of Set. *Xeper* ("kheffer") is an Egyptian verb which means "Come Into Being" or "Become". This word reflects the consciousness-worshiping nature of our religion and the source of ultimate responsibility in all things—the self.

STRUCTURE AND OPERATION OF THE TEMPLE

The deliberately individualistic atmosphere of the Temple of Set is not easily conducive to group activities on a routine or programmed basis. There are no congregations of docile "followers"—only cooperative philosophers and magicians.

Executive authority in the Temple is held by the Council of Nine, which appoints both the High Priest of Set and the Executive Director. Initiates are Recognized according to six degrees: Setian I°, Adept II°, Priest/Priestess of Set III°, Magister/Magistra Templi IV°, Magus/Maga V°, and Ipsissimus/Ipsissima VI°.

Recognition as an Adept II° constitutes certification by the Temple that one has in fact mastered and successfully applied the essential principles of Black Magic. The bulk of Temple systems are geared to attainment of, and subsequent support for the II°. That is the level of affiliation which most Setians are expected to hold: the Adept pursues continuing personal transformation and self-actualization. The III°–VI° are most accurately understood not as further benchmarks of individual attainment, but as specialized religious offices conferred by Set alone, and Recognized within the Temple according to his Will.
The design, care, and operation of the Temple are entrusted by Set to his Priesthood. All Initiates of the Priesthood are originally highly-qualified Adepts in the Black Arts and most of your contact with them will be in this context. Because they are responsible for the integrity of the Temple as a whole, however, they have the authority both to evaluate and Recognize Initiates' competence and, if necessary, to suspend or expel individuals who prove themselves incapable of maintaining Setian standards of dignity and excellence. The Priesthood takes all of these responsibilities extremely seriously, since it regards its name literally and its trust as sacred.

The knowledge of the Temple of Set is made available through four principal avenues: an extensive reading list, the newsletter *Scroll of Set*, internal publications by the Temple's various specialized Orders, and the series of encyclopedias entitled the *Jeweled Tablets of Set*. All are reproduced simply and inexpensively—usually in electronic form, sometimes as on-demand bound paperbacks—to keep costs down. The *Jeweled Tablets of Set* are not static documents, and are periodically revised to reflect new findings and areas of interest.

Recognizing the value and fellowship of a seminar environment, the Temple charters "Pylons" (named after the unique gates of ancient Egyptian temples).

While each Pylon is under the trust and responsibility of a II° Sentinel, they are emphatically not "congregations", but rather cooperative and interactive forums for individual Initiates.

The Orders of the Temple of the Temple of Set specialize in one or more particular fields of the magical arts and sciences. Such a specialization may be transcultural or oriented to a specific geographic area, time-period, or conceptual tradition. Participation in an Order is restricted to Initiates who have been Recognized as Adept in the principles of Setian philosophy and practice. Adepts are encouraged to affiliate with an Order reflective of their personal interests and aptitudes.

Setians have access to the Temple of Set's on-line forums and archives. However, the Temple is not an "on-line community": Setians attend annual international Conclaves as well as regional and local gatherings.
Individuals admitted to the Temple receive the *Crystal Tablet of Set*, which contains organizational, philosophical, and magical information pertinent to qualification as an Adept, as well as information on active Pylons and Setians open to contact. There is a two-year time limit for a new Setian to qualify for Adept Recognition. If such Recognition is not received by that time, affiliation is canceled.

Personal information furnished to the Temple in the course of admission or evaluation is not disseminated outside the Priesthood. You may apply the services and systems of the Temple as you wish, and as you deem most complementary to your Xeper; otherwise they will not intrude upon you.

AN IMPORTANT CLARIFICATION

Regretfully there still exist some individuals whose idea of "Satanism" is largely a synthesis of Christian propaganda and Hollywood horror movies. The Temple of Set enjoys the colorful legacy of the Black Arts, and we use many forms of historical Satanic imagery for our artistic stimulation and pleasure. But we have not found that any interest or activity which an enlightened, mature intellect would regard as undignified, sadistic, criminal, or depraved is desirable, much less essential to our work.

The Temple of Set is an evolutionary product of human experience. Such experience includes the magical and philosophical work of many individuals and organizations which have preceded us. Some of these were socially acceptable by contemporary or modern standards; others were not. Some made brilliant discoveries in one field of interest while blighting their reputations with shocking excesses or tragic failures in others. In examining the secret and suppressed corners of history for valuable and useful material, the Temple insists upon ethical presentation and use of such discoveries as it makes. Setians who are in any doubt as to the ethics involved in any of the fields which we explore should seek counsel from the Priesthood. All Setians are further expected to display a high measure of maturity and common sense in this area.

The Black Arts are **dangerous** in the same way that working with volatile chemicals is dangerous. This is most emphatically **not** a field for unstable, immature, or otherwise emotionally or intellectually weak-minded people. Such are a hazard to themselves and to others with whom they come into contact. The Temple endeavors to not admit them to begin with. If such an individual should gain admittance and later be exposed, he or she will be summarily expelled. In cases of doubt the Temple may be expected to place the burden of proof on the individual, for the sake of all Setians and the Temple's integrity.

The Temple of Set evaluates conventional religions as erroneous in principle and therefore unworthy of peer status. We feel no need to concern ourselves with their activities, nor for that matter to maintain any sort of "diplomatic relations" with them [as in councils of churches]. Our position is that they may serve a useful social function as purveyors of soothing myths and fantasies to humans unable to attain Setian levels of self-consciousness. Hence we ignore conventional religious organizations unless they intrude upon our affairs.

These warnings are not intended to be oppressive or intimidating, but they should be taken seriously. The Temple is a forum for the investigation of many subjects which conventional society finds odd, mysterious, and even extremely frightening. The Temple will be tolerated only to the extent that it is known to be pursuing its interests carefully, expertly, and responsibly. It occupies a delicate position in a world which is largely unhappy with itself, and which is ceaselessly searching for scapegoats. Hence the Temple must take care to maintain its social balance with prudence and dignity.

AFFILIATION

The key to philosophy is not reading about it, but practicing it. Abstract ideas are not enough; it is only through lived experience that Initiation occurs. Such experience is the mediator between the realm of consciousness and the world.

The First Degree (I°) of Temple affiliation is regarded as a "status of mutual evaluation" wherein the Initiate and the Temple can assess one another's merit from the standpoint of minimum investment and involvement. If a I° Initiate should decide that the Temple is not, after all, appropriate to his wants or needs, he is welcome to depart with our good wishes for satisfaction elsewhere.

Aspirants to the Temple should understand that it is not a club or fraternal society whose tokens may be "collected" along with those of other social affiliations, occult or otherwise. Membership in the Temple of Set beyond the I° precludes membership in any other religious organization.

Members or former members of non-religious occult organizations should understand that within the Temple of Set they will be expected to respect and observe the Temple's protocol, and that literature and other information from the Temple is not to be passed to non-Temple individuals or organizations without prior approval of the Priesthood.

Should you have questions which are reasonably pertinent to your serious consideration whether or not to apply for admission to the Temple, you are welcome to address them to the Executive Director of the Temple.

If you wish to apply for admission as a Setian I°, there are two avenues of approach available to you:

1 If you are in contact with a Priest or Priestess of Set, you may request him or her to sponsor your application. Complete the **application** for admission and mail the form, along with the first year's membership fee/card authorization (US$80), to the Executive Director, mentioning this sponsorship. If Priesthood sponsorship is verified, approval is automatic.

2 If you are not known to a member of the Priesthood, complete the **application** for admission form. Write a brief cover letter to the Executive Director introducing yourself, summarizing what aspects of your background you feel to be relevant, and stating your reasons for deciding to seek entrance into the Temple. Enclose the **first year's membership fee/card authorization** (US$80). The Temple will make a decision and respond to you accordingly. If necessary you will be asked for additional information. Should your application be declined for any reason, the fee will be refunded. Be as objective and candid as possible in your self-assessment. Attempts to mislead the Temple are a waste of time for all involved. If there are crucial areas of possible incompatibility, it is incumbent on the applicant to identify them before affiliation so that they may be addressed and, if possible, resolved.

The **first year's membership fee**, and the membership renewal fee (US$80/year), are intended to cover to cost of services provided. The Temple is a non-profit religious organization and its assets are used exclusively for benefits to its Initiates as a whole. There are no other regular or recurring fees, save that Orders and Pylons may set reasonable charges for their newsletters or other time/effort services. Special publications of the Temple and events scheduled by the Temple are customarily made available on a nonprofit basis to Initiates who are interested.

The only physical requirement for admission is that the aspirant be at least 18 years of age. Those below the age of 18 may **not** visit Temple functions, ceremonial or otherwise, whether or not they are relatives of Initiates. The Temple has **no** programs for children. It is our position that children and adolescents should not be indoctrinated into the assumptions and prescriptions of **any** suprarational system, whether it be our own philosophy or the faiths and superstitions of conventional religions. Rather their youthful years should be a time of **exclusively rational** training and education, giving them a sound and meaningful basis by which, as adults, they may consider and choose whatever philosophy or faith seems most meaningful to them.

If your application is approved, you will receive notification from the Executive Director's office, together with membership identification, certificate, Setian I° pendant medallion and access to the Temple's on-line publications, archives and forums.

The initiative is yours. The Temple of Set is designed to assist you in the ways we have found to be the most practical, productive, and factual. But, as versatile as the Temple may be, and as proud of it as we are, it is nevertheless a tool. You are the one who must put that tool to use in a way that will enable you to Xeper. Such is the Word of the AEon of Set.